PCPhoto

Digital ZOOM CAMERA HANDBOOK

ROB SHEPPARD

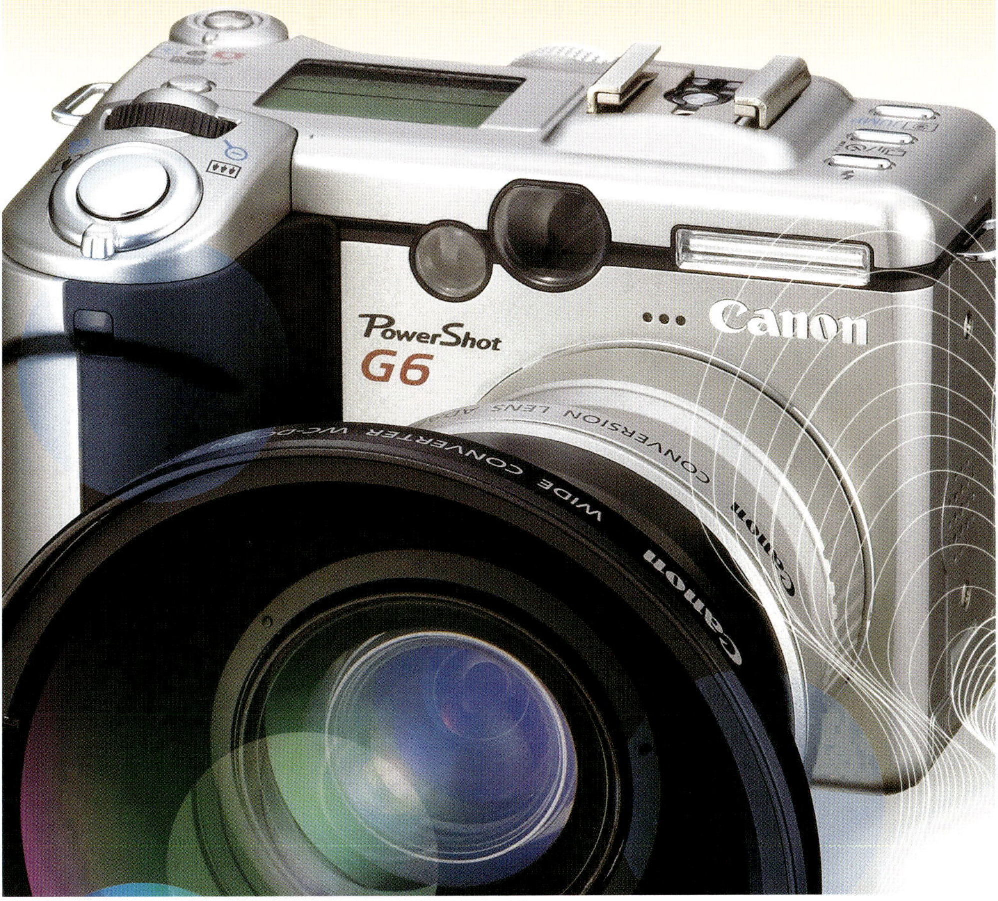

LARK BOOKS
A Division of Sterling Publishing Co., Inc.
New York

Book Design: Sandy Knight
Book Layout: Meredith Netzel
Editorial Assistance: Haley Pritchard

Library of Congress Cataloging-in-Publication Data

Sheppard, Rob.
PCPhoto digital zoom camera handbook / Rob Sheppard.
p. cm.
Includes index.
ISBN 1-57990-653-2 (pbk.)
1. Digital cameras--Handbooks, manuals, etc. 2. Zoom lens photography--Handbooks, manuals, etc. 3. Photography--Digital techniques--Handbooks, manuals, etc. I. PCphoto. II. Title.
TR256.S54 2005
775--dc22

2004019275

10 9 8 7 6 5 4 3

Published by Lark Books, A Division of
Sterling Publishing Co., Inc.
387 Park Avenue South, New York, N.Y. 10016

Distributed in Canada by Sterling Publishing,
c/o Canadian Manda Group, 165 Dufferin Street, Toronto, Ontario, Canada M6K 3H6

Distributed in the United Kingdom by GMC Distribution Services,
Castle Place, 166 High Street, Lewes, East Sussex, England BN7 1XU

Distributed in Australia by Capricorn Link (Australia) Pty Ltd., P.O. Box 704, Windsor, NSW 2756 Australia

If you have questions or comments about this book, please contact:
Lark Books, 67 Broadway, Asheville, NC 28801, (828) 253-0467, www.larkbooks.com

Manufactured in China

ISBN 13: 978-1-57990-653-5
ISBN 10: 1-57990-653-2

For information about custom editions, special sales, premium and corporate purchases, please contact Sterling Special Sales Department at 800-805-5489 or specialsales@sterlingpub.com.

contents

Introduction 6

- Chapter 1: The New Photography 9
  - Benefits of a Digital Camera 10
    - Low-Cost Pictures 10
    - Instant Feedback 11
    - Connecting with the Subject 12
    - More Freedom to Shoot 12
    - Quick-Change ISO Settings 13
    - Neutral Colors Remain Neutral 14
    - Adding Excitement 14
  - Digital Cameras Make Better Photographers 16
    - Instant Picture Review 16
    - Free Proofs 17
    - A Learning Tool 18
    - No Wasted Film 18
  - Digital Is Different 20
    - Sensor vs. Film 21
    - Sensor Size Affects Focal Length 22
    - No Film to Carry 23
    - White Balance Control 24
    - Flexible ISOs 25
  - Take Some Pictures! 26
  - The Quick Guide to Buying a Digital Camera 28

- Chapter 2: Digital Camera Features and Functions 30
  - Types of Digital Cameras 31
    - Totally Automatic Point-and-Shoot Cameras 31
    - Point-and-Shoot Cameras with Basic Controls 32
    - Compact Cameras with Flexible Controls 32
    - Advanced Compact Cameras 33
    - Megapixels and More 33
  - Compact Lenses for Compact Cameras 34
    - f/stop Limitations 36
    - The Sensor 37
    - Camera Speed 38
    - Autofocus 41
    - Metering 42
    - ISO Settings 43
    - Noise Problems 44
    - Noise Reduction Software 47
    - Camera Parameters 48
  - Maximize What You Have 49

- Chapter 3: Resolution and File Formats 50
  - Resolution 50
    - Understanding Resolution 51
    - Setting the Camera 53
  - File Formats 53
    - The Advantages of JPEG 54
    - Special Features of RAW 55
    - Choosing a Format 56
  - Moving Pictures 58

- Chapter 4: Get the Most from Your Digital Camera 60
  - The LCD Monitor 60
    - LCDs That Move 62
    - Edit as You Go 63
    - Advantages of In-Camera Editing 64
  - Exposure 65
    - Check Your LCD 65
    - Film vs. Digital Exposure 66
    - Understanding Metering 67
  - Exposure Modes 68
    - Program Mode (P) 68
    - Shutter-Priority Mode (S or Tv) 69
    - Aperture-Priority Mode (A or Av) 69
    - Full Auto and Picture Control Modes 70
    - Manual Exposure Mode 72
    - Why Use Manual Exposure? 72
    - Automatic Exposure Bracketing (AEB) 74
    - Exposure Compensation 74
    - Exposure Lock 75
    - Beyond "Good" Exposure 75
  - Using the LCD and the Histogram 76
    - How to Interpret the Histogram 77
  - Long Digital Exposures 78
  - Combining Exposures 79
    - How to Combine Two Exposures in One Photo 79

- Chapter 5: White Balance 82
  - The Color of Light 83
  - What is White Balance? 84
    - How the Camera Adjusts White Balance 84
    - Automatic White Balance 86
    - Getting the Most from the Presets 87
    - Custom or Manual White Balance 88
    - RAW Files and White Balance .90
  - About Metadata 90
    - How to Use the Metadata 91
    - Computer Access to Metadata .91

- Chapter 6: Memory Cards and Workflow 92
  - Types of Memory Cards 92
    - Memory Card Speed 94
    - Memory Card Capacity 95
  - Downloading Images from Memory Cards 97
    - Downloading From the Camera 97
    - Card Readers 98
    - Taking Your Card to a Lab 99
  - Clearing the Card 100
    - Erasing the Card 100

Reformatting the Card 100
Field Storage 101
Downloading to Your Laptop 101
Downloading to a Handheld Storage Device 101
Stand-Alone CD Burners 102
Protecting Your Images 102
CDs 102
DVDs 103
Simplified Digital Workflow 104

Chapter 7: Accessories and Flash 106
Lenses 106
Lens Speed 107
Beyond the Zoom 108
Wide-Angle Focal Lengths 110
Telephoto Focal Lengths 112
Getting in Close 114
Close-Up Mode 114
Accessory Macro Lenses 115
Modern Technology and Digital Camera Lenses 116
Special Glass 116
Aspherical Lenses 116
Image Stabilization 117
Lens Savvy 117
Angle of View 117
Perspective 118
Experiment with Your Focal Lengths 120
Depth of Field 121
Maximizing Image Sharpness 122
Proper Handholding Technique 123
Camera Supports 124
Tripods 125
Flash Made Easy 126
Basic Flash Exposure 126
Red-Eye Reduction Flash Settings 128
Easy Flash Options 128
Off-Camera Flash 129
Bounce Flash 130
Mixing Flash and Natural Light 131
Fill Flash 131
Slow Sync 133

Chapter 8: Picture Taking in the Field 134
Filters 134
Protective Filters 135
Polarizing Filters 136
Graduated Neutral Density Filters 137
Neutral Density Filters 139
Image Control with Depth of Field 140
f/stop 140
Distance 142
Batteries 143
Battery Types 143
Charging Batteries 144
Backup Batteries 145
Traveling with a Digital Camera 145

Glossary 147
Index 158

introduction

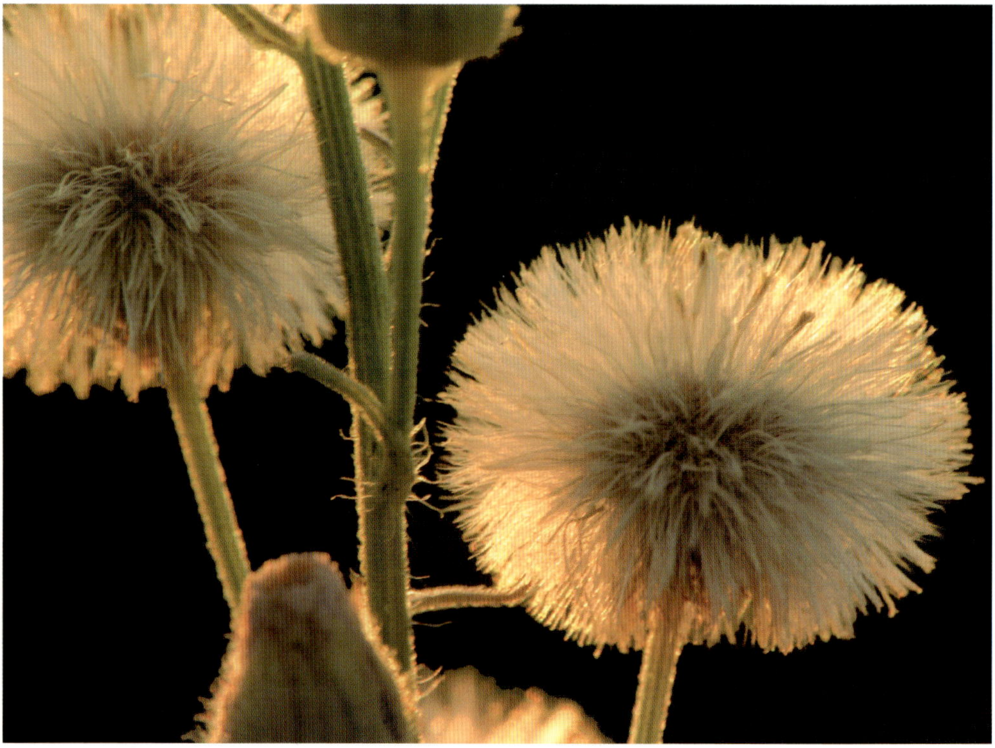

This book is about a remarkable group of digital cameras that do an amazing job. For lack of another name they are generally called digital zoom cameras. This is the second book in the PCPhoto Handbook series. The first book is the *PCPhoto Digital SLR Handbook*. While there are many similarities between these two books—a lot of information about digital photography is the same—there are also many differences. There are some significant differences between a digital zoom camera and a digital SLR.

There is no official designation for these highly capable units. Most of the cameras we will discuss in this book offer full control over exposure and focus, just like digital SLRs. They include a wide-range of focal length possibilities, even though they do not have interchangeable lenses. And all this comes in a compact, easy-to-carry package.

While these cameras are sometimes called "point-and-shoots," they are no more a point-and-shoot camera than a digital SLR that is set on a totally automatic mode. Others use the name "prosumer camera," meaning an above-average consumer camera that is not quite in the professional category. This is not a bad name, but not entirely accurate either. Some pros do use these cameras.

Until recently, a lot of serious photographers overlooked the digital zoom category, claiming to be waiting for the ideal digital SLR. They did not believe anything but a digital SLR would allow them to get the picture quality they were used to with their film cameras. And in a way, they might have been right. That's because these little cameras offer the possibility of getting pictures better than what you can get from an SLR design.

"How can that be?" you might ask. These little cameras aren't digital SLRs. Plus, they seem too inexpensive compared to the digital SLRs. Yet, I have been shooting with compact digital zoom cameras for several years, and I think they offer some fantastic opportunities for every photographer.

This came home to me in a photo workshop I was doing not too long ago. Some of the attendees had the new digital SLRs and several others were shooting with digital zoom cameras. The digital SLRs gave great results, no question about that. However, I actually saw more excitement and new enthusiasm about photography from people shooting with the digital zoom cameras. For example, one wonderful older gentlemen in the group had been photographing for over 50 years. He took a digital zoom camera—a Nikon Coolpix—into a field of flowers and came out beaming with a huge smile on his face.

Why do these cameras offer so much to photographers? First is the instantaneous response you get, the digital instant picture. You see a subject in two dimensions, just like a photograph, on the camera's LCD. And unlike the digital SLR, you actually see what the sensor is seeing before the picture is taken. This is fantastic because you are essentially working with a miniature photo and not just using the viewfinder to frame the subject. Plus you can review that photograph as soon as you take it and see if it is something you really like.

Also, compact digital cameras are fairly small, which makes them a pleasure to carry. It is also easy to get them into tight spaces. This makes a lot of shooting more spontaneous and lively. I once took a

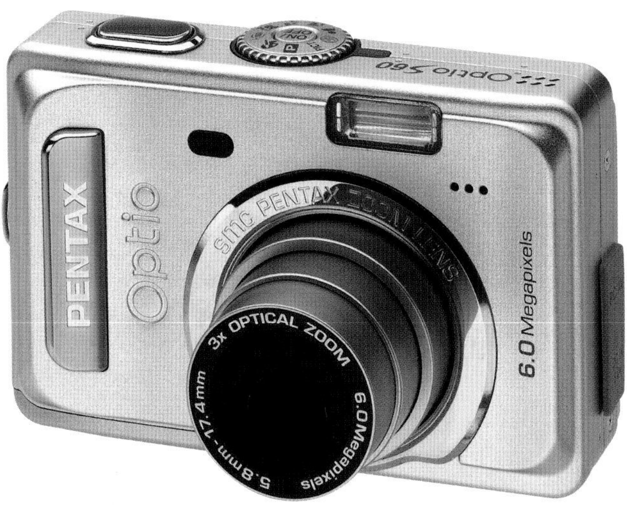

Compact digital zoom cameras—don't let their small size fool you. Many are packed with professional-level features.

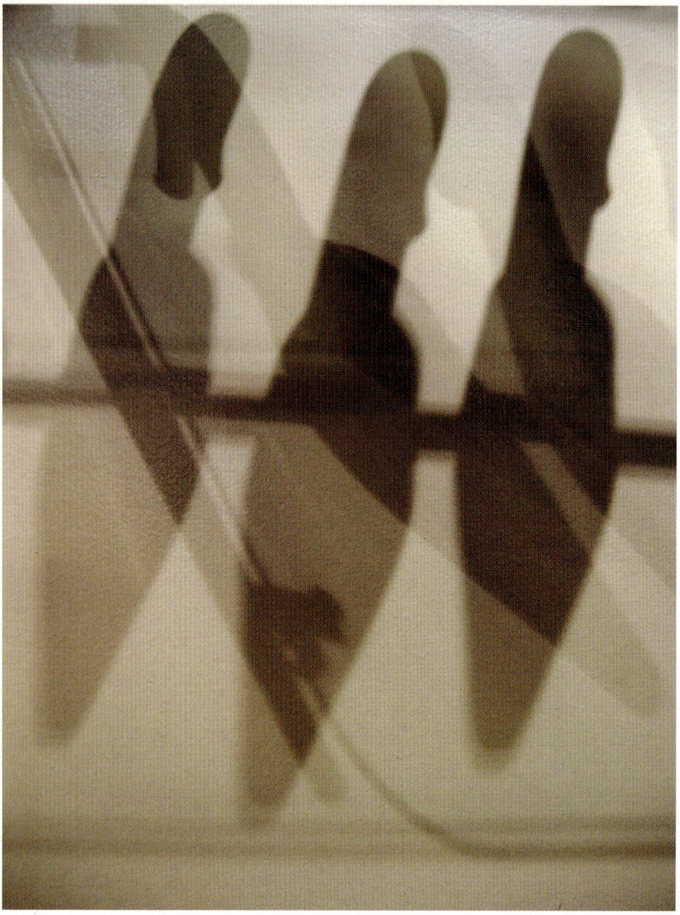

One advantage that compact digital cameras have over digital SLRs is that they are lighter and easier to carry. You can't take photos if you don't have your camera with you.

photo through a small arch in Nevada that required me to climb up some rocks. I could not get all the way up to the arch, making the use of a digital SLR impossible. But since I could see the picture on the camera's LCD, I just held the camera up as high as I could and took the photo.

Another creative benefit is the rotating or tilting LCDs found on some of these cameras. These allow you to put the camera into a space where you could not fit a large camera with your head peering through the viewfinder. For example, you can get wonderful photographs of flowers against the sky by putting the camera on the ground and tilting the LCD screen so you can see the image. Low-angle shots with a wide-angle lens offer some spectacular results. With these cameras you don't have to lie on the ground and contort your head and body to see through the viewfinder.

With a digital zoom camera, a few accessory lenses, and a couple of memory cards, you can travel very lightly and not be shortchanged in what you can do photographically. Such a package is not only more comfortable to transport but it can also increase your creativity and your fun with photography.

the new photography

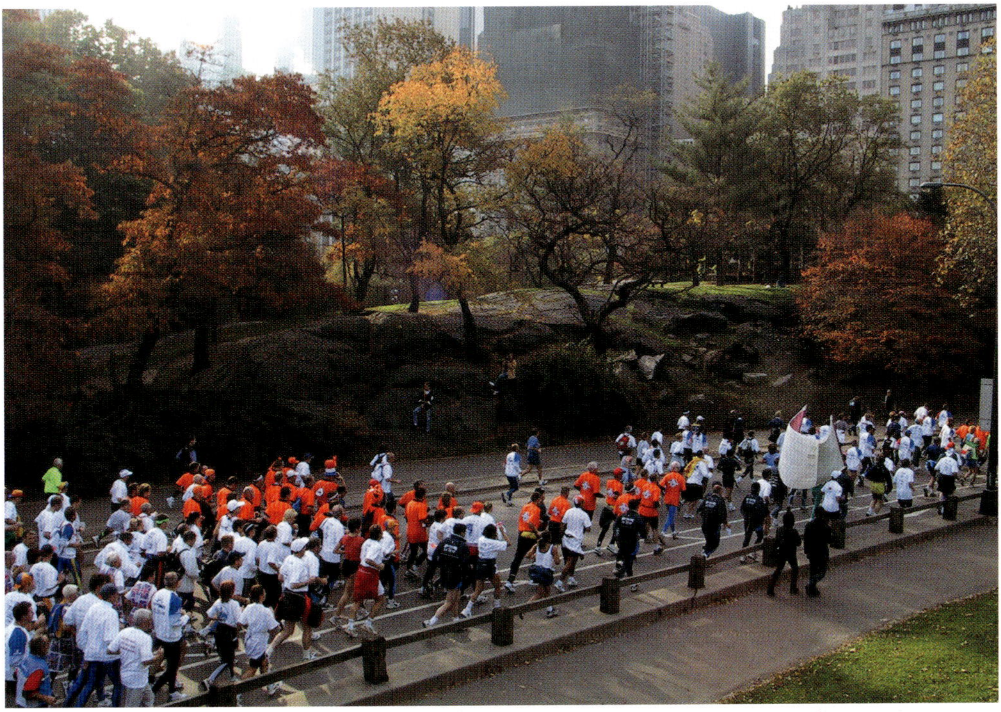

Photography can be a great deal of fun with a digital camera because you can take photos at any time in any conditions, without the worry or expense of buying and processing film.

Digital cameras have been around long enough that, today, they are neither a novelty, nor something alien to photographers. The first digital cameras were too often both. Some early digital cameras didn't even look like cameras. The designers of early cameras came from computer backgrounds and ignored the very important history of photographic technology. Initially, they did not take traditional camera design into account.

Today's digital cameras look and act more like traditional cameras. Yet, digital cameras are not the same as film cameras. There are a number of very important differences, including the addition of some new capabilities that truly enhance our picture-taking experience. This chapter examines the differences and similarities of film and digital cameras. It also offers you a quick overview of choosing and working with a digital camera.

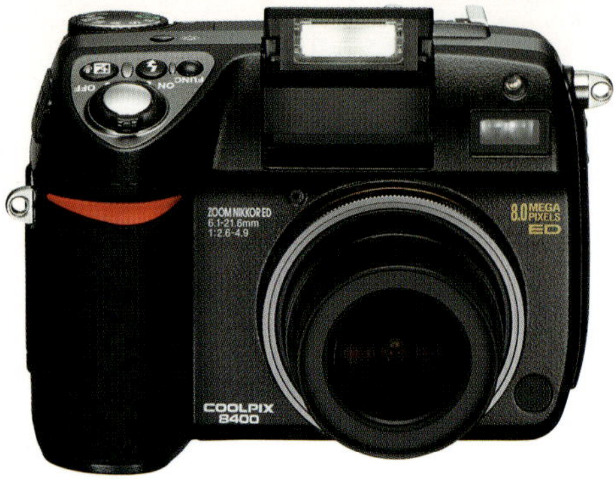

The Digital Advantage

- Low-cost pictures
- Instant feedback
- Connecting with the subject
- More freedom to shoot
- Quick-change ISO settings
- Neutral colors remain neutral
- Adding excitement

Benefits of a Digital Camera

The history of the digital camera is pretty amazing. While early models were available in the late 1980s, they were not cheap, nor did they offer image quality even close to that of film. Because of this, some photography experts predicted that these cameras wouldn't produce photo-quality images for a very long time, if ever. The real start of the digital camera revolution began in the mid-1990s, though even then, the cameras that an average photographer could afford had impractical designs, poor resolution, slow download times, and so forth. These cameras were produced for techno-gadget fanatics rather than for photographers.

Today digital cameras have transformed the marketplace. Film camera sales are on a steady decline while sales of digital cameras are exploding. People who say they will never shoot digital are becoming a very small minority.

There is good reason for this. Digital cameras offer some really terrific advantages over film. It used to be that film had a slight advantage in offering the chance to make larger prints, but this is not true today. Even a simple 3-megapixel camera can match the quality of 35mm film for prints as large as 8 x 10 inches. However, there are a few advantages to film cameras. For example, you can take very long exposures (such as those needed for star trails) without being limited by batteries. (There are even totally mechanical film cameras still available.) Even so, these advantages pale in comparison to the great benefits that digital cameras offer.

Low-Cost Pictures

When digital cameras first came out, shooting with them was expensive. The cameras were very costly and memory cards were high priced with low storage capacity. This has changed. Now, digital cameras are affordable, comparably priced to film cameras of similar capabilities, and memory cards are inexpensive, especially when you consider that you can reuse the cards again and again. Processing digital pictures is also less costly. Instead of developing and printing an entire roll of film, you can review your digital photos on the camera's LCD monitor, or a computer, and print out only the best ones.

This is a wonderful thing because you can't waste film! If you think a photo might be

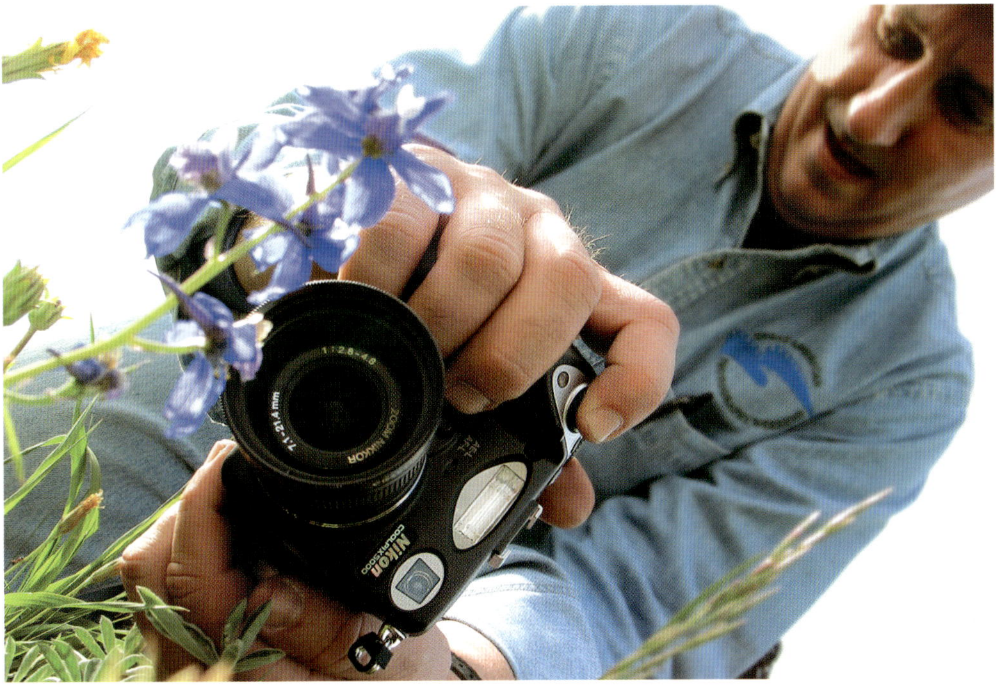

Since digital photos cost nothing to take, you are free to experiment and take photos you might not have even considered before.

interesting, take it. If you wonder what a certain setting on the camera will do, try it. You can't lose! I was working in the garden a few days ago and saw my cat sitting in the window, basking in the late afternoon sun. The light against the screen with the cat lit from behind wasn't some stunning photo sure to make the cover of *National Geographic* magazine, but it was fun and quite appealing. I took a break, went inside for my camera (knowing my lazy cat would not move) and took a whole series of photos. I did it because I could. If I liked the photos, great. If I didn't like them, I could delete them without worries. I experimented and learned from the experience in ways that would not have been possible with a film camera.

Instant Feedback

I love this feature of a digital camera. The LCD monitor is a tremendous resource. Once you discover how much it helps your photography, it is difficult to go back to shooting without it. It is true that Polaroid film does give feedback, but it is not something most photographers deal with, plus the Polaroid shot is rarely the final, high-quality image.

The non-SLR, advanced compact digital camera has a live LCD monitor. This allows you to see exactly what the lens sees. It is true that you can see through the lens with an SLR, but the live LCD gives a very different experience. You are now seeing an actual photo. You are not looking through a lens, at all, but at an image created by the lens. This really does affect how you look at the subject and can help you to compose photographs rather than simply sighting on a subject.

In addition, you can review photos after they are shot. This lets you check everything from composition, to exposure, to white balance, to use of flash. You quickly see if you got the photo you expected or if you need to make adjustments. You can identify and correct problems with your photos while you still have a chance to make corrections. This kind of feedback is impossible with film.

Connecting with the Subject

This may seem like an odd statement: a digital camera makes the experience of photography more natural and responsive. How can something more technical and automated offer something more natural?

The answer lies with the instant feedback of the LCD. Now you can take a picture of a subject, then connect the subject, the photograph, and your own feelings about the image all at once, all while you are still with the subject. This lets you respond to the subject while you are still taking pictures, and it's always exciting to see your results immediately. When using film, taking a picture and later viewing the final photograph can be unrelated experiences, often separated by days or even months. By the time you get your prints from the photofinisher, it is too late to correct a poor exposure or have your subject take a step to the left.

Digital photography gives you the chance to see exactly what your subject looks like in a photograph while still in the subject's presence! Translating the real world into a photograph can be tricky—things don't always respond well to the confines of a picture. This gives you the chance to see that and deal with the subject better while you still can. It also gives you an incredible connection with your subject.

More Freedom to Shoot

Many people are rediscovering photography with digital cameras. They are finding that digital cameras do not have the limitations associated with film. Using film can be restrictive. You have to choose the right film speed for indoor vs. outdoor photography. Plus, film colors are strongly affected by different kinds of light. Often, photographers just won't take the shot because the conditions aren't right. "I have the wrong film in the camera." "The photo just won't come out in this light." These common complaints are all too true. With film, you have to restrict your photography to conditions that you are sure about, or accept that you'll get lousy results in those marginal situations.

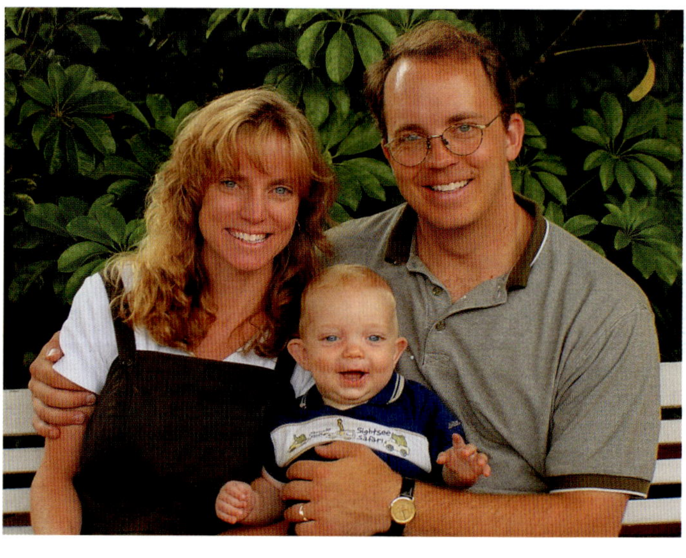

Group photos are a little tricky, especially with a baby. You have to make sure everyone is smiling and watch out for multiple sets of eyes to blink. With a digital camera you can evaluate each shot, instead of shooting a whole roll of film and hoping one picture looks good.

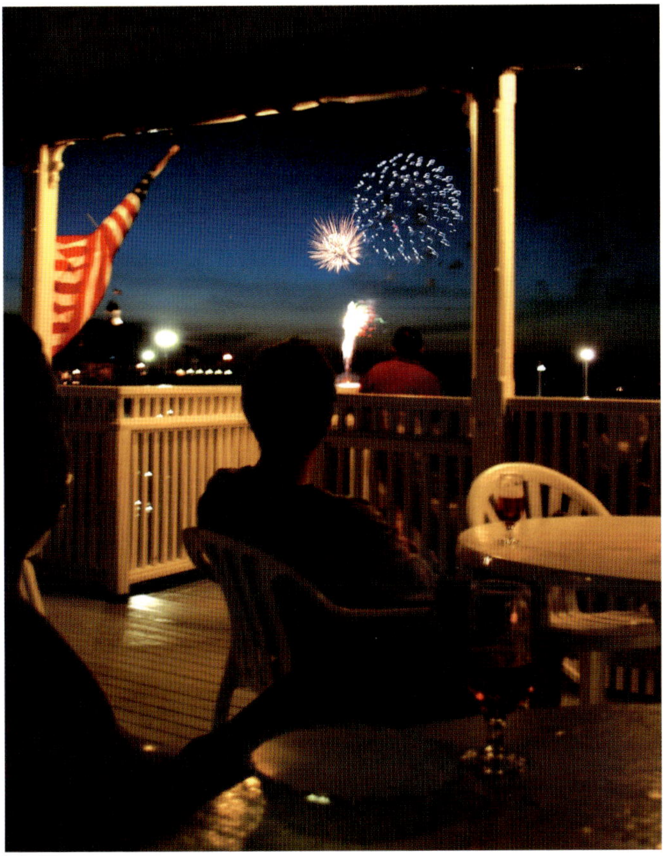

Consider all these advantages and the combination spells freedom. You are now free to shoot whatever you want, whenever you want, without restrictions of cost, color balance, film speed, and more. (© Mimi Netzel)

Digital photography changes all this. From the ability to change ISO, to the chance to adjust white balance, you have greater control over your results in a wide variety of conditions. You are no longer limited by film technology! You can make changes as you go, even from shot to shot if needed.

Consider all these advantages—the combination spells freedom. You are now free to shoot whatever you want, whenever you want, without the restrictions of cost, color balance, film speed, and more. One thing that I especially find beneficial is that, as you shoot, you are free to experiment. You can immediately erase anything you don't like, so no matter how wild your ideas, no one has to see them except you. Yet, you have the chance to get some new and exciting images that you would never get without such experiments.

Quick-Change ISO Settings

With a digital camera, you can instantly change its sensitivity to respond to different lighting conditions by adjusting its ISO settings. You could never do that with film without changing the actual roll of film. Now, a push of a button, a new selection in a menu, and you have the equivalent of a whole new roll of film. You can shoot outside in bright light using a low ISO setting, then step inside, switch to a higher setting, and you're ready to shoot indoors.

It is true that small digital camera sensors are more susceptible to noise at higher ISOs than digital SLRS. At this point in sensor technology, this is simply a fact of life. These photos will look grainier from the increased noise. On the other hand, you will be able to get the shot that might not

With a digital camera, you can now shoot in any light and still get great color. This would be considerably more difficult for the average photographer using film.

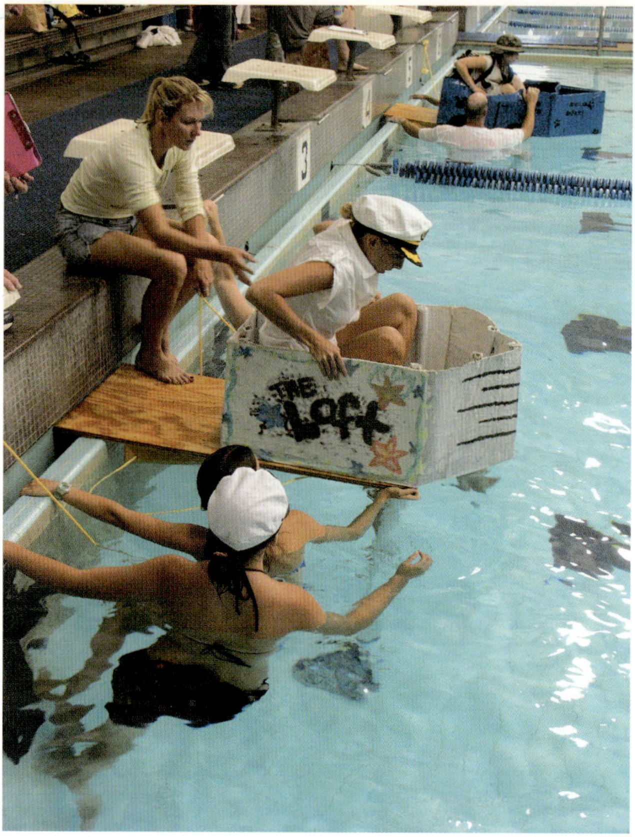

have been possible any other way. If you had used film, you might be in the middle of changing rolls when that great shot appeared, or maybe you didn't even try to change the film because it was inconvenient. The capability of instantly changing camera sensitivity is really a great benefit.

Neutral Colors Remain Neutral

One problem with traditional photography is that colors of light affect the photos differently than we actually see the light in the same conditions. Just think about all those old green photos shot under fluorescents—the scene never looked green to our eyes. We accommodate many different lights so that neutral colors stay neutral whether we see them outside under the sun or indoors with incandescent lights. Film can't do that.

With a digital camera's white balance controls, this all changes. Now it is possible to make neutral colors stay neutral under almost all lighting conditions, or precisely control what colors look like for creative effects. White balance is actually not a new control—it has long been a part of video recording. But, its application to digital photography has been a huge benefit to getting better color in photographs.

Adding Excitement

I started working with digital cameras when they were still just odd toys to most photographers. I thought they were exciting in many ways, but the traditional forms of photography still held most photographers' interest, including mine. And, to be honest, the traditional forms didn't offer anything new. Many photographers no

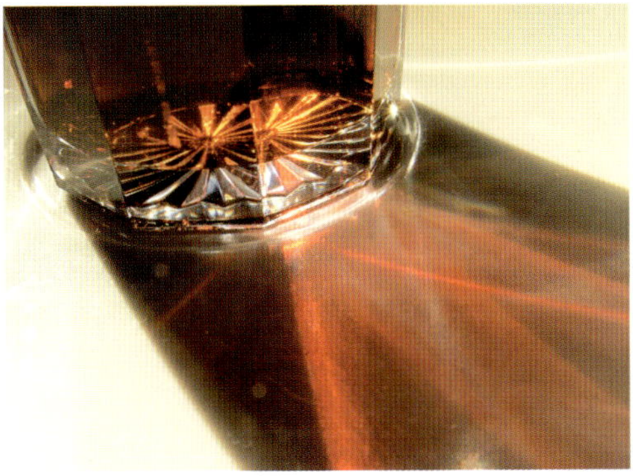

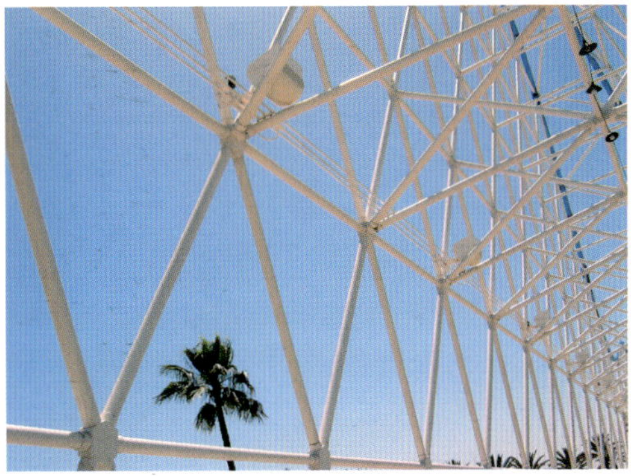

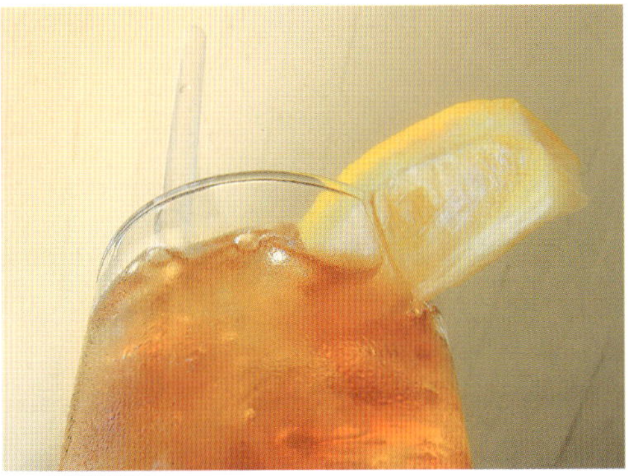

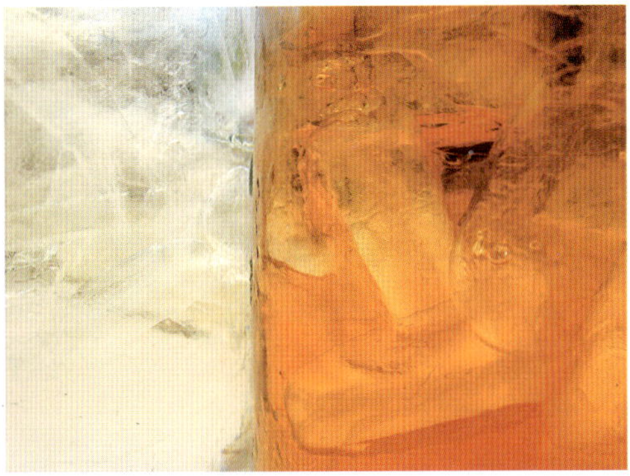

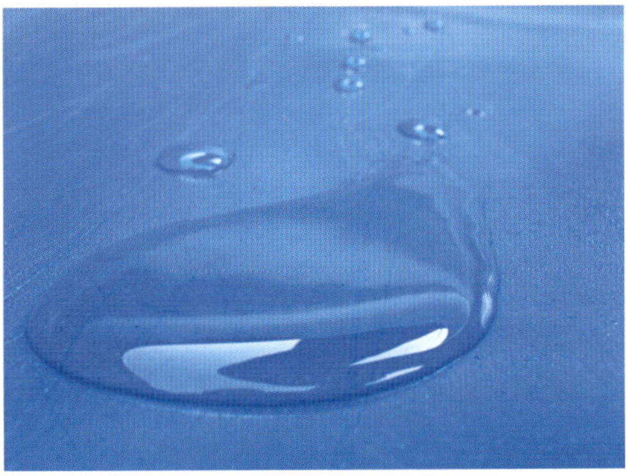

Freedom to try new things and take whatever photos you want is the hallmark of digital photography. Even the most basic camera will let you shoot indoors and out, from close-up to distant subjects.

longer explored photography because they were bored with the same old photos.

This new technology has changed people's attitudes quite dramatically. Today, digital cameras are exciting and extremely user-friendly, with some totally new ways of dealing with images. I have even had photographers stop me just to tell me that their interest in photography has been revitalized because they started shooting with a digital camera. The new technology has banished their boredom with photography, and they consistently tell me how much digital imaging has reinvigorated their desire to take pictures.

The reasons are pretty simple: lower costs, more freedom, instant feedback, better and more consistent results, and the ability to interact photographically with the subject. The combination of more possibilities for success with the ability to experiment at no cost (including getting rid of the bad images instantly) adds an air of excitement and fun to photography!

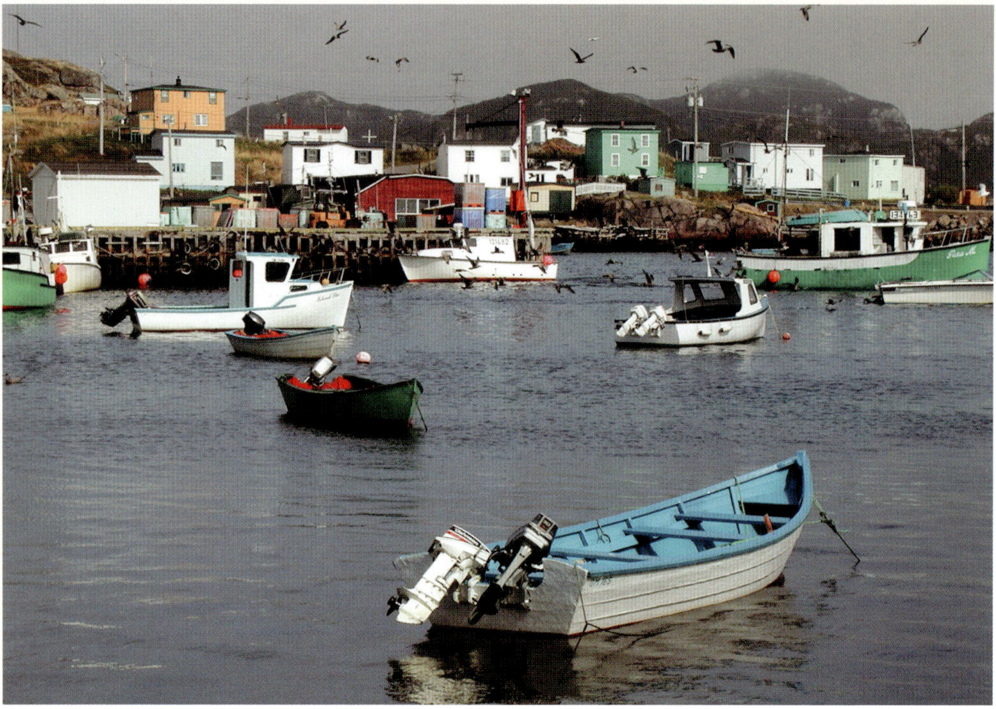

A digital camera has great potential for helping you become a better photographer.

Digital Cameras Make Better Photographers

A long time ago, I had a girlfriend whose grandparents showed long and boring slide shows of their vacations. The grandfather was always in search of a new camera that would give him better photos, as if he had little to do with it. Most serious photographers laugh at the idea that a new camera will automatically improve their photographs. After all, the photographer has control over the image, starting with picking the right subject, appropriate light, and creating a nice composition.

Yet, digital cameras have changed this idea in an interesting way. The photographer is still important, because photography was, is, and always will be a craft. While buying a new digital camera won't instantly turn anyone into a pro, the potential for making better images is great. This is no hype. Everyone I know who starts shooting with a digital camera discovers how their photos can get better through two unique features: the LCD monitor with its instant picture review, and the memory card, which eliminates the cost and limitations of film.

Instant Picture Review

We talked above about the instant feedback benefit of the LCD. Let's examine that a bit more, and how it might help a photographer improve his or her images. Every advanced digital camera has an LCD monitor, the instant giveaway that it is a digital camera. Watch people with these cameras and see how they hold them—not to the eye, but below the eye. They use the LCD as a "viewfinder." However, this is really a minor use in terms of what the LCD monitor offers the digital photographer. I am emphasizing it again and again because it is such a tremendous tool.

For a while, manufacturers of compact and point-and-shoot digital cameras were in competition to make the smallest digital cameras possible. To do this, they had to make the LCD monitor smaller and smaller. At one point, a company made a camera with an LCD monitor less than one-inch across diagonally! A marvel of miniaturization, to be sure, but essentially decoration for the camera, not something that could be really useful.

Manufacturers have begun to understand how important the LCD is for photographers, so they have started to make them larger. Size is important because the LCD is used to evaluate pictures. Later, I'll offer some tips on how you can make the most of your LCD monitor in all conditions. The latest cameras offer LCD's that are considerably brighter than they were a couple of years ago, but they can still be a challenge to use in bright sunlight.

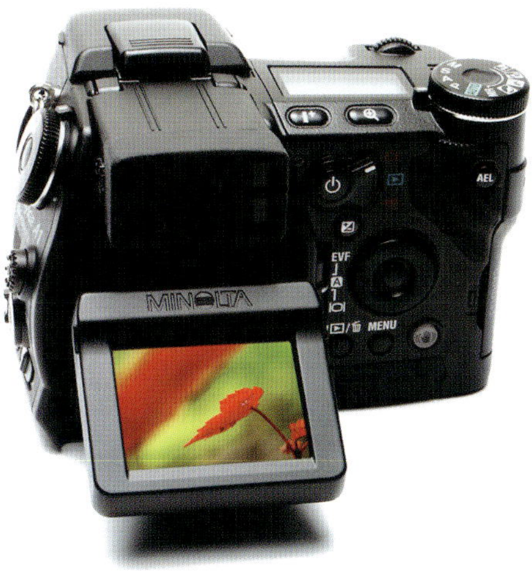

For both shooting and reviewing images, a large LCD monitor offers great benefits for the photographer.

The key is being able to see a photograph immediately after it is captured. This offers so many benefits, but the best is that you no longer have to guess or hope that you got the shot. Results can be viewed on the LCD. Any photographer, from beginner to pro, can benefit from seeing the photo immediately after taking the picture.

Free Proofs

When you go to a wedding or portrait photographer, they offer you proofs of the images they shot. This lets you evaluate the pictures so you know which ones you really want to purchase for posterity. The LCD lets you look at "proofs" of your images to see which ones you want to keep or what you need to do to make the photos better.

I know you have had this experience, because every photographer has: you take a lot of photos on a trip or at a party. Then, you take them to the processor, hoping for the best, but having no way of knowing if you really got the shots you wanted. You pick up the photos, full of hope, and find that some look great, but many are disappointing. Exposure might be off, your subject blinked, or maybe there is a tree seeming to grow from your subject's head that you didn't notice while taking the picture.

Sure, we all try our best, and depending on our level of expertise and experience, we have different proportions of acceptable photos. Regardless, we still find there are images that could have been shot better. The instant proofing that your digital camera offers changes this whole dynamic. You now know what you got and have the chance to change your shot while you are still at the location or with the subject.

This is not just an amateur's concern, either. Pros often shoot lots of film—varying exposure and composition—to ensure they capture exactly the image they need.

Advertising photographers typically shoot Polaroids before shooting film to check the lighting, exposure, and composition. Of course, a Polaroid cannot provide total peace of mind because it is only a test and not the real shot.

Thankfully, the digital camera changes all of this. Now, a quick look at the LCD monitor and you know immediately if your subject's eyes are open or closed. Are the eyes closed? Just take the picture again. You can check to see that no one is cropped out of the group portrait. You can see if you pressed the shutter release at the perfect instant, if the flash fired, and so on. This is a wonderful feature to use, whether you are photographing your child's soccer game, or a head of state.

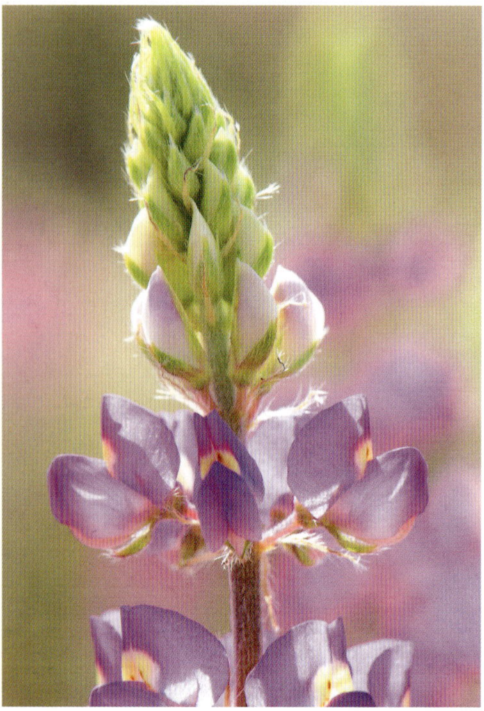

A quick look at your LCD will tell you if you got the shot—is the framing right, is the depth of field okay, is the exposure correct?

If you like to travel, consider what an asset this can be. You may only be in Venice a single day or maybe you are seeing a spectacular, one-of-a-kind storm over the Grand Canyon. Either way, you know you will not be back later to take another photograph. Being able to shoot and quickly review a "proof" of that shot on your LCD monitor is a tremendous benefit. You will be able to make corrections, adjust the exposure, or just take another shot from a different angle while you are there.

A Learning Tool

I really believe the LCD monitor on a digital camera is one of the best learning tools for becoming a better photographer that you could find anywhere. A beginning photographer can instantly see the results of changing the f/stop or shutter speed. The experienced photographer can try out blurs with slow shutter speeds and learn exactly what shutter speed will work for a particular subject and motion. The camera will show the exposure settings, so there is no guessing. Or maybe you've always wanted to experiment more with flash, but the results were so unpredictable that you gave it up. Now you can test all the possibilities, change everything from the angle of the flash, to the intensity, to the type of flash sync, and instantly view the results.

No Wasted Film

Years ago when I was learning the craft of photography, I started photographing everyone and everything. My parents wondered why I was "wasting so much film." When I photographed my lovely grandmother, she'd tell me to save my film for a better subject. Film was in finite supply, in a sense, limited by how many rolls I could afford. I had only a certain number of rolls of film with a specified number of photos on each roll.

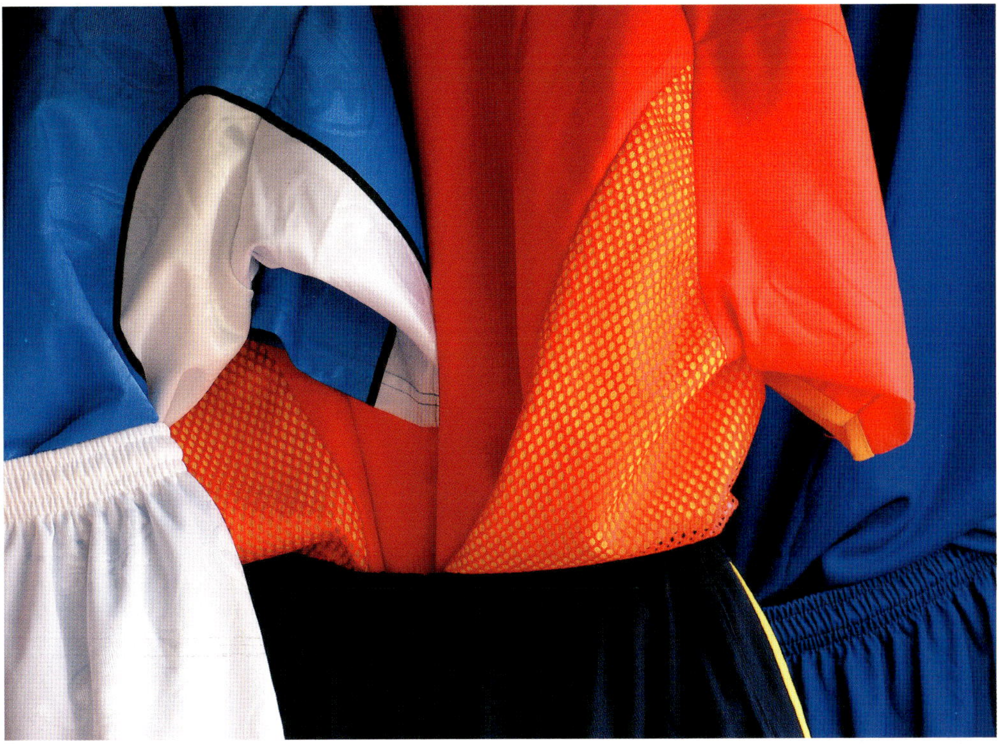

Shooting new things helps you learn and grow as a photographer.

This can result in a restrictive and dampening approach to picture taking. It is true that you become a better photographer by taking pictures, but how can you keep taking pictures when there are film limitations? Sooner or later, you restrict yourself by not taking a shot because you don't want to "waste film." In addition, it can be stressful when you realize you are running out of film just when the photographic action is at its peak. Even professionals experience this problem.

Digital imaging dramatically changes this. There is no film limitation. Larger memory cards have become very affordable, so you can take many, many pictures before filling one up. Plus, as you shoot, you can erase any images you don't really need or want to free up space on the memory card. This will allow you to take more photos from different angles, or maybe try some wild and crazy idea for a photo—you can't waste film! You can be as creative as you want without worrying about how much film you have left or how expensive it will be to process all the film you've shot. Just remember, once you have your digital camera and a memory card, there is no cost to trying new things.

Experimentation is the very essence of learning and growing as a photographer. You can try something different, see what it looks like, and then erase if it is awful. When you do, it's gone, never to be seen again by anyone. Yet, you might learn something from that awful shot that you wouldn't have had you never tried it. There is also the potential for discovering something new and exciting that might not have been discovered without the chance to freely experiment. You will even shoot fewer "I-hope-this-works" photos because you will know if the results were successful the instant you take the picture.

Digital cameras look like—and operate like—film cameras in many ways, but they provide a very different photographic experience.

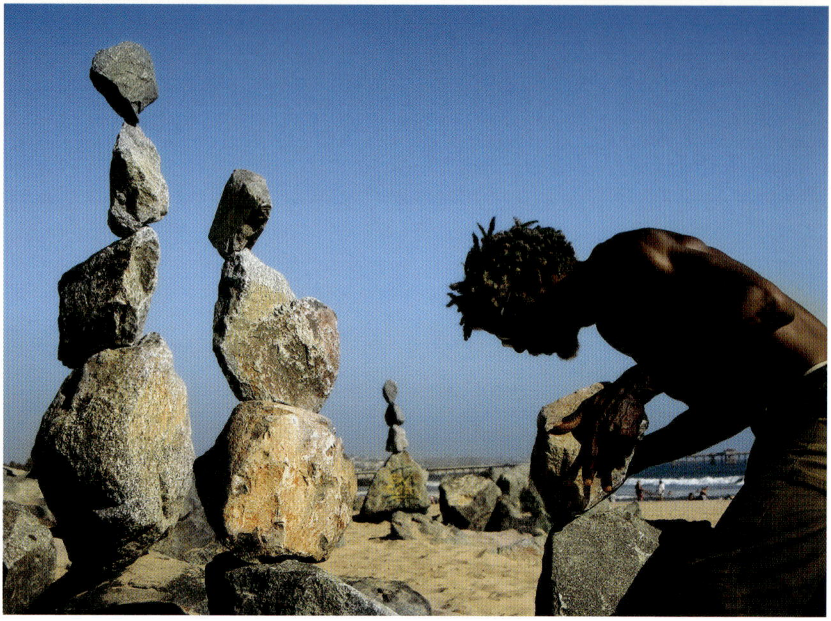

Digital Is Different

It certainly is true that photographs are still photographs, whether you shoot film or digital. In many ways, digital photography is identical to traditional film photography. Both use cameras that consist of a light-tight box with a lens to focus an image onto a light-sensitive medium. Both have ways to control the light coming in (exposure) and a viewfinder for the photographer to compose the image.

However, the experience of digital is different, as we've just discussed, and the capturing of images does change a bit with digital photography. Today, digital cameras are everywhere; they are even built into phones! But when they first caught the attention of photographers, a lot of people wondered what they might mean for photography. Would they be too different? The first digital cameras actually had designs that were much too "unusual," seeming to spring from the minds of designers who had little idea of what a camera was used for or what it needed to be.

People wondered if digital cameras meant learning something totally new. Did this technology mean that everything you knew about film was no longer true? Would digital replace film? Would something be lost if it did? Most of these fears are long gone. Digital cameras look and act like traditional cameras in many ways.

There was another barrier to digital camera acceptance that you still hear about today even though it is no longer true. Many technically minded people did the math relating to image resolution and concluded that true photographic quality required a camera with many more megapixels than anything available. It didn't help that the earliest digital cameras had terrible resolution, yet the folks marketing them hyped these cameras as having "high resolution."

As photographers began to work with digital cameras, however, they discovered that this film-biased evaluation of resolution was incorrect. There was supposedly no way a 3-megapixel camera could make an 8 x 10-inch print that matched the quality of film—but when a print was made, photographers found that a 3-MP camera could produce absolutely beautiful, true photo-quality 8 x 10-inch prints. It's true that if you put some of these pictures up close to your eye you might find some artifacts or image noise, but photographs are never meant to be viewed that way.

Size of an image, by the way, is always an important issue with digital cameras. Resolution is quite incomplete and rather meaningless without a reference to how an image will be used and the size at which it will be presented. Now we are seeing amazing 16 x 20-inch prints from 8-megapixel cameras. The ideas presented in this book can help you do that, too.

Sensor vs. Film

The light-sensitive sensor is a feature of digital cameras that film cameras don't have. It is like film in that it also reacts to light. However, a big difference is that film both senses the light and stores the image on its light-sensitive surface. With digital, the sensor "reads" the light, but the camera translates that information into digital data for storage elsewhere.

This is certainly interesting, but probably more useful for trivia contests than for picture taking. However, it is important to understand how a sensor responds to light and how it differs from film. Film "sees" detail equally when the light is in the middle of its range (where that middle is for a given scene depends on exposure). Film changes, though, in its response to the lightest and darkest parts of the image, gradually blending the middle tones into black and white, creating a very smooth tonal change.

Digital cameras tend to see light in a more linear way. This response, however, is quite variable, not because of the sensor, but because of proprietary image processing circuits that manufacturers put into their cameras. The sensor typically captures all tones throughout the exposure range, midtones may be seen the same as blacks and whites, However, there is much less of the tonal gradation seen in film's bright areas. Because of this, bright highlights in digital images often exhibit a sharp transition of tones in highlight areas. (The tonal gradation exhibited by film is missing.) An abrupt cut-off of detail in very bright areas is often a give-away that a digital camera was used.

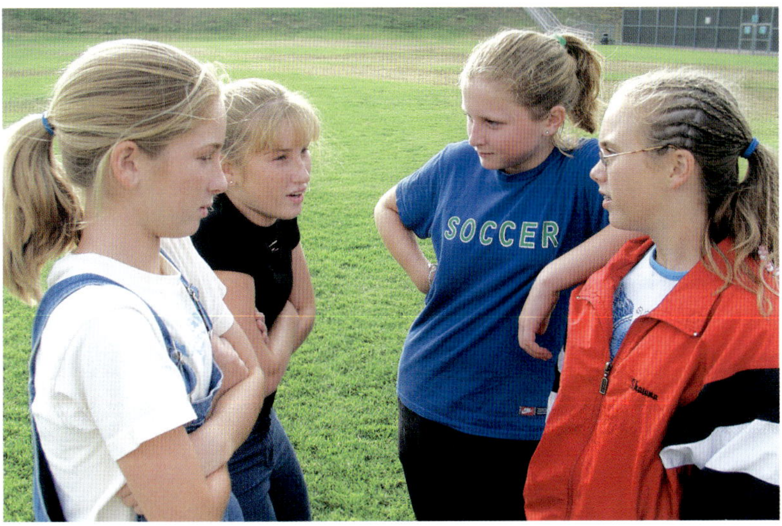

Image resolution has meaning only in relation to how an image will be used at a particular size.

This is important for photographers—we can expect overexposed highlights to lose detail quickly with digital cameras. This is similar to the way that slide film records highlights. It is interesting, however, that digital cameras frequently capture more detail in dark areas than slide film, making them react more like print film in the darker areas of the image. You will be surprised, if you are used to slide film, to see more detail in the shadows.

Note: With small digital cameras and their associated small sensors, dark areas can have more noise than the other areas of the photo.

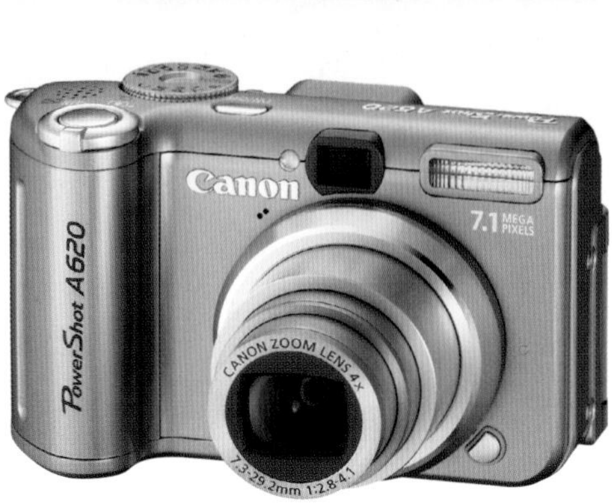

The actual focal length (7.3-29.2mm) is inscribed on the lens of this digital camera.

Sensor Size Affects Focal Length

A point-and-shoot digital camera has a very small sensor area compared to a frame of 35mm film. Typically, sensors are approximately 9 x 6.6mm (.35 x .26 inches), or 2/3-inch across diagonally. Many of the ultra compact cameras have sensors that are even smaller. This is a fraction of the size of 35mm film, which has a frame size of 36 x 24mm or 1.5 x 1 inches.

The area of coverage of a lens is independent of its focal length and is directly related to the film format or sensor size. With a 35mm SLR camera, a 50mm lens is considered a "normal" lens. It produces an image on the film that approximates a person's field of vision. When used with a small sensor, a 50mm lens becomes a telephoto lens recording only a narrow angle of view.

This means that a shorter-focal-length lens (wide-angle lens) must be used to give a normal angle of view for a digital camera. To get the 35mm film equivalent of a 28-80mm lens, for example, the camera might have a lens with an actual focal length of 7-20mm. That would be an extremely wide-angle lens for 35mm film.

This change in focal length affects three things: lens size, f/stop, and depth of field.

f/stop—Because the lenses have such short focal lengths, lens apertures get small. In addition, the reduced glass area affects what lens designers can do with f/stop availability. The result is that lenses on small digital cameras often don't stop down beyond f/8 or f/11. Lens designers limit that choice for quality reasons related to the size of the lens.

Lens size—The lenses on compact digital zoom cameras can be reduced in size because you don't need as much glass to give an image area that covers a small sensor. This affects the size of the camera as well as the lens, and has no effect on lens quality (other things being equal, such as f/stops and quality of glass used).

Depth of field—Short focal lengths typically give more depth of field. In addition, the smaller physical size of apertures will have an effect of more depth of field, too. This is a boon for those photos that need a lot of depth of field, but a real challenge if you seek a selective focus (narrow depth of field) effect.

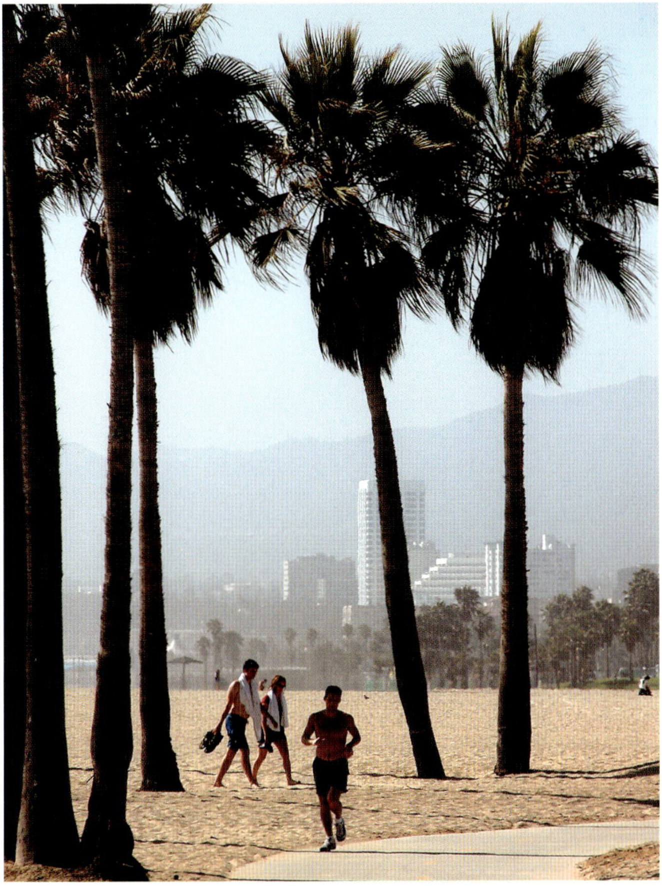

A digital camera offers great benefits for the traveler, especially since you no longer have to deal with the hassles of carrying film.

No Film to Carry

A 256 MB memory card will typically hold over a hundred high-quality JPEG images from an 8-megapixel camera and several hundred with a smaller resolution, such as 3 megapixels. That's equivalent to three to six (or more) rolls of 36-exposure film—all in a card smaller than a matchbook.

Think about how people shoot film. Most folks take many extra photos just to be certain they got the shot they wanted. Photographers will often shoot 3 or 4 extra photos of each subject, especially when using slide film. So now we are looking at 19–24 rolls of film compared to one little memory card. Think of the space all that film takes up.

Carrying enough film can really be a problem when traveling, especially with today's tight airport security. Photographers who always packed lots of film on trips now find they have extra space in their bags—sometimes a lot of space. They can take smaller bags with them, which are easier to put in the overhead compartment of a commercial jet. In addition, they have fewer security problems. Photographers could not keep film in checked baggage because of threats of damage from the scanners. While carry-on security doesn't have the same effect on film, multiple scans may result in fogging, especially with high-speed films In other countries, the effect can be worse. Film and security can be an annoyance or a disaster.

With digital cameras, this all changes dramatically, making travel and photography mix just like they should. Each small memory card has the same image capacity as many rolls of film, takes up very little space and is easily tucked into your carry-on bag. Gate security machines have no affect on memory cards. The cards are small and cause no security problems, so keep them with you to ensure your photos are not lost in transit.

White Balance Control

White balance is probably the biggest departure from film of anything digital. It represents a totally different way of dealing with the color of light and the benefits of this feature are great. We'll examine how to best use white balance later in the book. In this chapter, we're going to look at how white balance changes the photo experience compared to film. It really does, and this is very important to understand.

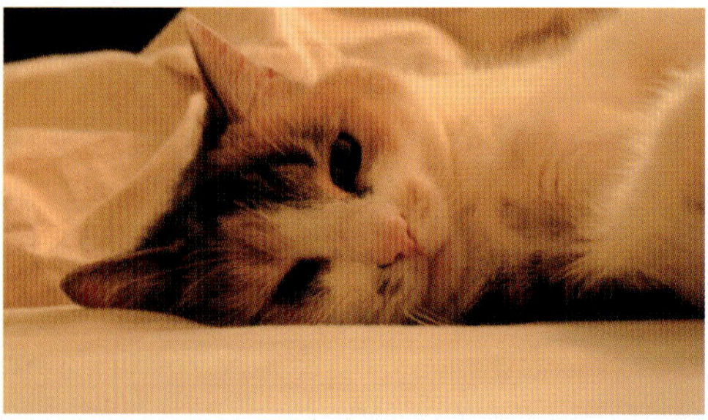

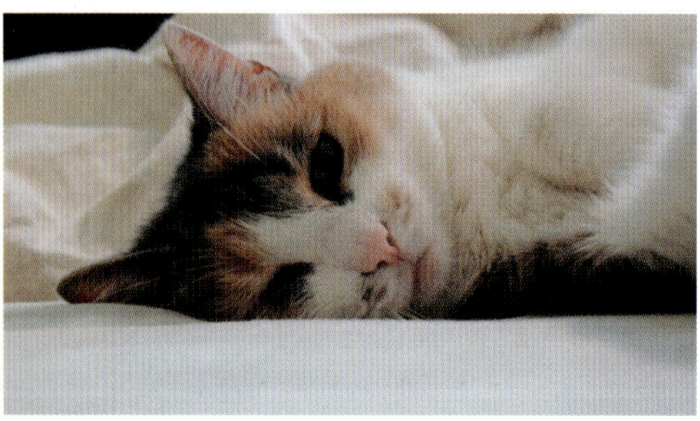

Set white balance to match the lighting conditions. If you use the Daylight setting when shooting indoors, you'll get a photo with a warm cast. Use the white balance setting for incandescent light to prevent this. (© Mimi Netzel)

First, though, you need to know that different types of light have inherently different colors. Our eyes and brain interpret these changes and compensate for the way we see colors whether the light is fluorescent, incandescent or daylight. On film, these conditions apear as extremely different colors of light. If you've ever shot film under fluorescents, the results were probably photos with an overall green cast.

Film can only be balanced for a single type of light, and any other light will give the scene a color cast. Use a daylight-balanced film indoors, for example, and it looks like you dipped the resulting picture in orange soda. Pros who shoot in business or industrial situations always carry an extensive set of color correction filters to deal with the varying lighting conditions. Print film handles different types of lighting better, but often requires major color corrections in the printing.

A digital camera adjusts its sensitivity to the color of light so that the camera responds more like our eyes. White balance refers to the way videographers would use a white card to actually balance their cameras to the color of light. The purpose of white balance is to make neutral colors neutral and the rest of the colors more natural. The camera isn't quite as tolerant as our eyes, so slight variations in a scene's light can affect it even with white balance tricks. Still, it does work quite well.

White balance is a common feature on all digital cameras. The digital camera today can examine a scene, automatically check the light for "proper" white balance, and select a setting for those conditions. More importantly, white balance presets can be chosen to match specific light conditions, or, in some cases, the camera can be custom balanced to match the light. In any case, no filters are needed, no light is lost due to filtration, and you can see through the lens with no darkening of the viewfinder from filters. All huge advantages!

Flexible ISOs

Film speed, measured with an ISO number, tells you how sensitive a film is to light. This is predetermined by the manufacturing of the emulsion, although it can be altered in special circumstances by the exposure and processing. This sensitivity rating was established by the International Organization for Standardization. It is a standard agreed to by countries throughout the world, and is used universally by manufacturers.

The important thing about ISO and film is how varied films with different ISOs relate to each other. Low numbers—50 or 100—represent less sensitivity. High numbers—400 or 800—show that a film is more light sensitive. The numbers are mathematically proportional so that, when two films are compared, doubling or halving a number represents twice, or half, the sensitivity, or speed, of the film. Once you choose a particular film, you must use the whole roll at that film's specific ISO setting.

This does not apply to digital cameras. Technically, they do not even have true ISO numbers because they do not have the same standards as film, and because their sensitivity changes based on processing circuits in the camera. They have what are called ISO equivalents, though most cameras do abbreviate this to ISO. The equivalents are pretty close to true ISOs in film, but if you use multiple digital cameras, you may discover exposures are slightly different even at the "same" ISO. This discrepancy is because manufacturers do their own bit of interpretation on the numbers since there is no central testing standard.

What actually happens with a digital camera when the ISO setting is changed is that you modify the sensitivity of the sensor's circuits. Using a higher ISO setting is like turning up the volume on the radio when a station's signal is weak. This can result in static, or in the case of a digital camera, noise. But the really great thing is that you can now change film speed at the touch of a button. You can be indoors, photographing your child's party with an electronically chosen ISO setting of 400—and you don't need to use flash! Then, you follow the kids outside to play and change to ISO 100. This is a huge benefit! Since one camera can handle multiple situations, you don't need to carry along a ton of extra film in case you need the speed of different emulsions. And you don't need to load a new roll of film or switch camera bodies.

There is one very big difference in film and digital cameras as to how ISO is set by the camera. In most automatic film cameras made in the past 20 years, ISO is set automatically when you put the film into the camera. The DX code—the silver and black checkerboard pattern on the side of the film canister—tells the camera what ISO speed to set. This means that you don't have to think about ISO once you load the film, unless you want to manually override the film speed.

Digital cameras don't work like that at all. You never use film or anything else that has a specific sensitivity to light. With a digital camera, you may have to choose the ISO. (Some automatic picture control modes on certain digital cameras will automatically set the ISO.) For standard auto and manual exposure settings on digital cameras, you must deliberately choose and adjust ISO settings.

Since a digital camera and its sensor do not have a true ISO that matches film, manufacturers have developed ways to make the sensor respond similarly to a film's sensitivity. Practically speaking, if you set a digital camera to ISO 400, it will respond to light in a way that is very close to that of ISO 400 film in a traditional camera.

Take Some Pictures!

As you read through this book, you will discover many ways that you can get more from your camera. To get you started or to offer a review, here are some basic elements of digital photography that will help you to get going quickly with any digital camera. Of course, there are many features and advanced controls available in digital cameras on the market today. You'll have to read your camera's manual to learn all of them. However, there are basic features common to any digital camera. If you understand them, you can quickly start taking pictures with any camera.

Remember, when shooting digital, you still need to pay attention to:

• **Light**—Without light there is no photograph, regardless of the recording medium you use.

• **Exposure**—No amount of computer manipulation can make a badly exposed image look as good as one that was shot well; blacks, whites, and mid-tones must be captured correctly, or the image will not look good.

• **Sharpness**—Good lenses and proper techniques ensure optimum sharpness. Image processing programs do have sharpening tools, but these are designed to pull existing sharpness out of a photo—they cannot make a fuzzy image appear tack sharp.

• **Depth of field**—This is affected by the point of focus, the focal length, and the f/stop, not digital technologies. It is true that depth of field is affected by the small size of the digital camera sensor, because these cameras use shorter lens focal lengths for equal image size, which result in more apparent depth of field.

• **Exposure**—Autoexposure in today's digital cameras is very good. It is true that the lower priced cameras may offer less sophisticated metering systems, but most of the advanced cameras have intelligent exposure systems that rival the best digital SLRs. For many photographers, the camera meter and its automation are all you need for most photographs, and are certainly adequate to get started using any camera. The P or Program mode is probably a good place to start. With it, you can immediately start taking photos with a high percentage of good exposures. In addition, on most advanced digital cameras, you can adjust the shutter speed and f/stop on a shot by shot basis in P mode for more control (if you need to do this for all shots, use a different mode, such as Aperture-Priority or Shutter-Priority mode).

• **Exposure compensation**—Find your camera's exposure compensation adjustment control. On older cameras, this may be buried in a menu, but on most new cameras, it will be accessible from a button. This control allows you to add or subtract exposure a little at a time until it looks right on your LCD monitor (some cameras even have a live histogram to help with exposure—more on that later). With a film camera, you had to guess if you had the best exposure. With digital, you can review your photo right after it is shot, then use the exposure compensation to make the exposure darker or brighter (– or + compensation) for your next picture.

• **White balance**—White balance is something totally new for the photographer accustomed to film. This is a digital technology that allows the camera to adjust for the color of light so that whites and other neutral colors remain neutral. This is an amazing thing for anyone used to the bad colors that could result when film was exposed under fluorescent or incandescent lights. Now, photographs taken under those conditions with a digital camera can look great.

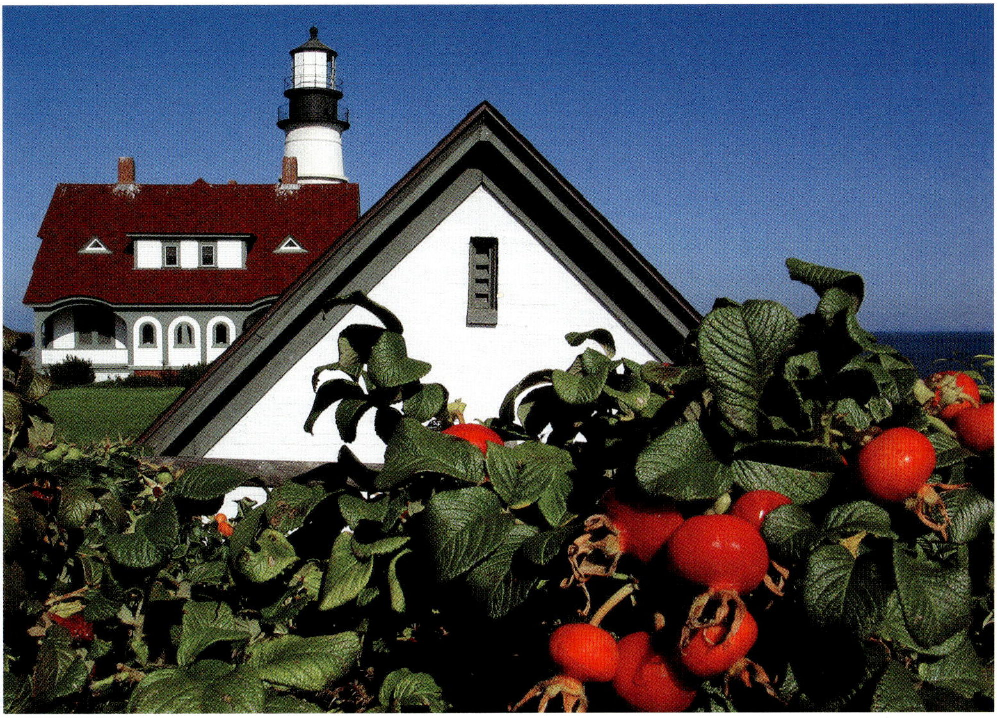

The basics are are important with digital too. Pay attention to exposure, lighting, sharpness, and depth of field.

• **ISO**—Film photographers were always limited by film-speed issues. Once a film was chosen and put into a camera, you were stuck with it. Changing films to change film speed was possible, but a major pain. Now, with your digital camera, ISO sensitivity can be adjusted anytime you want on a shot-by-shot basis. You can use a slow speed outdoors, change to a fast setting when you step inside, and then change again when you go back outside. Experiment with your camera and see how adjusting the ISO affects the rendition of the scene.

• **The LCD monitor**—The LCD monitor on a digital camera offers a huge benefit. Some photographers seem to be afraid to use it because it drains the batteries. Take my advice: the advantages are worth it! Buy some spare batteries! This is just too valuable a feature not to use. The LCD monitor lets you preview exactly what your photo will look like, plus you can get a review image on the LCD right after the exposure. Many cameras offer a quick review to instantly go back to the last image you shot. To see all of your recorded images, use the playback feature (a dial, switch or button—it depends on the camera). Use the LCD to check exposure, or to see what a composition looks like.

• **Autofocus**—The autofocus feature on digital cameras is very sophisticated, which is good, because manual focus systems on these cameras can be hard to use. The camera will choose the focus point that correlates to the closest part of the subject or scene. Many cameras will allow you to select different focus points as needed, including continuously variable focusing areas that can be set anywhere on the image. Many cameras offer two types of autofocus: single shot (the most common—meaning the camera will not fire until it has achieved focus) and continuous (where the camera constantly exposes images as the autofocus works to keep up with a moving subject).

The Quick Guide to Buying a Digital Camera

With the rapid pace of digital camera introductions, many photographers find it difficult to keep up with the latest features. Buying a digital camera can be a challenge since they come in such variety with considerable cost differential. In addition, it is easy to lose track of key buying criteria in the heat of the buying moment. If you don't already own a digital camera, read through this book and you'll understand how digital cameras work and what features you may need.

I have put together a quick list of things you might want to remember when shopping for a digital zoom camera. There are some things to think about that are unique to this camera type. I recommend you purchase equipment from a camera dealer who has experience with digital cameras, and especially the advanced compact models. These cameras are often sold at mass merchandisers but, all too often, the salespeople have no knowledge or training on important features of the cameras. There really can be many nuances to each camera that a good salesperson will know. Many features on cameras have no standardized form so this can be important.

Camera Shopping Considerations

1. **Megapixels**—Remember that resolution mainly affects your maximum image size. More megapixels will capture more detail but, unless the photo is made into a large print, they might never be seen. One issue that is unique to compact digital cameras is that the higher megapixel cameras often offer the most advanced features, so even if you don't need the megapixels, you may want the camera for its other features.

2. **Camera system**—Manufacturers of digital cameras each offer different systems of add-on lenses, flash units, and other accessories. You need to think a little about what you might need in your photography before going with a particular brand to be sure that the camera can use the accessories you need. If you already own a good set of filters, for example, you may want to see how easily they can be attached to the camera you are considering. On the other hand, you might discover that your existing flash does not give you what you want in your digital photography and a different camera system may be better suited to you.

3. **Electronic viewfinder (EVF)**—This is a feature that is completely new to most photographers unless you have shot with a camcorder. (Camcorders use a similar viewfinder.) The EVF uses a miniature LCD monitor that displays the image as it is seen throught the lens. It can take a little getting used to. When buying a camera with this feature, there are several things to be concerned about: pixel count (more pixels mean a smoother image on the monitor, fewer pixels can make the monitor appear grainy), refresh rate (as you move the camera around, how quickly does the image update), brightness and contrast (can you see the image in bright light?), how easy it is to change between the EVF and main LCD monitor, and color (is image color displayed accurately in the camera's viewfinder?).

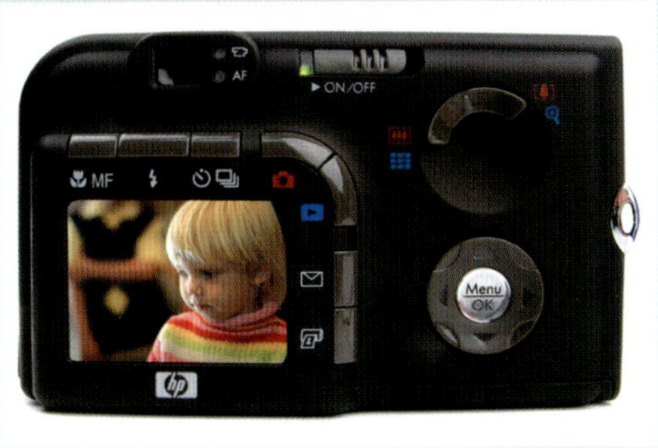

When evaluating the camera's LCD monitor, consider the size, brightness and contrast, color accuracy, and ease of use. These characteristics are important when taking pictures, and also for reviewing the photos you've taken.

4. **LCD Monitor**—We've spent a lot of time praising the LCD monitor. It really does improve the digital experience. Some small cameras have a monitor that is just too small to be useful. Make sure the camera's LCD has good size, color, brightness, and contrast, and that it is easy to view.

5. **Internal processing**—While some compact digital cameras do offer RAW file capabilities, high quality JPEGs work very well for most purposes. However, it can be worth looking at how a camera handles images before recording them as JPEGs. Data from the sensor is processed by unique computer chips in the camera that can affect things like color, digital noise, speed, and more. Unfortunately this processing isn't always easy to discover about a camera, so look carefully at the literature from the manufacturer and ask questions of the salesperson.

6. **How does it handle**—To me, this is an extremely important aspect of a camera purchase. How do you and the camera fit together? The compact digital cameras are very different than digital SLRs in one way—none of them match in size or form! You really have to hold the camera, try the controls and see how it fits you. A chart of features will never tell you this. You are buying this camera to use, and if you don't like the way it feels or handles, you won't use the camera as often as you would if you loved it. I guarantee that you will get better results from a camera you like than from a camera that is awkward to handle or use—even if it's the latest feature-rich pro camera.

7. **Ease of use**—You would think sometimes that manufacturers worked together to design digital cameras—not to make them consistent in their controls, but to figure out how to make them arbitrarily different! Controls on digital cameras are not consistent in either design or position. Since we all handle cameras in different ways, how these controls feel to you will be quite subjective. This goes back to handling the camera. You need to experience how easy it is to find and use the controls. Also, check that the menus are clear and easy to read as they can be critical to the use of the camera.

8. **Features you need**—Think seriously about the types of photographs you are most likely to take. This book should give you some ideas of what features will most likely affect your use of a camera. You may find that your needs demand specific features or controls. Pay attention to these needs because they will affect how well you can use your camera. Some special features that may need particular attention will include close-focusing distance, minimal shutter lag, noise reduction for long exposures, built-in flash controls, second-curtain flash sync, slow flash sync, bulb exposure and so on.

digital camera features and functions

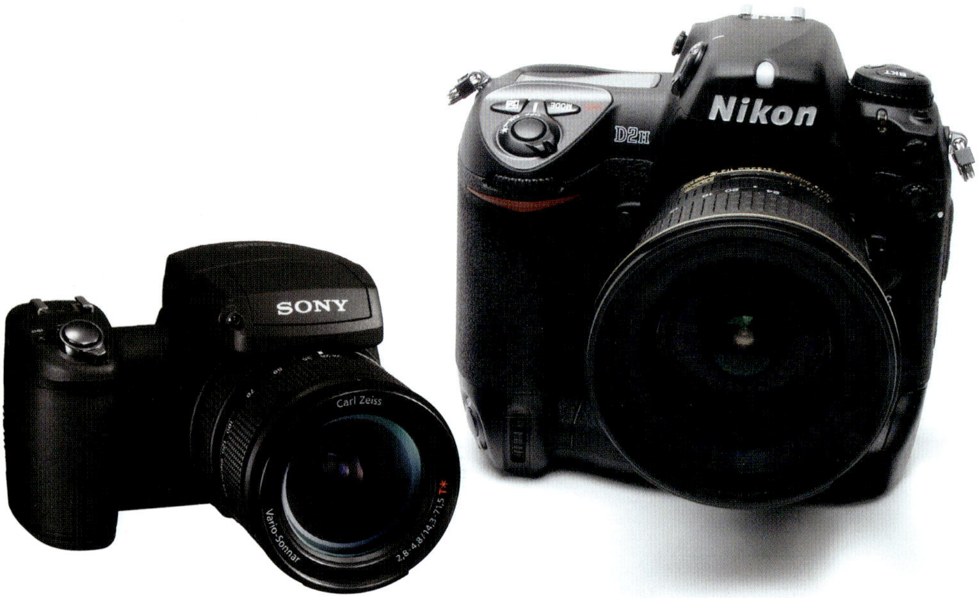

The compact digital camera on the left offers a great deal in a far smaller package than a digital SLR.

Digital cameras come in a variety of designs—camera designers seem determined to do things differently than the competition, even if the cameras have the same functionality. With digital SLRs, the designs are based on the conventional single-lens-reflex camera style, so they all look pretty much the same. Not so with the rest of the digital camera market. They range considerably in size and shape.

All digital cameras have some common features, no matter what the brand, though the expression of these features will often vary. There are a number of key features that you should know about, as this will help you better understand how digital cameras work, how to get the most out of your camera, and how to evaluate different models when you want to buy a new camera.

Types of Digital Cameras

Digital cameras can be grouped by type, such as SLR or point-and-shoot, or categorized by the target market, such as pro cameras, advanced amateur cameras, and family or mass market cameras. It so happens that pros will use all types of cameras and many amateurs buy the pro models. These are simply designations used by manufacturers to define the market so that they can produce cameras that meet the needs of diverse photographers.

Looking at non-SLR digital cameras gets a little tricky. There are no neat categories. Even though an advanced, full-featured compact digital camera is sometimes referred to as a point-and-shoot (because it looks more like a point-and-shoot than an SLR), such cameras are often packed with sophisticated features.

Some people have tried to describe different cameras as viewfinder (cameras with an optical viewfinder) or EVF (electronic viewfinder) cameras. While this difference is distinctive, it really doesn't tell you much about a camera's capabilities the way the category SLR does. I believe this is one reason why many photographers kept waiting for the ideal digital SLR before they made the leap to digital.

Another way of looking at these cameras might be price. That would be great except for two things: prices of digital cameras keep changing, and camera capabilities don't remain static either. A price criteria that worked one month could be completely off the next. And there is no way we could do anything related to price in a book because books have such a long lead time before they reach bookstores.

We do need some way of examining the differences among digital cameras, so we can talk about features and how they apply to photography. We'll use a four-tier grouping of non-SLR digital cameras based on their capabilities:

1. Totally automatic point-and-shoot digital cameras

2. Point-and-shoot digital cameras with basic controls

3. Compact digital cameras with flexible controls

4. Advanced compact digital cameras

Totally Automatic Point-and-Shoot Cameras

The simple, totally automatic, point-and-shoot camera is designed for the mass market buyer who is a casual photographer. While these cameras can be small and inexpensive additions to a camera bag, they are really not made for the photography enthusiast. They have some severe picture-taking limitations that don't really affect the casual user. The simplest point-and-shoots often don't allow settings to be changed. The camera only needs to be

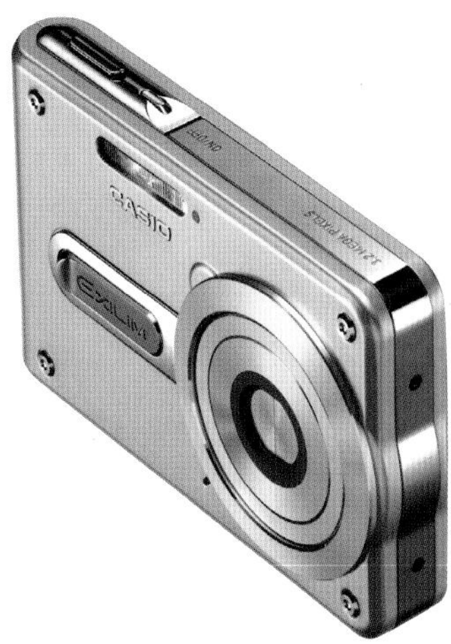

Totally automatic point-and-shoot cameras are small and easy to use, but the ultra compact models don't have much room for user controls.

turned on and off—everything else is automatic. The buyers of these cameras don't want to do anything except push a button to take a picture. These cameras have fewer megapixels and lower quality lenses because the people who buy them don't expect to make large, high quality prints. Camera speed and processing capabilities are limited and lag time is usually very noticeable. These cameras are designed for light usage.

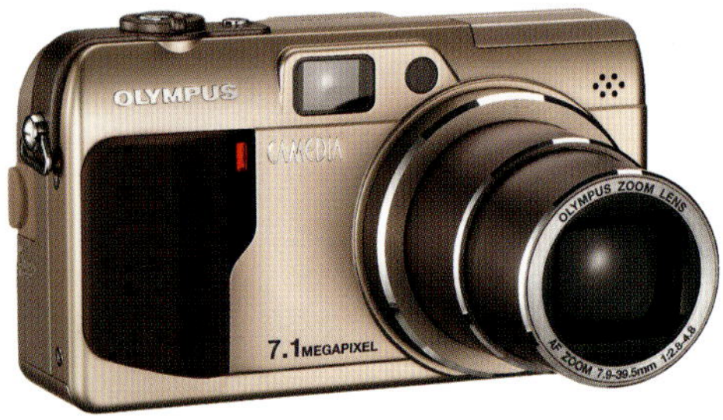

Today, even very small digital cameras offer a great deal of control and excellent image quality.

Point-and-Shoot Cameras with Basic Controls

Point-and-shoot cameras with basic controls are also designed for the mass market buyer who is a casual photographer. They can be a small and inexpensive addition to a camera bag to be used by family members of a photo enthusiast. They do offer some control beyond just turning the camera on and off, but they have picture-taking limitations that might disappoint a more serious photographer. They are generally best suited for the casual user. The cameras in this group have fewer megapixels than the more advanced categories, but sometimes include better quality lenses and often come in extremely compact designs, making them cameras that can literally go everywhere. Camera speed and processing capabilities are limited, and lag time is usually very noticeable. These cameras are designed for light usage.

Compact Cameras with Flexible Controls

The compact digital camera with flexible controls usually offers a significant step up in capabilities. Of course, all of these camera groups are based on compact designs, but this particular group has controls like those found in much more expensive cameras, but their size is still small. Some true, mini-pocket cameras even fit into this category. All are designed for the amateur, but they also appeal to more sophisticated photographers. Some of the features include choices for white balance, ISO settings, exposure modes, multiple focus modes, focal lengths (including some very long telephoto zooms) and other photo controls. These will offer a range of megapixels, depending on the price, and definitely include better quality lenses. Some very specialized features are often found in this group, such as weather- or water-resistant qualities. Camera speed and processing capabilities are improved, although they may still have a noticeable lag time. These cameras are designed for moderate usage. Much of the information in this book applies to this category.

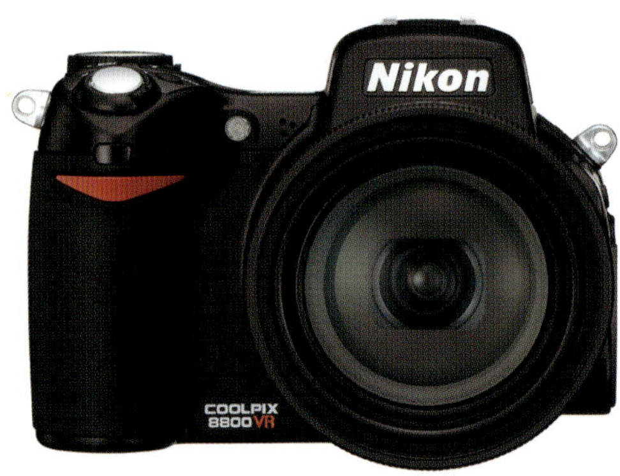

Modern digital cameras often mimic the look and feel of film cameras because that design works!

Megapixels are important, but so are things like lens quality and internal processing capabilities.

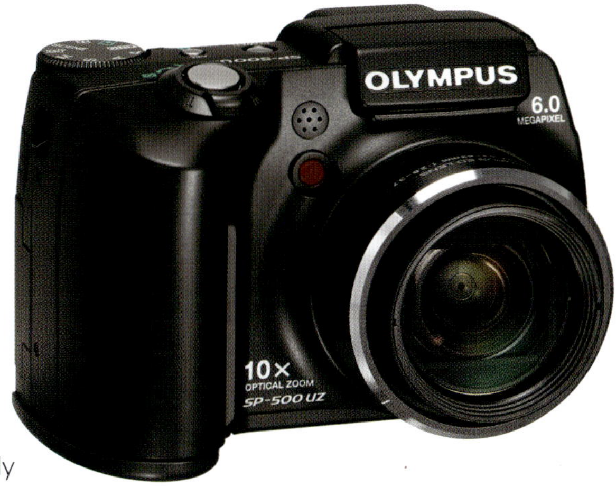

Advanced Compact Cameras

The advanced compact digital cameras are what this book is really all about. They offer a significant step up in capabilities. Their features and controls equal those of digital SLRs in many ways, but their size is still small (although no true pocket cameras fit this category). All are designed to appeal to sophisticated photographers, but they also include features to make the cameras extremely easy to use. Most offer settings that allow the camera to act like a point-and-shoot. These cameras can produce superb results, even for the most demanding photography enthusiast. They offer a choice of image capture sizes and formats. They include a wide range of choices for white balance and ISO settings. They offer various exposure modes, including full manual plus specialized modes that affect exposure, color and sharpness. Their autofocus is an improvement over the other camera styles we've discussed, plus the advanced compact cameras may include manual focus. They have both built-in and external flash capabilities. These cameras offer excellent optical quality, often featuring pro-level lens elements such as low-dispersion glass (called ED, LD, or SLD glass). Camera speed is the best of anything short of a digital SLR, and the processing capabilities are superb. While there is still a slight lag time, it is manageable. Advanced compact cameras are designed for moderate to heavy usage (meaning heavy usage by a photo enthusiast, not a photojournalist).

Megapixels and More

With all the marketing hype out there about megapixels, it's easy to think that megapixels are everything. Unfortunately, it isn't that simple. Megapixels are directly related to resolution, which is such a confusing topic that there is an entire chapter in this book devoted to it.

For now, let's take a quick look at what megapixels really mean to the photographer. They do offer increased resolution, which doesn't mean arbitrarily sharper photos, but rather more detail that can be expressed in larger photos or prints. A 4 x 6-inch print made from a 2-megapixel image will look very similar and perhaps even identical to one made from an 8-megapixel image if the only difference is in the megapixels. It is only when large prints are demanded from these same images that the higher number of megapixels will show its clear advantage.

However, manufacturers typically have made the highest megapixel cameras their flagship digital cameras. This means they include the best features, such as

The size of a print affects the number of megapixels needed to capture detail. If you want larger prints, you need more megapixels. A 3-megapixel camera will easily produce a full 8 x 10-inch print.

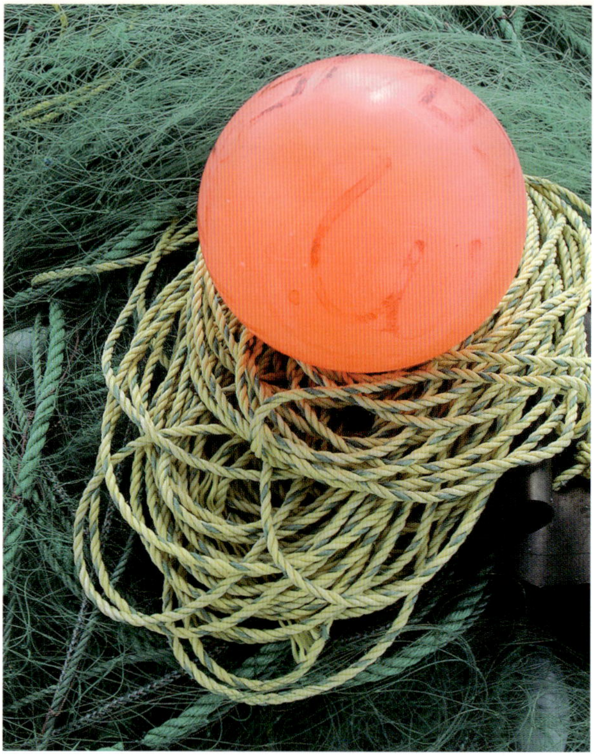

pro-quality lenses, advanced flash capabilities, the latest in EVF and LCD technologies, a wide array of accessories, and more. While you might not need the added megapixels if you are mainly printing snapshots, you may be interested in some of the features that these advanced cameras offer.

Compact Lenses for Compact Cameras

If you look closely at a compact digital camera's lens, you'll notice two things—the lens is physically small and the focal length is quite short, considerably different than you might expect from a 35mm SLR or even a point-and-shoot 35mm camera. As I noted earlier, the size of the lens affects more than just compactness of the camera body. Understanding the basics of lens designs can help you get the most from your digital camera.

To start, lets look at some of the reasons for the size of the lens. Obviously, camera designers want to keep their cameras small. New lens design technologies allow camera manufacturers to pack a lot of focal length into very small zoom lenses and still maintain high quality. It wasn't that long ago that lens designers could barely make some of these zoom ranges in any size, let alone in such small packages.

But that's only part of the story. The sensors in compact digital cameras are quite small compared to 35mm film. While there are some variations, here are some typical sizes for these small sensors:

8 megapixels: 8.9 x 6.6 mm (0.35 x 0.26 inches), 2/3-inch diagonal

3 to 5 megapixels: 7.2 x 5.3 mm (0.28 x 0.21 inches), 1/1.8-inch diagonal

2 to 4 megapixels: 5.4 x 4.0 mm (0.21 x 0.16 inches), 1/2.7-inch diagonal

Obviously, these are very small areas. Lenses only need to produce an image on that small area, so they don't need to be as physically large. The smaller the sensor, the smaller the lens needs to be. As lenses decrease in size, focusing mounts and other parts of the lens structure diminish physically as well.

In addition, there is a change in the focal length needed to create a "normal" image on the sensor. If you look at the actual focal lengths matched to the smallest sensors, you'll see such designations as 7-21mm. For anyone used to 35mm film cameras, that seems like an extraordinary wide-angle lens. Yet, it acts like a standard moderate zoom on a digital camera. To understand how focal lengths relate to the size of the imaging area, we need to look at image formats.

Film formats are based on size differences of the actual image captured by a lens. APS format is the smallest, commonly used film format; 35mm is larger; then come the medium format film sizes (6 x 4.5 cm, 6 x 6 cm, 6 x 7 cm); and finally the large formats (4 x 5 inches and bigger). Each format requires a larger camera and a different range of focal lengths. Consider, for example, the normal focal length lens for each film format. A normal lens has an angle of view that is similar to our eyes when viewing a subject from a moderate distance. A 50mm lens is a normal lens for a 35mm camera, an 80-90mm lens is normal for medium format, and a 150mm lens is normal for 4 x 5-inch film.

If you could take a 75mm wide-angle lens made for a larger format camera and put it on a 35mm camera, you would see a telephoto effect on that format. The focal length never changes, yet the magnification of the subject within the format does change. The reason is simple; the 35mm film only captures a small portion of the image, while the 4 x 5-inch film captures a much larger portion of the image.

The same thing happens with digital cameras. The size of the sensor is much smaller than a frame of 35mm film, so shorter focal lengths are required to cover the same part of a scene on the imaging area. It is also impossible to know exactly what a digital camera lens' focal length really does without knowing the image sensor size. This is where focal length equivalents come from. Anyone who has used 35mm film cameras for even a little while has an

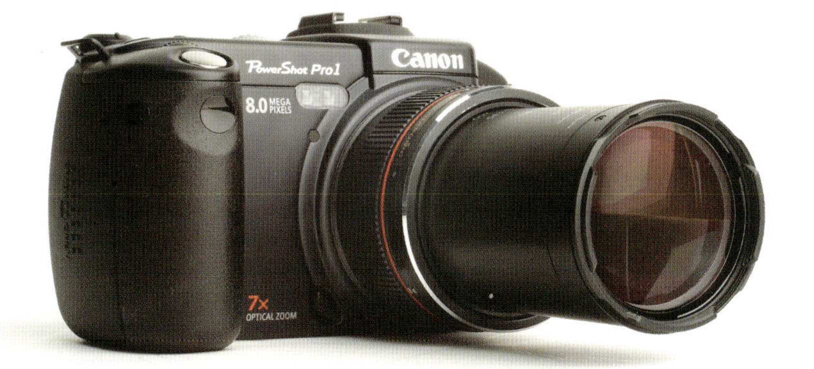

Lens designers are making very high quality zoom lenses that have a wide range of focal lengths for digital cameras.

idea of what focal lengths mean to that format—what's wide, what's telephoto, and so forth. So the industry uses a convention of explaining focal lengths for the small digital sensor format as "equivalent 35mm focal length." Some cameras even have both real and equivalent focal length markings on the lens.

The small sensors and lenses do limit the wide-angle side of camera zooms. Recently, manufacturers have been offering cameras with 28mm as their widest equivalent focal length, a distinct improvement over the more common 35 and 39mm lenses of the recent past. Manufacturers have tried to compensate for restrictions at the wide-angle end of focal lengths on their zooms by offering quality wide-angle accessory lenses that will increase the wide-angle capabilities by, typically, a factor of 0.7–0.8 times the focal length.

f/stop Limitations

One thing that has surprised many photographers is the shortened range of f/stops that the compact digital cameras offer. Typically, they do have fairly large aperture settings, such as f/2.4–3.2. (This range indicates a variable f/stop that changes as the focal length of a zoom lens changes.) The smallest aperture is typically f/8 or maybe a maximum of f/11. This is far below the standard f/16, f/22 or even f/32 of a 35mm format lens. This becomes a concern because obviously you can't use f/stops you don't have and that may affect exposure and depth of field.

The reason there are no smaller f/stops is because of the focal length and physical size of the lens. Reduce the size of the lens and the f/stop is reduced in size as well. But once it gets too small, problems occur; the worst is diffusion. A very small lens opening will create diffractive effects, meaning that light bends around the opening and reduces the sharpness of the image. Most digital cameras have significant diffractive effects once the aperture is smaller than f/8. Camera manufacturers don't want to sell cameras that give poor results, so they don't use f/stops smaller than f/8.

This did cause a problem with older cameras because the shutter speeds were often not fast enough to compensate for wider lens openings in bright sun. Some cameras actually had built-in neutral density filters to compensate when needed. Today more cameras include very fast shutter speeds, but an ND filter can still be helpful to reduce the light.

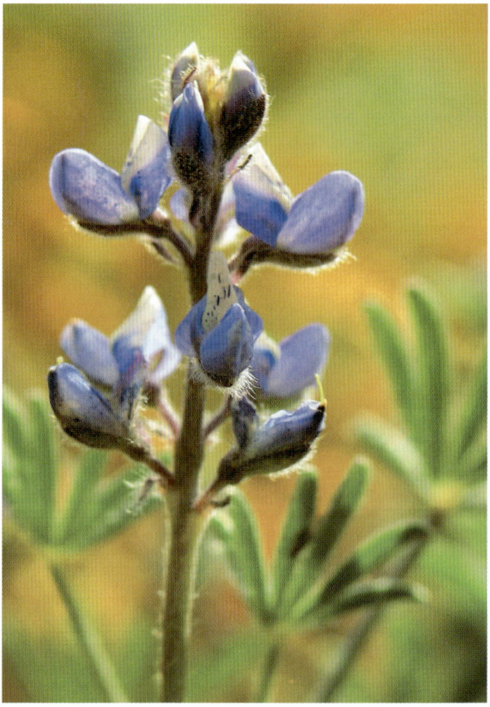

Shallow depth of field is more difficult with small digital cameras, but can be achieved with telephoto focal lengths and close-ups.

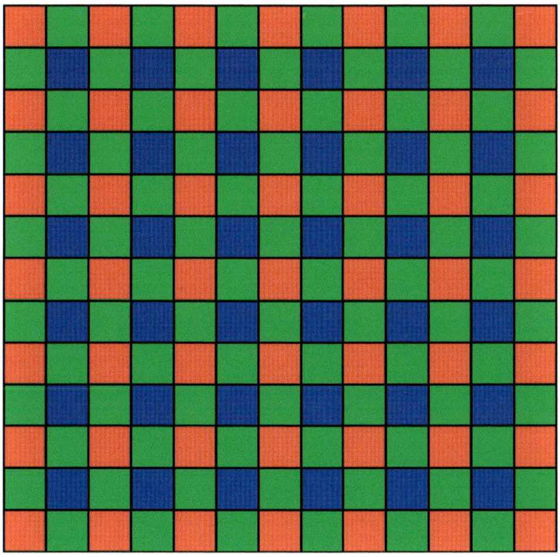

Most sensors use this checkerboard arrangement—the Bayer pattern—to filter light into its red, green, and blue components. Each pixel receives and records only the primary color of light transmitted by the filter. This method of color capture requires the camera's software to interpret image information and make adjustments to color and sharpness.

The depth of field issue is a different one. It is true that f/8 will give you less depth of field compared to f/16 on the same lens. However, the f/8 of a small digital camera is on a rather short focal length. Depth of field is affected by focal length, and shorter focal lengths have more depth of field. The f/8 minimum aperture of a short lens will match the depth of field you might get with the equivalent focal length used with an SLR. With a compact digital camera, the problem is not always about getting more depth of field, but can be about ways to creatively limit depth of field. Confining sharpness in depth by using a selective focus technique can be more of a challenge. We will look at ways of working with depth of field later in the book.

The Sensor

The sensor is a key element of any digital camera from the smallest mini-camera that fits a shirt pocket to the most advanced pro camera. It is the light-sensing part of the camera that reads the scene as focused by the lens. Sensor engineers have some distinct challenges: they must create a light-sensing device that acts like film by having a wide tonal range, that works well in both bright and low light, that meets the same exposure time and ISO speed expectations as film, and that offers clean, clear images without digital artifacts. (Artifacts are details added by the technology that were not present in the scene—for example, film grain is an artifact of film.)

Because sensors are so technical, they can be difficult to discuss in a book like this. Truthfully, understanding some of these details is more important to an engineer designing them than a photographer using a digital camera. But, I will try to give you an overview of sensors so you can better understand how they work in a camera.

First, all sensors are an array of tiny light receptors, or photodiodes, that produce electricity when stimulated by light. They represent the smallest picture element (hence pix-el, or pixel). Sophisticated circuitry attached to the sensor interprets and amplifies the signals coming from different pixels in order to build a photograph. All sensors are physically slightly larger than the "effective pixels" (the actual area being used by the camera for photography).

Color is captured in a unique way. Each pixel senses the amount of light in terms of black and white, but not color. A pattern of tiny filters is laid over the pixels so that they can then "see" colors. Most sensors use what is called a Bayer pattern. This has a pattern that is 50% green, 25% red, and 25% blue. It looks like a checkerboard of green, where the black squares would be, and alternate red and blue for the red squares. Scientists developed this pattern based on the way we see light and color and it works very well.

There can, however, be a problem with this pattern because every pixel does not see all three colors (red-green-blue, or RGB). Potentially, this can result in color inaccuracies and color moiré patterns in very fine details. Practically, this is rare because of some very sophisticated filter technology (low-pass filters in front of the pixels) and camera false-color reduction algorithms developed by sensor engineers.

Foveon, Inc. developed a special chip that avoids this color issue entirely by creating a sensor with layers so that each light-sensing photodiode sees all three colors. The result is a sensor that, theoretically, can define color details better. In addition, Sony created a unique sensor with four colors, red, green, blue, and emerald, that is supposed to render colors more accurately. The success of these two technologies is hard to predict. Neither has surpassed the Bayer pattern as the color technology of choice for digital camera sensors.

Two types of sensors are presently available for digital cameras: CCD (charge-coupled device) and CMOS (complementary metal oxide semiconductor). However, at this point, almost all compact digital cameras use CCD sensors. (The Foveon chip—a CMOS sensor—is only used in one camera at the time of this writing.) When digital cameras of any type first came out, CCD sensors were the only choice available to camera manufacturers. They have a history of solid performance, consistent production, low noise, and a high signal-to-noise ratio (which means less noise in the image). They are easier and less expensive to produce in quantity than CMOS sensors, making them the manufacturers' choice for compact camera models. This could change in the future.

You may have noted that some small, compact digital cameras have sensors similar in megapixel size to (or even better than) those of a digital SLR. But, there are differences that go beyond megapixels. An ultra-compact digital camera has only a limited amount of space for the sensor, so there is a need for small sensors. However, some compacts are certainly big enough to handle a physically larger sensor, but they don't because of cost. Sensor prices go up dramatically as they increase in size, which definitely affects the camera price.

To have a high pixel count on a small-sized sensor, the pixels have to be increasingly smaller as megapixels increase. With its smaller pixels, the small sensor will handle a narrower exposure range, giving it less latitude. In addition, such a sensor has less light being gathered by each sensing element, so it potentially has more of a noise problem. It is harder to get a clean, noiseless image from a small camera. This is why noise can be a big challenge in low light and with high ISO settings. Many manufacturers include elaborate noise processing algorithms in their cameras that help to reduce the effects of noise at the higher ISO settings.

Camera Speed

Camera speed involves five separate issues: boot-up time, shutter-lag time, sequential photo capture (the "drive" speed), buffer capacity, and how fast image data is written to the memory card. All five factors play a part in how quickly a camera can take pictures.

Boot-up time is that short delay between when the camera is turned on and when it is ready to take a picture. This speed has decreased dramatically since digital cameras first came out. Some of the latest compact digital cameras are ready almost immediately, making this much less of an issue. Still, some cameras may need a little

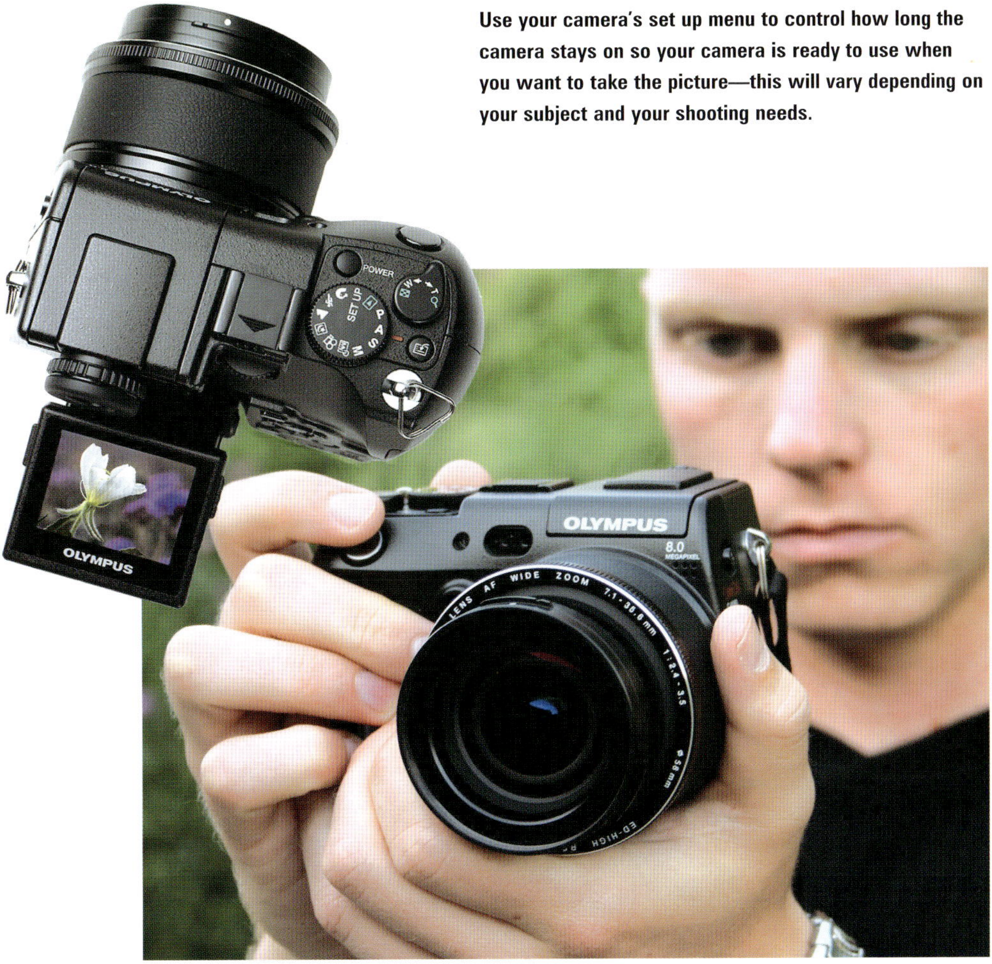

Use your camera's set up menu to control how long the camera stays on so your camera is ready to use when you want to take the picture—this will vary depending on your subject and your shooting needs.

time to power up their circuits, and the amount of time depends entirely on the specific camera model. No generalizations can be made.

While you cannot change a camera's boot-up time, you need to be familiar with how long it takes for your camera to be ready to shoot. If you are photographing an event, such as a baseball game that has peaks of activity and lulls, you need to be sure your camera is ready to shoot when the action happens. If your camera has a noticeable boot-up time, I would recommend that you extend the time delay before the camera goes to sleep if your camera offers this option. An "awake" camera will be ready for shooting. Having the camera at the ready at all times can quickly drain your battery power, especially if the LCD is in use. On the other hand, the LCD is a valuable part of the digital camera experience, so be sure you have extra batteries.

Lag time, the time between when you press the shutter and when the shutter actually goes off, varies tremendously among digital cameras. In some cameras, this can be a significant issue, with the time delay affecting what you can and cannot take pictures of. Practice taking pictures of action so you know how much you have to anticipate the action (shooting a beat early). You can also try using the continuous shooting function and hope to catch the right point within the sequence.

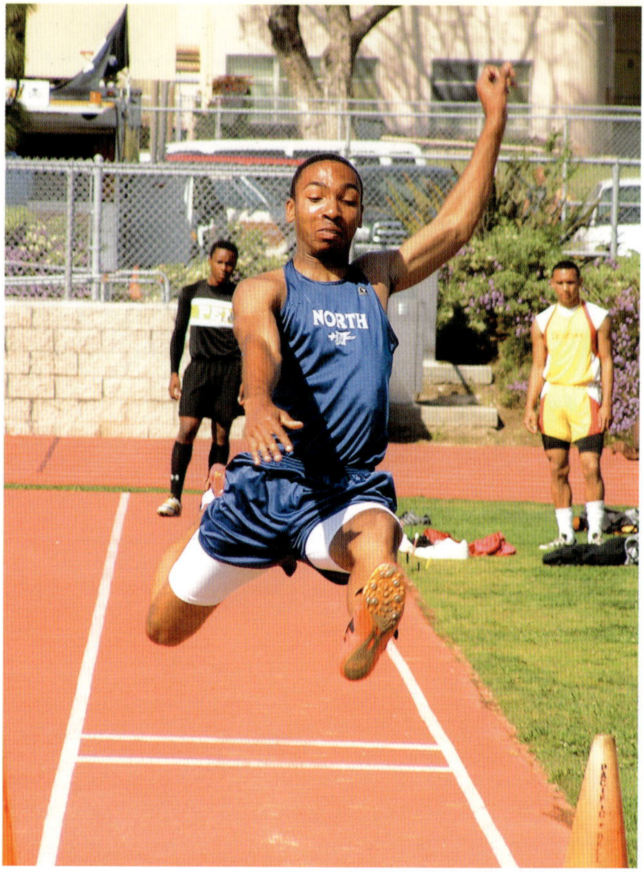

Most small digital cameras have a shutter lag—a short delay between when you press the shutter and when the shutter actually goes off. With practice, you can anticipate a subject's movement and shoot slightly before the peak action.

How fast a conventional camera could take pictures was a function of the motor drive that advanced the film. This feature is often still called "drive speed" although there is obviously no motor drive involved. The speed depends on how fast the camera can capture the data from the sensor and move it to the internal buffer. (The buffer is built-in memory that stores image data until it can be downloaded onto a memory card. This is all done automatically.) With high megapixel cameras, this becomes an increasing challenge because of the amount of data involved. Low-priced digital cameras typically have speeds of one to two frames per second (fps), while specialized pro SLRs designed for action can shoot eight fps or more. Drive speed is affected by shutter speed, as well. Using faster shutter speeds will allow the fastest drive speed.

Once the camera's internal buffer is full, the camera cannot take pictures until data is transferred to the memory card. You hold down the shutter and the camera takes photos one after another until it just stops—this is normal. On the compact digital cameras, the buffer is relatively small and you might only get six to ten photos before the buffer is full. Check your manual, or simply do a test by holding down the shutter on the continuous setting until the camera stops. It doesn't matter what subject you use—you'll probably just erase the shots afterward. You'll want to know the buffer size before you try taking photographs of action.

Memory card speed is promoted rather heavily by memory card manufacturers. It can affect how quickly images get cleared from the buffer, but only if the camera is designed to handle that speed. On the fastest digital SLRs with high buffer capacity, the speed of the card can make a significant difference in how many photos can be taken before the camera stops to catch up. On the average digital camera, there is usually minimal effect if any (unless you compare an old, very slow card with a high-speed card of today). It is important to know that memory card speed has no effect on how fast a camera can actually take pictures.

Autofocus

Autofocus (AF) is an amazing technology and a relatively modern development in photography. Cameras today, both film and digital, low-priced and high-priced, have the incredible ability to focus quickly and accurately on the subject. The camera's AF sensor examines a scene then works with a microprocessor to determine focus. Every company has its own proprietary algorithms, and in addition, cost plays a factor in what kind of AF system can go into a camera. Autofocus performance has a number of important attributes: speed, number and location of sensors, single vs. continuous focus, and light sensitivity. Advanced cameras usually perform better, but this is not simply a matter of camera price, since newer AF technologies can allow the latest, lower-priced camera to beat an older, more expensive camera.

Speed of the camera is affected by the type of autofocus selected: single or continuous. Not all cameras will allow this choice, and then you get whatever the camera comes with. In single-exposure autofocus, the camera will not take a picture unless it has focused on something—this is fine for most subjects, but can be a problem with moving subjects. With cameras that only have single-exposure AF, you'll often get frustrated because the camera won't let you take a picture if it has trouble focusing on movement. With continuous focus, the camera fires as it is focusing. Advanced cameras even use a feature called predictive AF that helps the camera to keep up with the action. This is most common with digital SLRs and is not very common with small digital cameras.

Subjects in motion can be a challenge for autofocus. On most compact digital cameras, you have to anticipate the movement and lock focus before you have to take the picture. (Most cameras lock focus when you depress the shutter release halfway.) If you try and focus on a subject in motion, the camera may not have the subject in focus when you really want to take the picture. It is possible to get very good shots even when the action is quick, but you must anticipate the action and "pre-focus" by locking the AF on the point where you expect the action to be. This takes a little practice, but the neat thing about digital is being able to review action shots on the LCD. You can check your shots and learn quickly how to best capture the action.

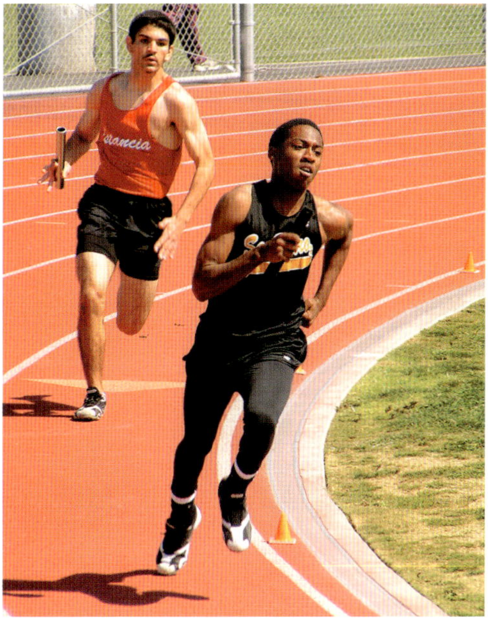

For moving subjects, your camera's autofocus may not react as quickly as needed. Instead "pre-focus" on a point, then release the shutter just before the subject reaches that point.

Location of the actual sensors in the image area also affects how the autofocus will work. More advanced cameras will have either a group of sensors across the viewing area or variable sensing over the whole scene, which makes it difficult for the subject to elude detection. Some cameras even let you set the specific sensor area to match the composition you want. At times, you may need to move the camera around a little so the camera picks the spot you want for focusing. Low-priced cameras may have only a single central AF sensor. The photographer may have to do more work by always centering the subject, locking focus, and recomposing the image.

Lighting conditions can also affect autofocus operation. Low light levels can make it very difficult for the camera to achieve focus. (This is most problematic with telephoto zooms on the smallest cameras. These lenses are typically very slow and limit the amount of light reaching the AF sensor.) Even the least expensive of the more advanced cameras typically have an AF-assist beam—either infrared or visible light—emitted by the camera in dark conditions. Be aware if your camera uses visible light, as it can be inappropriate, rude or even dangerous in some situations.

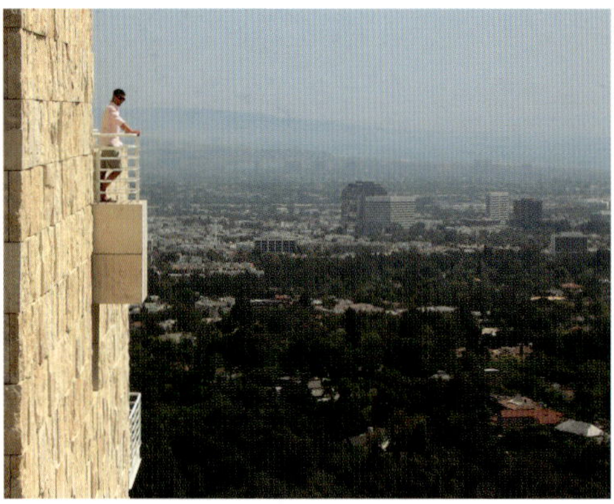

On most cameras, you can focus on an off-center subject by first pointing the camera at the subject, then locking the focus by pressing the shutter halfway.

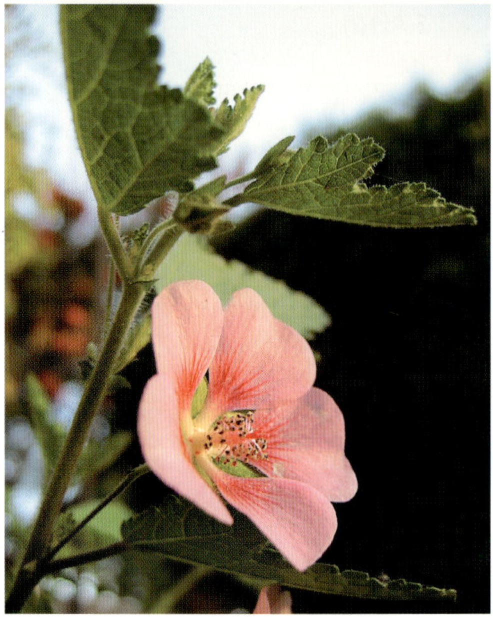

Autoexposure is usually quite good, but you may want to confirm its accuracy by checking the LCD monitor.

Metering

Autoexposure with modern cameras, both film and digital, has become so accurate that it seems like metering is now a non-issue. Yet, there is a difference between a good exposure and a really great exposure. To get the most from your camera, there are some things you need to understand about metering in order to make the best decisions about autoexposure. It still works best with some thought and control from the photographer. We'll go into more detail about this a little later.

Remember that you have a great tool in the digital camera to help with exposure—the LCD. You always get to check on your picture to see if your exposure works for you or not. (The LCD is not a perfect rendition of exposure, but with practice, you will learn to interpret your camera's LCD so you can get a quick, overall judgment of exposure.) We'll spend more time on metering and the LCD later.

ISO Settings

ISO is an international standard from an organization called the International Organization for Standardization. In film, it refers to the sensitivity of the film and is an important standard so that you can depend on a 400-speed film from one manufacturer to be very close to a 400-speed film from another. In addition, simple math tells you how each film speed relates to another, such as a 400-speed film being twice the speed (or sensitivity) of a 200-speed film.

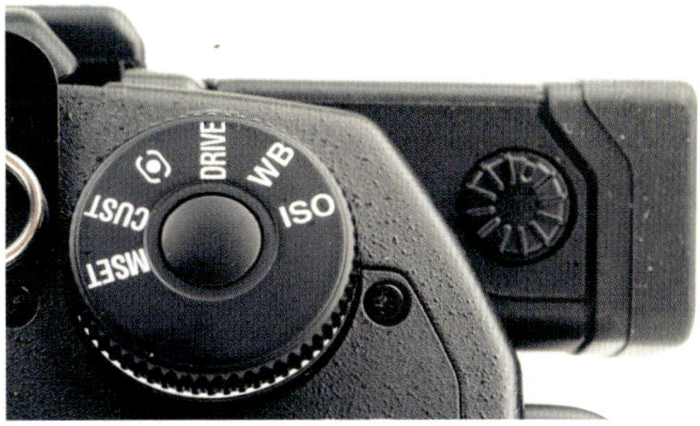

Digital cameras offer you many quick image controls, including the ability to change ISO from shot to shot.

Technically, as explained earlier, digital cameras do not have a true ISO because sensors are not like film. Instead, there are ISO equivalent settings. Still, these settings do make the camera react like the ISO of film, so that a 100 setting is half the speed of a 200 setting. But the sensor does not change, only the circuits reading the sensor data do. They alter how the sensor data is read so that it becomes more or less sensitive to light. (Technically, the signal is amplified, but the result is as if the sensor changed its sensitivity.)

ISO settings in digital cameras do not have a specific international standard, nor have manufacturers agreed to a specific standard. They do compare their settings to real film speeds, but interpretations are made. This is why you may find that two brands of cameras can have the same ISO settings, yet have slightly different exposure readings. Experiment with your camera to see if any adjustments need to be made to compensate for your way of metering and the ISO setting. I find, for example, that some of my cameras require exposure compensation. Otherwise, the straight meter reading of a scene produces an image that seems dark to me.

Why would you choose different ISO settings? With compact digital cameras, it is usually better to use the lowest ISO setting you can. That offers the highest quality with clean tonalities (little noise) and the best color. However, there are times that you really do need the higher ISO settings. Here are four key things to consider when choosing ISO speed: image quality, aperture setting, shutter speed, and flash needs.

Image quality—Low ISO settings offer very clean images with little or no noise (noise is like film grain). This makes them render fine details and tonalities extremely well. In addition, "clean" images offer purer color. The small sensors on compact digital cameras have challenges when dealing with higher ISO settings. Noise quickly becomes apparent. For optimum image quality, use the lowest ISO speed possible. However, there are times when a higher ISO speed can mean the difference between getting or missing the shot.

Aperture setting—When you need a certain shutter speed, when handholding the camera or photographing a subject in motion, changing the ISO can give you more aperture options. Higher ISO's allow for smaller f/stops and greater depth of field, while lower ISO settings require wider lens openings resulting in less depth of field.

Blurs can be fun to experiment with, but if you want a sharp image at dusk, a higher ISO setting will help.

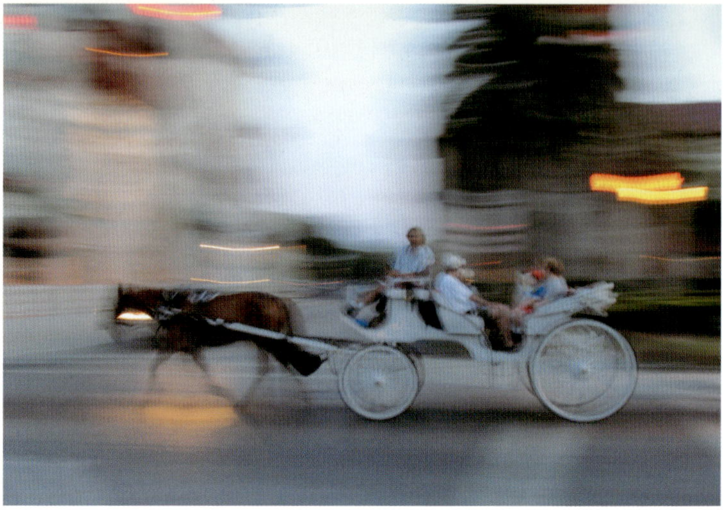

Shutter speed—Higher ISO settings let you use faster shutter speeds. This can be extremely helpful when handholding your camera, especially when using the telephoto setting of a zoom lens on a small digital camera. At the longest focal lengths, f/5.6 or even smaller may be the maximum aperture. Faster shutter speeds will also capture action better. Lower ISO settings let you choose slower shutter speeds, which can be useful for blurred action.

Flash needs—Any given flash unit, whether built-in or an added accessory, produces a finite amount of light. This light affects how you can use the flash—what f/stops can be used, the maximum subject distance that the flash can illuminate and so forth. The increased sensitivity of higher ISO settings give you more range for your flash, smaller lens openings can be used, the subject can be farther from the flash and so forth. Lower ISO settings usually make fill-flash easier to use in bright conditions because they aren't as sensitive to the ambient light.

Noise Problems

A clean, noise-free photograph can be a beautiful thing. Noise looks like grain and, if too strong, can detract from the photo. Yet, grain has long been a challenge for the photographer. High-speed films have always had a trade-off of more grain. Fast high-quality films have extremely fine grain and helped to propel the small format of 35mm into dominance of the film world.

Noise in an image will be seen as tiny specks of random color and light. This can become very obvious in certain images, especially in large areas of smooth tone, such as sky and out-of-focus areas. It can obscure fine detail and alter colors, but sometimes it can add an interesting effect. It may or may not affect apparent sharpness, since our evaluation of sharpness can be influenced by the sharpness of the noise. Noise typically shows up most strongly in dark areas of the image.

It helps to understand some of the key digital camera factors that cause noise. Plus, you'll need to know what factors have a remedy so you can decide how much you can control the noise. There can be trade-offs for certain features of the camera, such as using a high ISO even though it will increase noise.

1. **Sensor noise**—Small sensors have smaller pixels than larger sensors used in digital SLRs. Small pixels don't gather light as well, so when

their signal is amplified for higher ISO settings, noise increases. In addition, dark scenes that require long exposures can be a problem for similar reasons, although the latest cameras tend to have very good noise reduction circuits for this condition.

Solution: You have no control over the sensor itself (more expensive digital cameras often control noise better in their processing circuits). However, if you shoot in bright light and restrict the use of higher ISO settings, you will minimize the noise in the image from the sensor.

2. **ISO settings**—As mentioned in the previous section, noise increases with ISO.

   Solution: Use the slowest ISO speed possible. If you want to play with noise effects, try high speeds. With a given brand and model, you can depend on noise increasing with ISO speed, but how much can only be determined with testing.

3. **Exposure**—Underexposed images can cause problems. Lightening the image can make any noise more visible. Digital camera sensors don't like underexposure.

   Solution: Be sure you have enough exposure. It is important to expose images well so that dark areas contain enough image data. (You can always darken them in the computer if needed.) You want to avoid having to over-enhance them to bring out detail. In low light situations, bracket exposure to ensure you have an image with minimal noise.

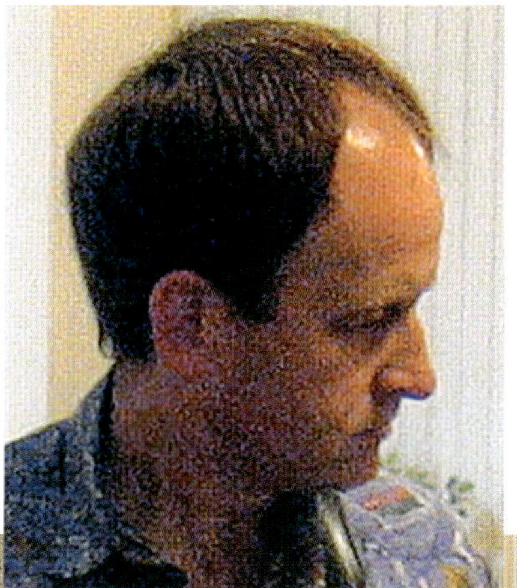

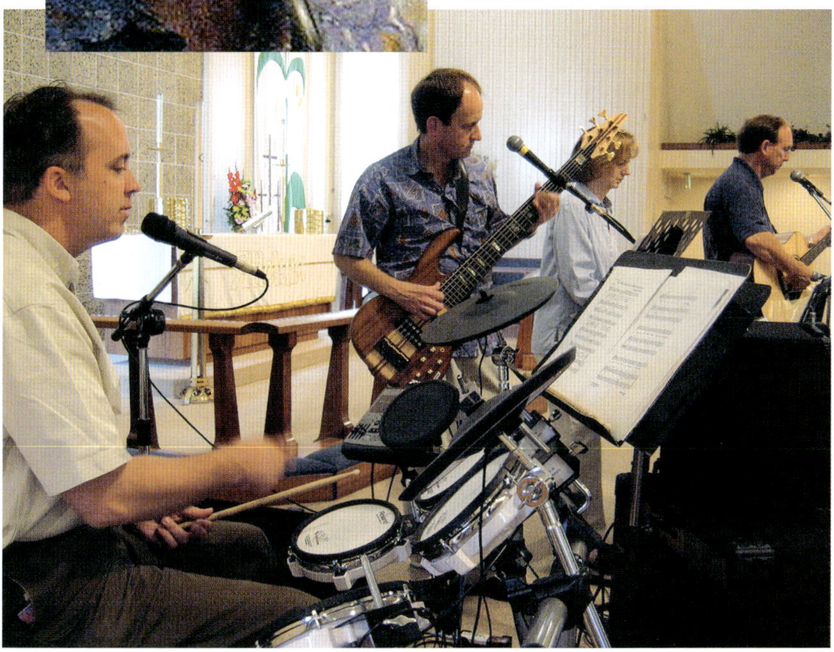

A higher ISO setting will let you get the shot in low light, but be aware that image noise will increase dramatically.

4. **JPEG artifacts**—Too much JPEG compression in the camera, or repeatedly opening and saving a JPEG image in the computer, can create little blocky artifacts that look like chunky grain. This can be very noticeable in the sky or across any single-colored area with minimal detail. In addition, JPEG compression can accentuate other noise in a digital photo.

   Solution: Set your camera to its highest quality compression even though that does mean larger file sizes. Don't try to cram as many photos on a memory card as you can by using the higher compression levels available on your camera—buy a larger card. Once your images are in the computer, save your image as a TIFF or Photoshop (PSD) file. Don't continue to use JPEG as your working format.

5. **Digital artifacts**—Areas, such as sky, made up of a subtle continuous gradient often exhibit digital artifacts. A digital camera must give the illusion of the gradient, yet it cannot produce continuous tonal change since it uses discrete bits of data (pixels). This can cause a grain-like pattern, especially in images taken with low-megapixel cameras. With the latest digital cameras, this effect may not be very noticeable initially. However, it may be intensified when the image is adjusted in the computer.

   Solution: Out-of-focus areas and large expanses with a slight tonal change emphasize artifacts because the translation of these smooth gradations to individual pixels is difficult. Be aware of what your camera can do and, when working on images in the computer, avoid extreme changes in Levels, Hue/Saturation, and sharpening of these areas, as the adjustments will accentuate the noise.

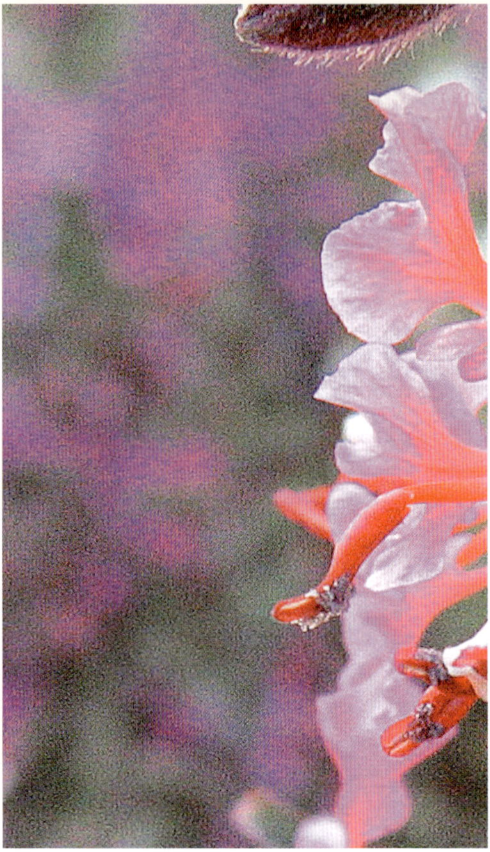

6. **Sharpening**—Indiscriminate sharpening and oversharpening, both in the camera and in the computer, can overemphasize noise to the detriment of a photo. All too often, when the entire photo is sharpened, little-noticed noise suddenly becomes very ugly.

   Solution: Use the computer for all image manipulation. Don't process images with the camera's software. Skies and out-of-focus areas that show digital noise should not be sharpened. Selectively sharpen only the focused parts of the photo. You might also try setting the threshold higher in Photoshop's Unsharp Mask tool to reduce the sharpening effect on grain.

Noise looks like grain—you can see it in the magnified section (left) of this floral image (right). In this shot, the noise occurred unnecessarily due to the use of a high ISO setting when one was not needed.

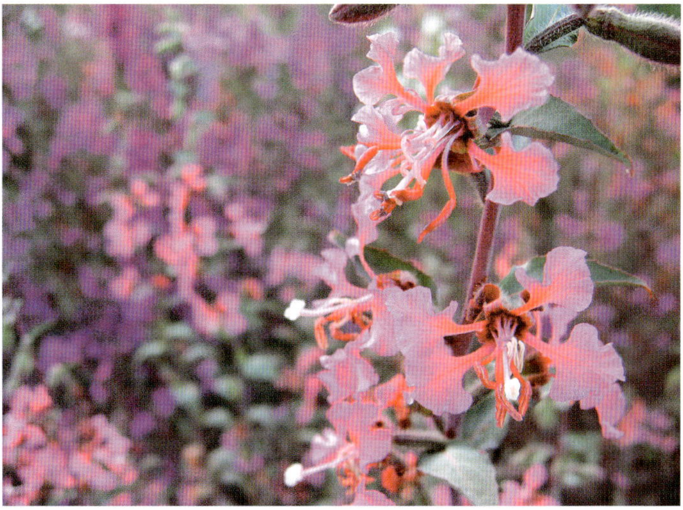

7. **Image processing software**—Image processing software, like Photoshop, can actually increase the appearance of grain or noise due to the use of certain processing controls. Overuse of Hue/Saturation, for example, will dramatically bring out undesirable noise effects in the photo.

   Solution: Work on a copy of your image. Use the software's preview and watch for the appearance of unwanted noise. Avoid over-processing the image color because it can enhance the color and tonal differences in grain or noise.

8. **Heat**—If you read the fine print in many digital camera manuals, you might notice that heat can cause an increase in noise. This is one reason why very long exposures pick up more noise. As the sensor "works" during the exposure, its temperature will increase. But any time the camera is overheated, noise can be an increased problem.

   Solution: Keep your camera as cool as you can. Never leave it in a hot car, especially before you shoot. In hot climates, shade the camera from direct sun. You might even consider using an inexpensive cooler to keep the temperature of your camera lower. Don't put ice in the cooler (that might cause other problems, such as condensation), but a couple of bottles of room-temperature water will help maintain a moderate temperature inside the cooler.

Knowing the causes of noise allows you to focus on technique in those specific areas. You will rarely completely eliminate the problem with standard photographic or digital procedures, however, by paying attention to the details outlined above, you can improve your results.

Noise Reduction Software

There are a couple of excellent software plug-ins to help reduce noise in digital photos: DIGITAL GEM and Dfine. Kodak's DIGITAL GEM is very simple and easy to use (www.asf.com and www.kodak.com). Dfine, from nik multimedia, Inc. (www.nik-multimedia.com) offers more flexibility and adjustment capabilities, which makes it more versatile. This added functionality comes with a steeper learning curve.

Camera Parameters

Many cameras offer a choice of several settings for sharpness, contrast, and color. These features are typically found in the camera menu or custom functions menu, although your camera may or may not have these particular choices. They are usually included with higher-priced cameras, but there is no consistent way of predicting which types of cameras have this feature. Check your camera manual.

In general, the default settings of digital cameras employ moderate contrast and less color saturation as compared to film, with little or no added sharpening. This varies among different camera models though. You can get your camera to imitate the look of certain types of film by tweaking the contrast and color. One problem is that these settings alter the image capture, so their effects are built into the photographs.

The default settings work well for most photographers. However, these settings offer some interesting possibilities if you are willing to make some changes to the camera's response to a scene. Look for ways to change sharpness, color saturation, and color tone in the camera menus. Here are some ways to use these settings:

Personal preferences—If you find that your camera consistently makes photos that are not saturated enough, or too warm or cool, check the parameter settings to see if you can tweak them to better suit your preferences.

Direct printing—If you have a printer that allows direct connection to a camera, you may find that adding some sharpening and increasing color saturation can be helpful when you print directly from the camera.

Gray days—Try setting more contrast, increased color saturation and warmer colors to add zip and warmth to photos taken on overcast days.

Portraits—You may find that adjustments that reduce contrast, decrease color saturation, and add warmth improve your photographs of people.

Experiment—Try different settings with your favorite subjects and see if you prefer particular results.

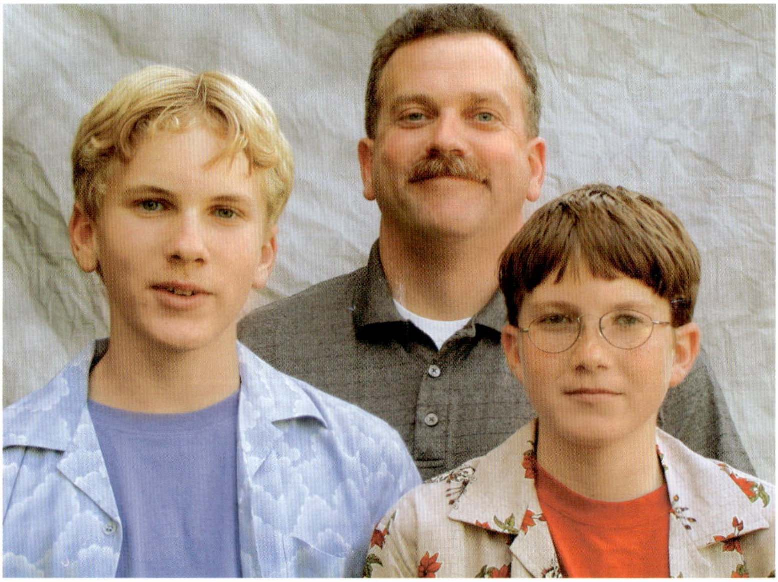

Some higher-priced cameras allow you to adjust image parameters, such as increasing color saturation and adding warmth to a portrait.

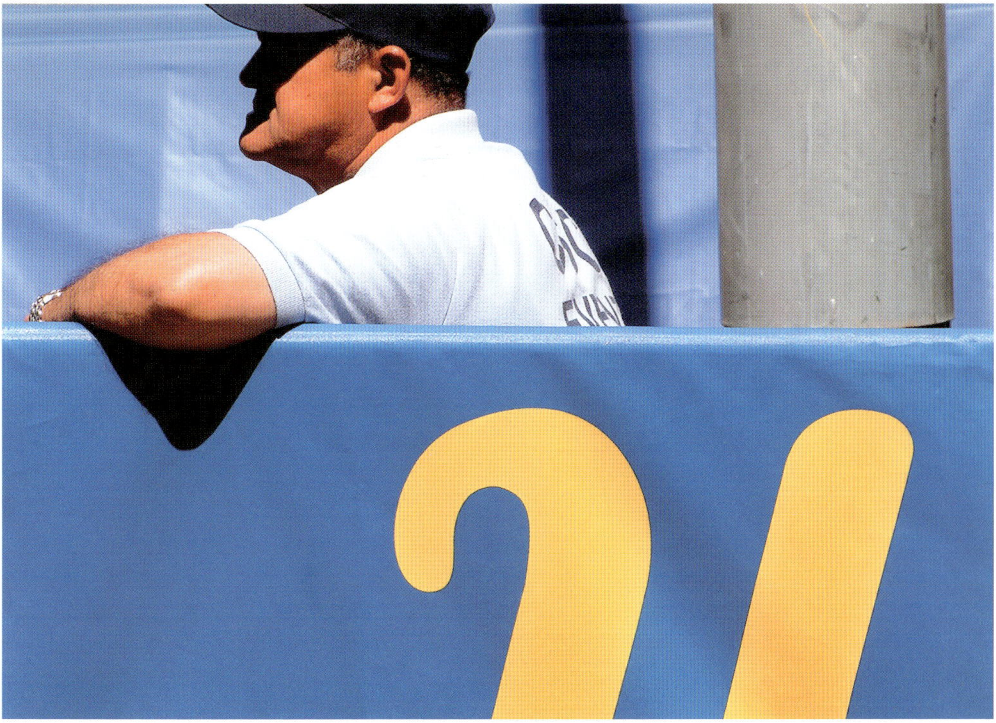

A great thing about a little digital camera is that you can take it with you everywhere and when an interesting image presents itself, you can get the shot without worrying about film costs or processing.

Maximize What You Have

A downside of photography magazines (including *PCPhoto*) is that they report on all the camera gear that gets introduced. That's certainly good to help photo enthusiasts keep up with what is going on in the industry. However, the problem is that photographers learn about all the new features that their camera doesn't have, or features in cameras that are out of their price range. I love learning about all the new things that cameras can do, but on a personal level, I try to assess if they are practical for my photography needs.

My feeling is that you should make the most of whatever camera and system you have. Cameras today are good products that offer much to photographers. If you find that your system does not allow you to get the types of photographs you need, certainly that may be a reason for upgrading to a new camera. Still, for most of us, spending more time with our existing camera, learning to work within its limits can be a great benefit. Use your camera—play, experiment, take pictures! You'll learn what it can and can't do so you won't frustrate yourself trying to make it do something it doesn't do well.

Have fun with your gear, no matter what type of camera you own! You can take photos at any time, see them immediately for instant feedback, yet spend no money on film or processing.

resolution and file formats

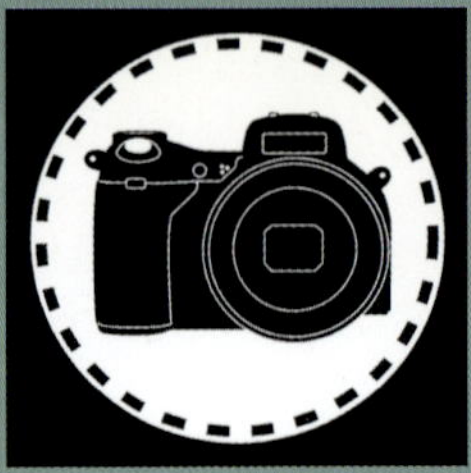

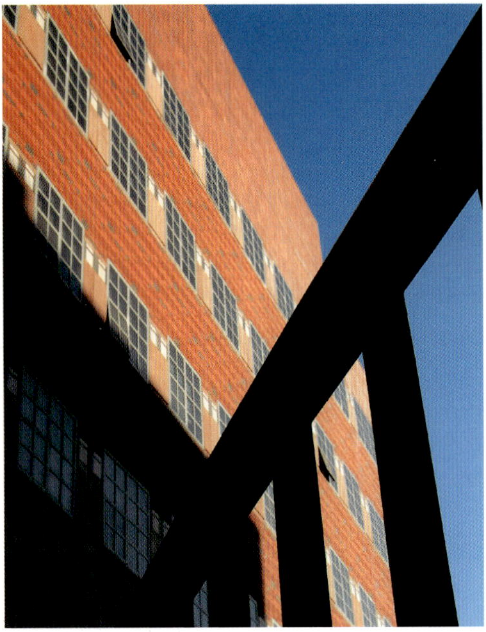

Resolution of a digital camera ultimately affects the size at which the photo can be used.

You already know a bit about resolution—more resolution allows you to make bigger prints, for one thing. You may also be intimidated a little by resolution—many photographers are. It is not a very "photographic" concept. Camera resolution and image formats are two confusing aspects of digital photography. While there is plenty written about these topics, there is also a lot of misinformation. Yet, in order get the most out of your digital camera, you need to understand enough about resolution and file formats to make the right choices for your photography.

Resolution

Resolution is especially difficult because the term can refer to at least three different things: area resolution, linear resolution, and printer resolution.

Area Resolution—This refers to the total number of pixels in a digital photo file. The height and width of the file are given—for example, 3000 x 2000 pixels. It is directly related to the megapixels of a camera. Multiply the pixels in the example and you get a total of 6,000,000 pixels, which is equal to 6 megapixels.

Linear Resolution—This is the number of pixels per linear dimension (usually inches), which is expressed as ppi (pixels per inch) or dpi (dots per inch). Technically, ppi and dpi are not the same, but they have become interchangeable in general use. Sometimes you may even see both used: 180 ppi/dpi (180 pixels/dots per inch). Linear resolution is meaningless without the image size or dimensions for reference, such as 8 x 10-inches at 200 dpi.

Printer Resolution—This is very confusing since the resolution of a printer—such as 1440 dpi—is a separate measurement that is determined independent of camera resolution. The outrageous resolutions (4800 dpi or higher) for printers are mostly marketing hype. These will not necessarily give better photo quality prints than lower resolutions. We won't be discussing printing much in this book, but you can learn more about printing in books on that topic like the *Epson Complete Guide to Digital Printing* (also published by Lark Books).

Understanding Resolution

With a digital camera, our first concern is the overall, or area, resolution. This tells us how much data we have to work with. It is very important to understand that resolution is not an arbitrary quality issue. Resolution affects image size more than anything else. One misunderstanding is that megapixels equal sharpness. You can have a very sharp image from a 3-megapixel camera and an unsharp photo from a 6-megapixel camera. You can also make 4 x 6-inch prints from 3, 6, or even 12 megapixel cameras and they will look essentially identical in sharpness.

Increased resolution gives you more detail—revealed in larger prints. On a basic level, you need approximately 2 megapixels for a print up to 5 x 7-inches, 3 megapixels for an 8 x 10, 8 megapixels for 16 x 20. These numbers are somewhat conservative but will give true film-quality prints from a photo ink jet printer. Since digital camera files can be so "clean" (meaning without grain), the image files that they create can be printed even larger with exceptional results.

However, you can make larger high-quality prints with more digital data—larger digital files that come from cameras with higher resolution. Anyone who needs to create images that can be used at large sizes with the highest quality printing must use the highest megapixel cameras available today.

Digital photos are typically printed at image resolutions of 200–300 ppi/dpi. This is not printer resolution, but the actual linear resolution of the image. The variation is due to the way different printers deal with the digital photo and its resolution. Almost all ink jet printers on the market today will

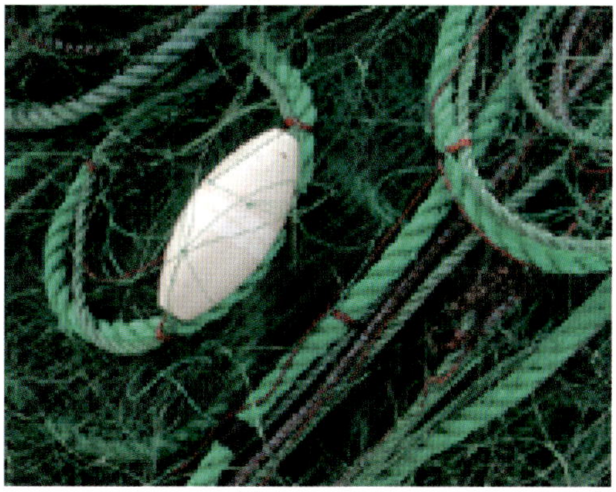

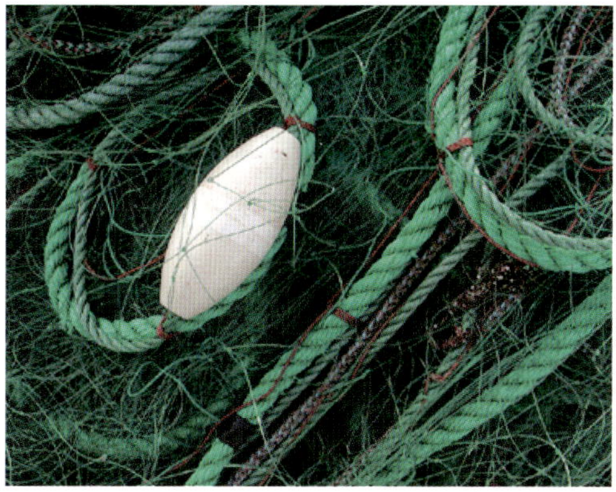

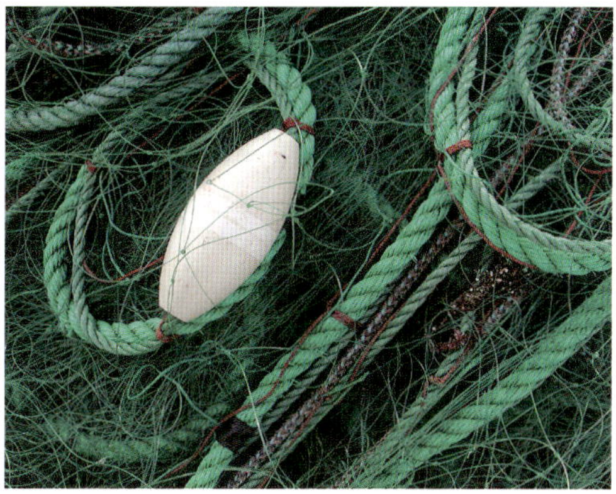

If the image resolution is not high enough for output at a particular size, the photo will look unsharp. Once you have a high enough resolution, increasing the resolution has little effect. The images are at 72 ppi/dpi (top), 150ppi/dpi (center), and 300 ppi/dpi (bottom).

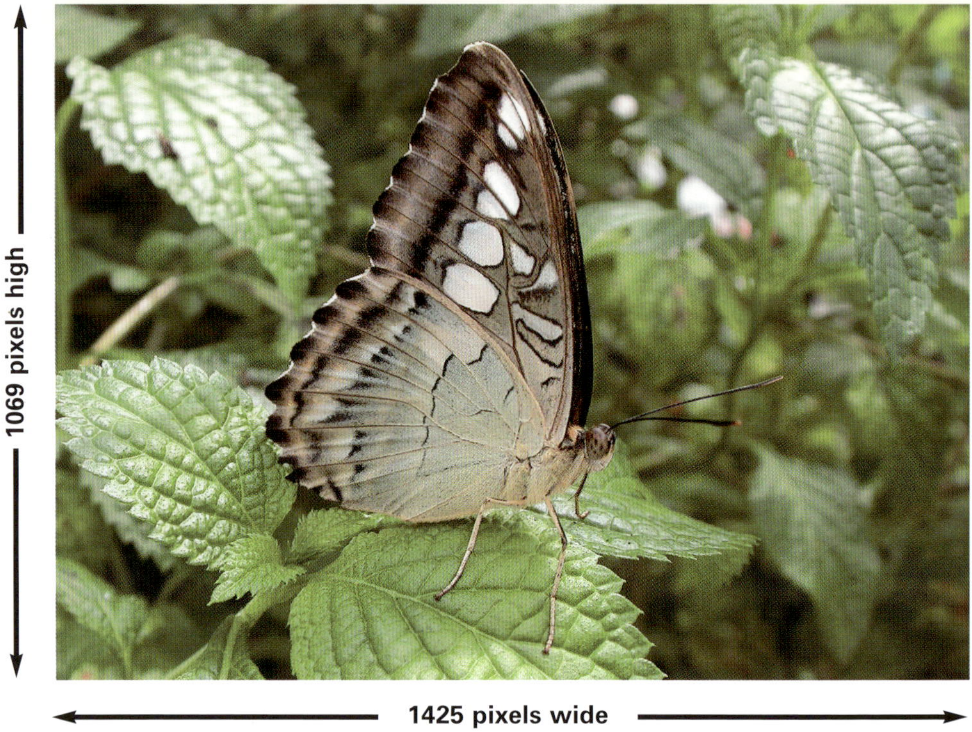

The area resolution of this image is 1425 x 1069 pixels. At a linear resolution of 300 dpi (used for printing here), this image measures 3.5 x 4.72 inches. At 200 dpi, the image size would be 5.3 x 7.1 inches. The original file from a 4-megapixel camera was 2272 x 1704 pixels. The image was resized to fit the page of this book.

print beautiful images with an image resolution of 300 dpi. Most photo printers, however, will give acceptable quality at 200 dpi (sometimes less). This spreads out the available pixels for making larger prints.

Consider a 6-megapixel camera with an area resolution of 3000 x 2000 pixels (these numbers are used just to make the math easy). At the linear resolution of 200 pixels per inch (200 ppi/dpi), you can print an image as large as 15 x 10 inches in size. (3000/200 = 15 and 2000/200 = 10). But, if you had to print the image at 300 dpi/ppi, the resulting image would be approximately 10 x 6.5 inches (3000/300 = 10 and 2000/300 = 6.6)—a significantly smaller photo. How do you know which works best with your camera and printer? Test them both and see.

Unfortunately, digital camera manufacturers have not been consistent with how they associate a particular linear resolution with the camera's images. It would make sense to use a "real" linear resolution like 300 dpi (commonly used in the publishing industry) or 200 dpi (used with printers), but that sort of "sense" is not part of the camera making industry. A resolution of 72 dpi is commonly used, but this is puzzling. It is a web resolution and not an appropriate resolution for any type of printer. With that hypothetical 6-megapixel camera, a 72 dpi image would be approximately 42 x 28 inches, which is too large for most uses.

An image of this size won't fit on any web site and it can't be printed with any quality. What were they thinking? Before printing any digital camera files, you will usually

As the menu shows along the bottom of the screen, this camera gives the user a choice of five JPEG file sizes, plus RAW format file capture. The JPEG files are differentiated by image resolution, with the largest size being 3072 x 2304 pixels.

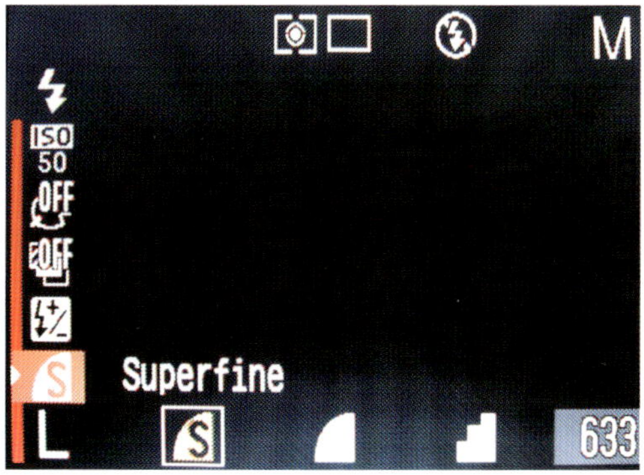

The user then sets the amount of compression to be applied to the JPEG file. (RAW files have no compression.) Use the lowest compression setting as much as possible for the best results.

need to adjust the linear resolution. This is found in the Size, Resize, or Resample choice in image-processing software. Some printing programs will do the resizing automatically. The image must be resized because printing an image at too high a linear resolution (such as 600 dpi) can actually reduce the quality of the print. The printer cannot output an image at this high resolution and discards some of the data. Also, this can slow printing down because the computer must process more data than is needed for the print.

Setting the Camera

With your digital camera you may be able to capture images at several possible resolutions. Most of the time you should use the maximum resolution offered by the camera. This delivers files with the most potential; you will not be limited to small-sized prints. Plus it gives you the resolution you paid for. You can always reduce the size of an image, but increasing the pixels in a low-resolution image will never give you good quality.

If your need is only to display photos on the Internet, it is more efficient to shoot at a resolution that is less than maximum. This will give you smaller files that transfer faster, take up less space, and can be worked on quickly. If your photos are only going to be viewed on the computer (e.g., selling on eBay or documenting possessions for insurance purposes), shooting at the highest resolution is not necessary.

File Formats

File formats are the types of image files that your camera creates. This information can also be confusing, especially since you'll often hear contradictory advice about which format is best to use.

TIFF (Tagged Image File Format)—This is an ideal format for photographs—once they are in the computer—but it is not ideal for the camera! TIFF files are uncompressed full-data files that retain image details when used as a working file format in the computer. However, they are large files that slow down the camera, hog memory card space, and offer no real advantage for image capture. This is why most cameras no longer offer this format.

JPEG (Joint Photographic Experts Group)—JPEG is an international standard for extremely smart compression technology that offers a small file with superb detail. Technically, JPEG is a compression scheme and not a true format, but it is effectively considered a format. The amount of compression can be varied and, while the higher compression gives smaller files that fit easily on the memory card, those files start to lose important data. JPEG is a "lossy" format which means data is lost as the file is compressed. At high-quality (low-compression) settings, most of the lost data is redundant and can easily be rebuilt when the file is uncompressed. At high compression levels more data is discarded—including some information that is necessary for displaying tonal gradients and other fine details. The JPEG format can work great, but it should be used at the highest quality settings most of the time.

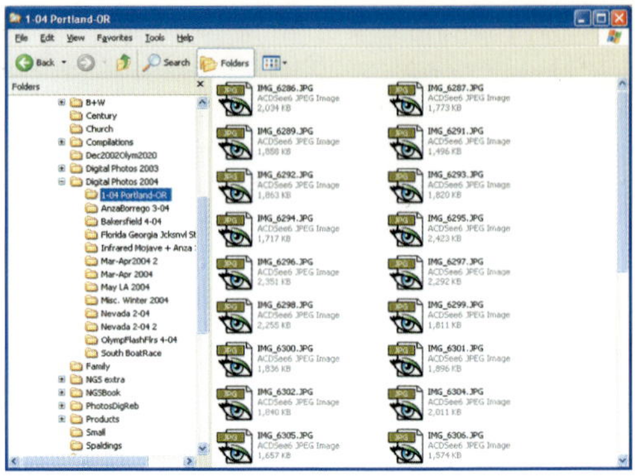

JPEG is a common digital image format that has excellent quality when used at low compression levels.

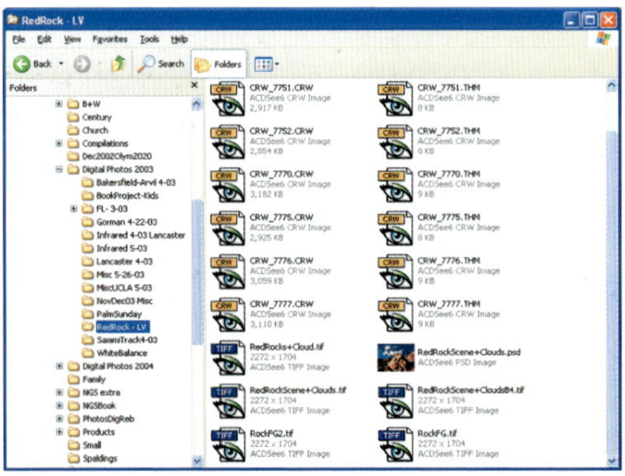

RAW image files offer more adjustment capabilities than JPEG, but can also require more processing and a more complicated workflow.

RAW—This type of file uses data as it comes from the sensor with little processing. It is a "full-featured" file in that it offers more color data than a JPEG file. RAW is a 16-bit file format that easily holds the 12 bits of color data that today's digital cameras capture. (A common misconception is that since a RAW file is based on 16-bit color, it is using 16 bits of data from the sensor; sensors today provide 12 bits.) JPEG is an 8-bit file that holds much less color and tonal information—especially in the darkest and lightest areas of a photo. RAW files are proprietary for each camera manufacturer. You need special software to read these files and to process them.

The Advantages of JPEG

When you save your photos as JPEG files from the camera, there are advantages and disadvantages. One disadvantage is loss of detail, especially if too much compression is used. It's best to use the highest quality (lowest compression) setting. While a JPEG file also contains less color and tonal information on a mathematical basis than a RAW file, for most photographic purposes the difference is not important.

In addition, JPEG offers some special advantages. Nearly all advanced compact digital cameras have unique processing chips built into the camera that examine the data coming off of the sensor and (using highly refined algorithms) process that information to get the most out of the image as captured by the sensor. These processors will look at the same data that is recorded to RAW files, but do some work on image qualities like tonality and color in order to record a better image file to JPEG. In essence the camera smartly converts the 12-bit file captured by the camera into the best 8-bit file that JPEG can record.

Special Features of RAW

Not all compact cameras offer RAW format capture. When RAW is available, the files offer the ultimate in total data to the photographer along with the ability to have complete control over that information. Up until a couple of years ago, this was not as great an advantage as it should have been. There were few software programs available that could work with 16-bit files other than the camera manufacturer's conversion software. This often made RAW file processing slow and tedious—plus the conversion software varied considerably in how much adjustment could be made.

That limitation is no longer the case. Manufacturers' software has gotten faster and offers better control. Image processing programs, like Adobe Photoshop, can now convert RAW files and work fully with 16-bit files. (They used to have strong limitations in that program.) A big advantage of a 16-bit file is that the extra data increases the capability to adjust the image and reduces the chances that banding (or posterizing) will occur. A JPEG 8-bit file can offer great quality, but if you make major changes to it (big adjustments in color or tonality), gaps will occur which cause banding across gradients. When this occurs, the tones no longer blend seamlessly and will have obvious looking step patterns. This is much less likely with RAW.

RAW files are terrific when color is off, too. With the extra information to work with, the conversion software can often make better color adjustments. Most RAW conversion software will allow you to change the white balance—just like you were changing it on the camera—in addition to making more precise color adjustments in actual color temperature or color tints.

If you need really big files interpolated above the camera's file size (e.g., to make larger prints than with the camera's normal file size), 16 bit is the best way to go. Most conversion software allows you to do this

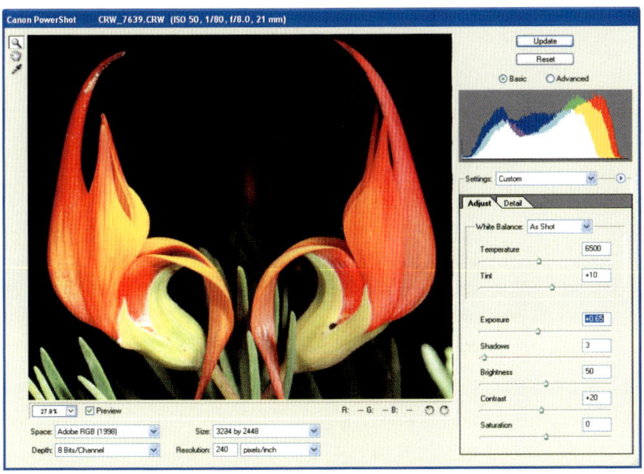

RAW files need special software programs but you do gain increased control over your changes to an image.

ramping up of size in the software while you are still in the conversion stage, and Photoshop offers enlargement algorithms that work on 16-bit images. The reason for this advantage is the amount of additional image data. Remember, more file data gives the computer more information to interpolate up in size.

Choosing a Format

It's the battle of the digital age. Everyone is weighing in with more than simple opinions. The sad thing, I think, is that many photographers feel forced into using RAW when it is not appropriate for their needs and may make their photography less fun and more work. Since RAW can be better for certain things, some experts want everyone to believe it is the only way to go for all photography with digital cameras. This makes the JPEG user feel inferior. I have even heard photographers say that they don't want to use JPEG because it is an "amateur" format with poor color and tonality. That could not be further from the truth. Look at the photos throughout this book. Almost every one of them, with just a few exceptions, originated as a JPEG because I personally prefer working with that format.

I have shot for magazines, including *Outdoor Photographer* and *PCPhoto*, with images printed across two-page spreads and completed several books that were produced with digital photos, including the *Epson Complete Guide to Digital Printing* and *PCPhoto Guide to Digital SLRs*. Only a scant few photos in these publications came from RAW files.

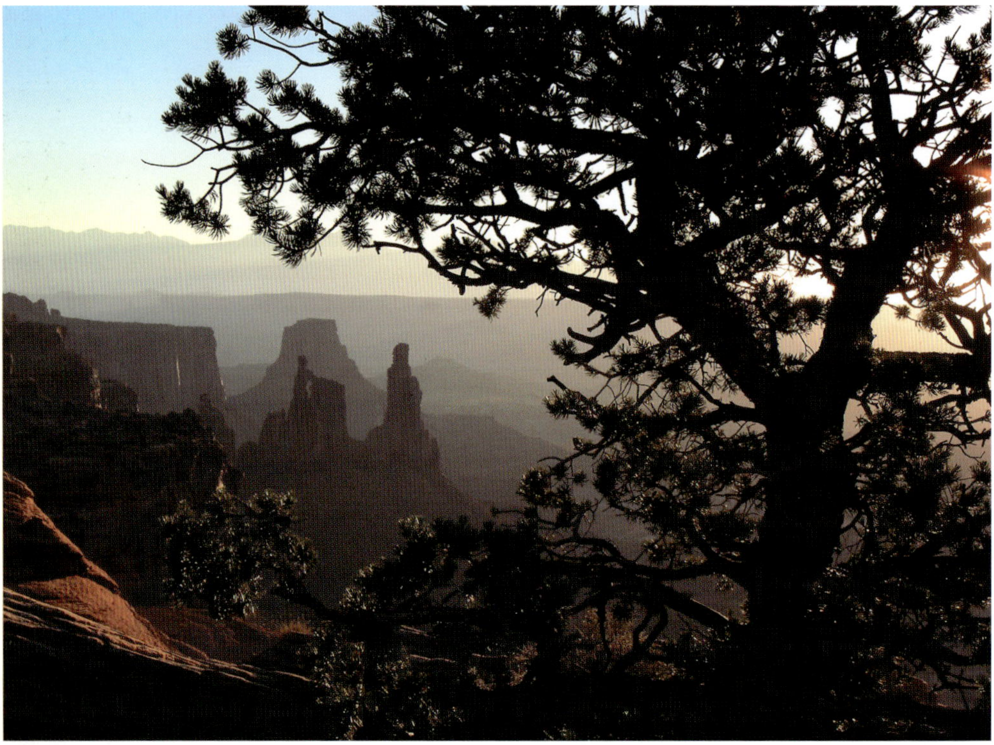

The photos on the opposite page are details from the center of this image. You will not see any real differences between the TIFF and high-quality JPEG files. If you look carefully, you will see some detail degradation in the other shots.

The only thing this really says is that I like working with JPEG and can get the publication-quality results I need. Several of my good friends in the nature photography industry would not consider shooting anything but RAW. They say they like the extra flexibility they get to process the image after the shot. They get more exposure latitude, the ability to easily readjust things like color balance and the capability of making higher quality enlargements if the file has to be interpolated up in size.

Still, some amateur photographers wonder about the world of professional photographers. Don't they rely on RAW files to be published in high-quality applications? Yes, that is absolutely true for some pros. But I can also tell you from working with a lot of pros that many of them shoot JPEG files that end up being used in high-quality applications, too. The point is simple: Pros use both formats for their work and achieve beautiful results from each of them.

What is important is the photography you do and your way of working, not what some other digital photographer wants you to do. If you were used to shooting snapshots with film, JPEG is a good way to go. If you love the darkroom and processing film, RAW is a great continuation of that process. Coping with problematic lighting that needs every little nuance of tone and color? RAW may give you the best results. You have tons of images to handle? JPEG may be the most efficient. Notice that I said "may"—there are no absolutes about these formats, it is about you and what you need from your photographs.

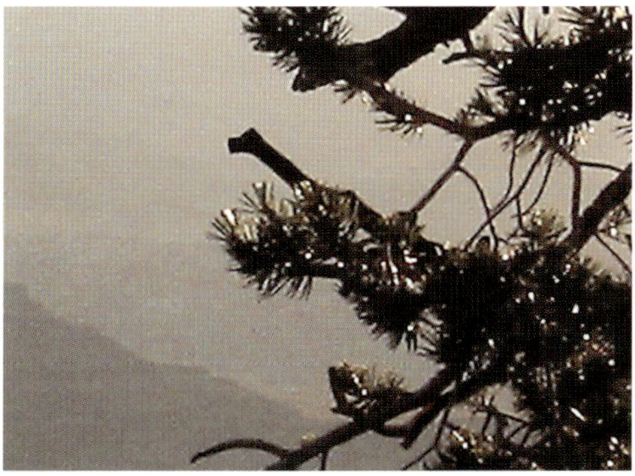

TIFF

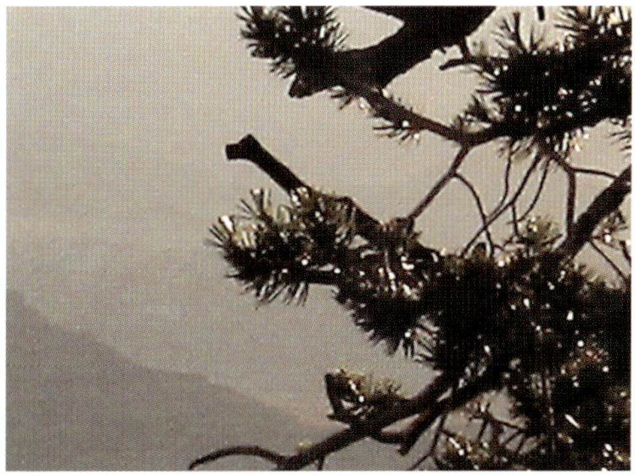

High-quality JPEG

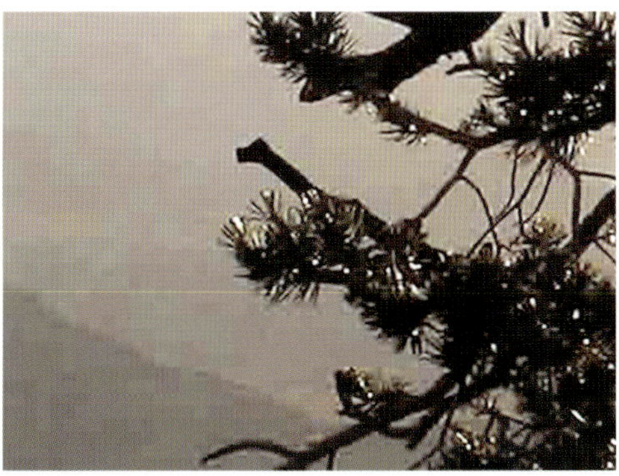

Low-quality JPEG

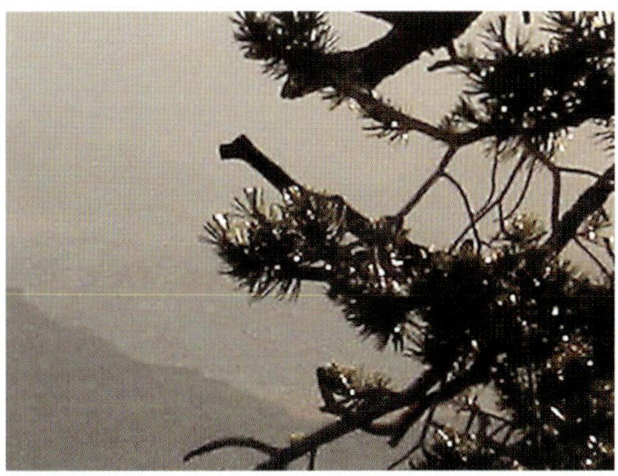

JPEG file saved multiple times

JPEG and RAW should be considered ways of working as much as formats. The key is how you like to work and what results you need. You have to test the formats for yourself and see what fits your photography. Don't be intimidated by didactic people who seem to think that anyone who doesn't work the way they do is wrong and should be corrected. Whatever choice you make should be based on your real-world photographic challenges. Whichever format works best for you is the best choice.

One thing to keep in mind is that RAW has the infamous good news and bad news. The good news—you have more choices on how to control your photos. The bad news—you have more choices on how to control your photos. RAW can actually slow you down tremendously if you want to see every choice and what it does for the photo, regardless of the actual speed of the computer or software.

Like many photographers, you may like certain aspects of both JPEG and RAW. Unfortunately, for most digital cameras, it is not a quick process to make the changeover. It is usually a series of button and controller choices that walk you through a menu to make the change.

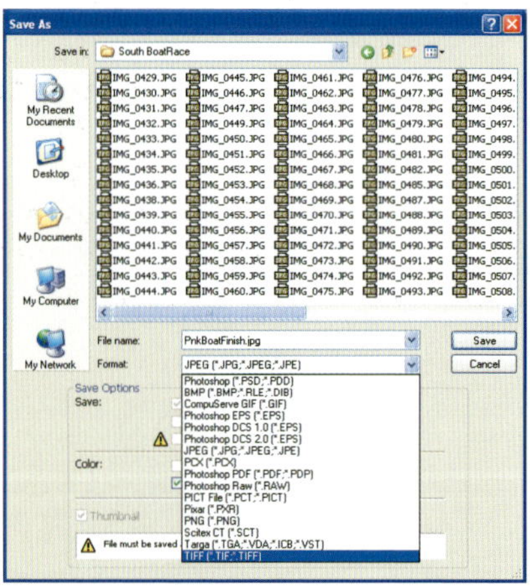

JPEG files should first be saved as either TIFF or the software's native image files (Photoshop in this case) before you make any other adjustments.

What if you could choose each format as you shoot? Maybe even after the shot was made? Canon has a control that lets you do just that. It would be nice if all camera manufacturers offered this, and if Canon included it on all their cameras. Here's what happens: in the top-of-the-line Canon PowerShot cameras, you can decide if a photo should be JPEG or RAW when it shows up on "Review" on the LCD right after you take the picture. You shoot in high-quality JPEG, then simply hit the Function button when the photo appears on the LCD after releasing the shutter. At that point, the camera asks you if you want to save the photo as a RAW file and you say yes. This lets you start to take a JPEG photo, then change your mind and take a RAW photo almost instantly. This is a great feature that should be on more cameras.

Moving Pictures

Most small digital cameras offer a neat little feature—video capture. You can actually shoot videos with the camera. It is all recorded to the memory card. This is not something that is available on digital SLRs.

The quality varies as well as the maximum length of the recording. In video, a resolution of 640 x 480 is standard; this is the standard for all television programs. The lowest quality video recorded by digital cameras is 160 x 120 and will play on your computer screen in a small window. This size is not large enough to give any decent quality on a television. Another common resolution is half the standard at 320 x 240; this will look okay on TV, almost as good as VHS, though still not at optimum video quality. The highest resolution is the television standard of 640 x 480.

The reason for these resolutions is size—the lowest make videos that take up considerably less space on your memory card or hard drive. For example, you can store the following amounts of video on a 1 GB card: 16 minutes at 640 x 480, 45 minutes at 320 x 240 and 109 minutes at 160 x 120. Another thing that affects storage is the type of file format used by the camera. QuickTime and AVI use more space than MPEG—all formats work well for video, though QuickTime and AVI can be easier to edit in some software.

Frame rate is another important issue. The standard frame rate for video is 30 frames per second. That requires processing time and more storage space if done in a digital camera. This is why you'll find video there at a lower frame rate, such as 10–15 fps. This will look a little choppier than the standard 30 fps, but it will keep file sizes smaller. If you can shoot at 640 x 480, 30 fps, you will gain the highest quality, best looking video, but this can use up space on your memory card in a hurry. Because camera processing is so intense on these files, the camera may have to quit recording after a short time to catch up. This is why video from a digital camera may be limited to a short duration.

Digital camera videos can look great, but, at the moment, is certainly not a replacement for a camcorder. A camcorder will allow you to always shoot at true video quality for as long as you want. In addition, the miniature microphones on a digital camera don't offer a lot of quality compared to those on a camcorder, plus you can add external mikes to most camcorders for the best sound.

Still, for many photographers, video built into a digital camera does offer the chance to take high-quality video quickly and easily. It is ideal for snapshot videos, to grab quick and easy video of the kids, and more. Plus, downloading the captured video is easy—just use a card reader and drag and drop the files from memory card to hard drive. My daughter and her friends recently used a digital camera to make a video for school and she loved being able to download and edit it so easily.

The real advantage is that the video is on a memory card so you can download it directly into your computer. There is no "capture" of the video playing at real time from a camcorder. You can literally drag-and-drop your video files from card to hard drive and start editing immediately.

An interesting variation on video is a sequence of shots made with an intervalometer feature. A number of advanced digital cameras have included this unique way of shooting. If you remember seeing time-lapse photography in nature shows on the Discovery Channel, you have seen an intervalometer at work. This is simply a special timer that triggers the shutter at set intervals. You can usually set such controls for anything from a picture a second to a picture an hour. The camera typically shuts itself down in between long intervals and wakes up for the shot, then sleeps again.

These photos can be viewed as separate images, but you can watch them as a fascinating look at something changing over time. This type of sequence shooting has made growing seeds seem alive, flowers explode into bloom and buildings rise to full size in minutes. It can be a fun tool to play with. You simply lock the camera down, focused on the subject. Give extra compositional room for something growing. If you want to transfer this to video, think about the time you want the event to appear, then consider you will have 30 frames per second, so you want something that will give 30 shots multiplied by the number of seconds in which you want the completed sequence to occur.

get the most from your digital camera

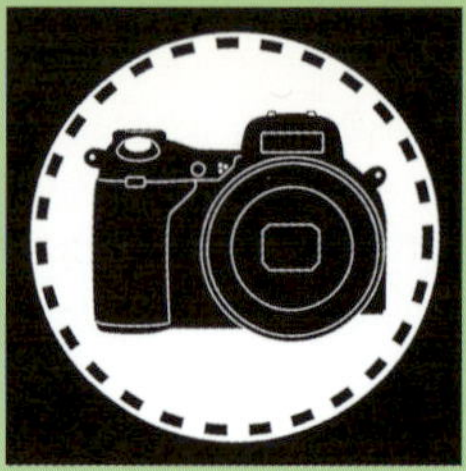

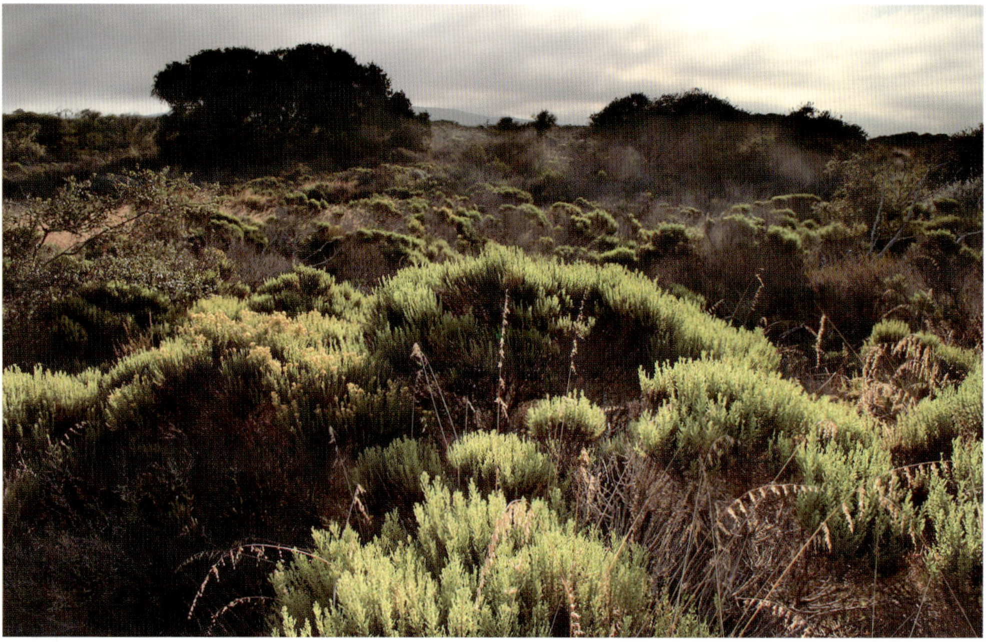

The LCD monitor has truly revolutionized picture taking for many photographers. There is no longer the "hope-I-got-it" attitude. Instead, just check the shot and re-shoot if necessary.

The LCD Monitor

If just one thing were identified as the key to changes in photography due to digital cameras, the LCD monitor would definitely get the nod, no questions asked. The ability to see the picture immediately after capture gives instant feedback on how well you are doing. You can see if the composition looks good. Was the exposure right? Did the subject blink? Even a beginning photographer with the most basic of digital cameras can quickly see how the photo looks and make adjustments.

Another great feature of the compact digital camera is its "live" LCD. You now see photographers holding a camera out so they can look at its LCD while shooting. This feature—the ability to see what the sensor is seeing at all times—is not found in digital SLRs because of the mirror used to reflect light from lens to viewfinder. A live LCD lets you view the image, before you take the picture, so you can judge composition, white balance, exposure, and so forth, which can be very, very helpful. Let's look at the example of white balance. When using the LCD monitor as a viewfinder, you see immediately if the white balance is not correct, so you can fix it right away.

In addition, the LCD has made professional techniques more accessible to all photographers. For example, look at flash photography. You never would have thought of doing anything sophisticated with a little camera. Yet, even if the only flash available is the one built into the camera, the digital camera gives more choices on how and why to use the flash. You don't have to worry about wasting film. Even pros have had major challenges with flash. Although their flash had modeling lights that supposedly showed what the flash would do, one could never be sure of the light unless some test Polaroids were shot to see what the camera was truly getting.

Now with the camera's LCD, you gain something truly better because you see the real photo in the LCD, not a substitute that has to be retaken with the "real" film. Now anyone can use flash and check the results to be sure they got the shot. And you can use this tool at any time and in any light.

The LCD monitor has truly revolutionized picture taking for many photographers. There is no longer the "hope I got it" attitude. Instead one just checks and reshoots. Again and again, photographers find that they love being able to respond to both the subject and the photograph at the same time. It allows you to make changes while the subject is still there. This is truly a godsend with travel photography when you are at a location of a lifetime and probably won't be returning soon. The LCD is like insurance because you know that you got the shots you wanted.

But sometimes the LCD panel isn't used as effectively as it could be. It can be hard to see in certain light, it requires a conscious effort to use it all the time (although many of the compact digital cameras make it so convenient compared to the viewfinder that many photographers just naturally use it), and it increases drain on the battery. I have heard people recommend that you never use the LCD for shooting, only for reviewing, and then only sparingly, just because of battery use. I believe that is bad advice and keeps one from really benefiting from a digital camera. Being able to use the LCD the battery power used. The latest cameras have new circuitry that increases the battery efficiency, making the LCD all the more inviting. With digital, it's so easy and you get such valuable information, so why not check?

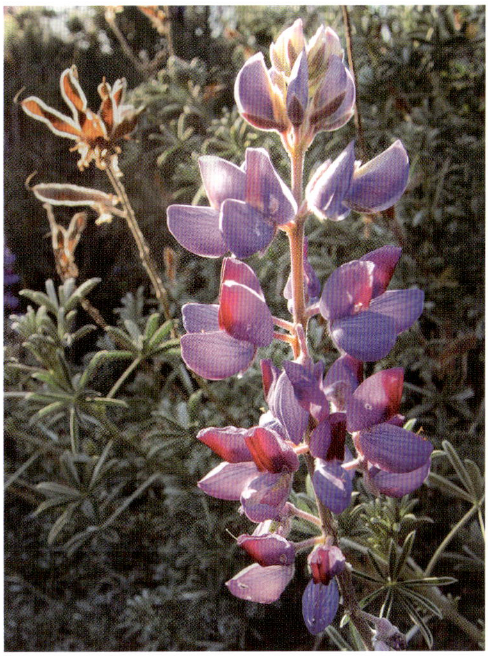

With the LCD monitor, you can check exposure before, during, and after the shot! Continue to check as the light changes, because you can see what is happening in the live LCD view. The LCD is not a perfect rendering of what your image will be, but with practice you can learn to accurately interpret the image you see.

LCDs That Move

While this feature is pretty standard on video cameras, the tilting or swiveling LCD has been a real innovation on digital cameras. It is a great benefit and top compact camera models include a variation on this design. This offers the photographer a great way of ensuring that the LCD can be seen. Stuck flat on the back of the camera, the traditional LCD is great as long as you can position yourself so you can see the back of the camera.

Tilting LCDs pop out from the camera back and tilt up and down so that you can see the screen from any angle. Instead of holding the camera out in front of your face, a position that can cause sharpness problems because of camera movement or "shake" during the exposure, you can hold the camera at chest level, keeping your arms close to your body for more support. Yet, you can see the LCD (and the scene) quite well. It is actually easier to shield the camera LCD with a hand when in this position, too. It is like using an old-time twin-lens reflex camera, but with all the technology of today.

Low-angle, and even ground level shots, are now simplified. Tilt the screen up and you can put the camera at flower level, for example, yet you don't have to lay on the ground to see the view. If your camera is on a tripod, you can put it at any height and see the LCD without contorting your body to use the viewfinder or a back-mounted LCD.

You can even go high. Tilt the screen back and hold the camera over your head to photograph over a crowd. Or if you set the camera on a tripod, there are times you cannot easily get to the viewfinder or back-mounted LCD because of the terrain or because of the height of the camera. You can still easily see an angled LCD and your shot. This offers some really great advantages to giving you the most flexibility possible in setting up a creative shot.

A few cameras, notably models from Canon and Nikon, have an LCD monitor that flips out from the camera back, then swivels and tilts for an infinite number of positions. This offers a couple of advantages over the strictly tilting LCD. First, it allows you to see the LCD when you are

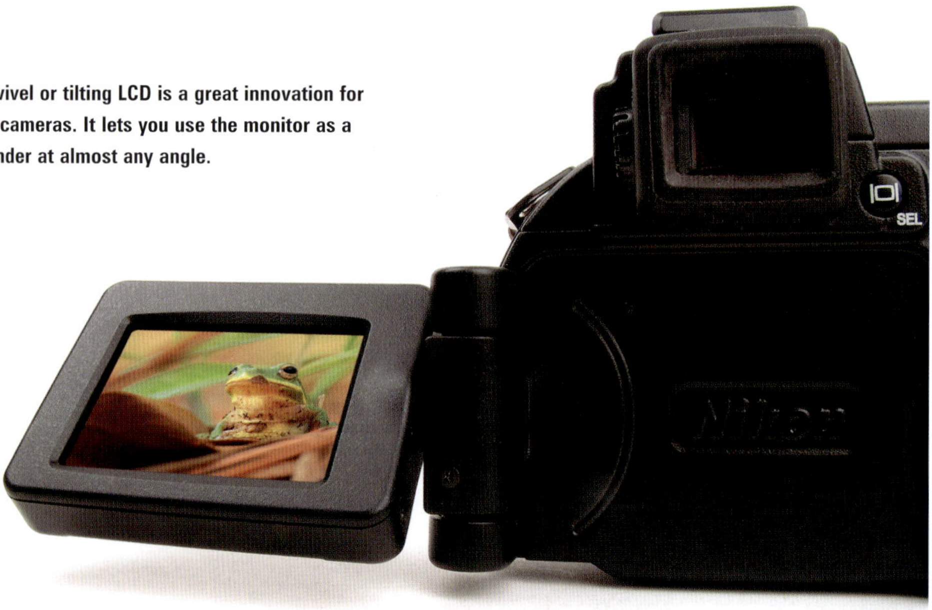

The swivel or tilting LCD is a great innovation for digital cameras. It lets you use the monitor as a viewfinder at almost any angle.

shooting a vertical with the camera and using the viewfinder is inconvenient. You simply flip the monitor out and swivel it into position. The other thing a swivel monitor can do is to pivot completely so that you can see the LCD from the front of the camera. This lets you take a self portrait. However, it also lets you take pictures in a tight spot. You can literally put the camera up against a wall with the LCD facing outward, and still see what the lens is seeing.

Edit as You Go

The review function of your camera lets you access your photos at any time. For me, this is very important. I like to check them as I shoot to confirm that I have captured the image exactly as I wanted to, and I can edit as I go. You may, however, hear some photographers tell you never to do this. They believe that if you edit as you go, you may remove photos that might have been keepers.

The ability to edit as you go is certainly very convenient and easy. You simply call up an image on the LCD, evaluate it (you may want to enlarge it to check sharpness) and then keep or trash it. You may want to safeguard some images so they cannot be easily erased—most cameras offer a "lock" function for that purpose. It is usually in the playback menu, but you may have to consult your camera manual to see where it is on your camera

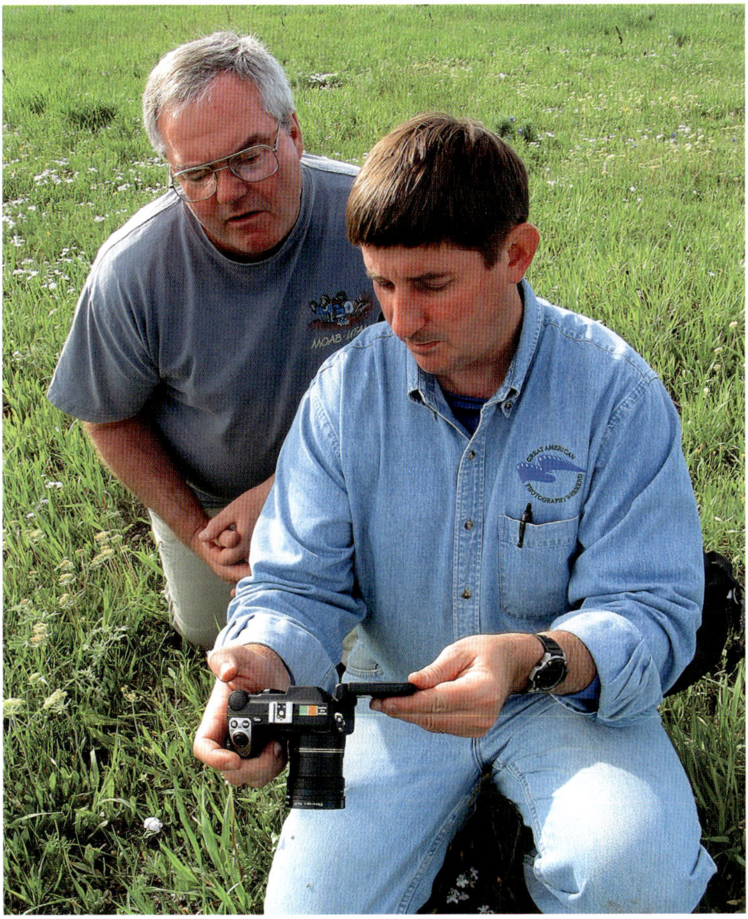

By reviewing your photos and editing as you go, you can confirm that you are getting the images you want.

Advantages of In-Camera Editing

1. **Exposure and composition check:** Being able to see what your image looks like with your exposure and composition choices is vital. You will quickly know if you should continue with the same choices or try something new.

2. **Improvement:** Increasingly, photographers are finding that looking critically at photos while shooting improves subsequent pictures. Long-time pros have told me this is a big advantage for them and gives them a newfound excitement for their photography. You could keep all the shots after looking at them, but I believe that when you delete the "bad" shots, you not only clear them from the memory card, but you also clear them from your mind. You can focus on what is working for you, since that is what stays on the card and in your memory.

3. **Reduce clutter:** If you keep all your photos as you shoot, you're more likely to just move them all to your computer and you'll end up with a lot of junk to deal with later. Where do you put them? How do you organize them in the computer? You could toss them into a file and forget them, but then they just take up hard-drive space. Filling your computer with loads of mediocre photos that you'll never go back to can be overwhelming. Take a few minutes to edit.

4. **Trends:** As you look at your photos you will begin to notice trends in your picture taking. You may see a tendency to always capture subjects at certain angles. You can adjust your shooting based on that understanding. Or maybe you'll notice a thread of an idea beginning to develop as you review a large group of images. I find it really interesting to work with composition by taking some photos, checking how they look, and then seeing what new shots I can make.

5. **More complete coverage:** In the film and video industries there is always a lot of talk about "coverage" (or capturing the subject from different angles, varied distances and so forth). News photographers will do this to be sure they bring back their best photos for publication. By looking over your photos as you go, you can evaluate your coverage of the subject. This means you are more likely to get more photos you really want to keep. You won't later be disappointed that you missed a key picture. This will instantly upgrade the quality of your photography.

6. **Pride:** As anyone who takes a lot of photos knows, it can be disappointing when you review photographs from a shooting expedition. Some great photos stand out, but it's normal to find a lot of junk that doesn't quite make it, sometimes seeming to mock your ability as a photographer. When the final selection of photos you bring home are ones that you can take pride in, it's very satisfying.

7. **Less work later:** With a lot of images comes the challenge of editing them down to a reasonable number to work on and keep. This editing job is time-consuming and can mean that photos sit unedited or unused for months. Even if you edit just a little as you go, you make your job much easier later.

8. **Memory cards:** As memory cards get larger and less expensive, storage space will become less of an issue. Still, cleaning up the trash is a good habit that will optimize the use of your cards.

Exposure

Exposure has become so automatic that you can get really good results without understanding exposure or metering. Cameras and their metering systems do their job remarkably well—even low-priced cameras can be surprisingly good. Yet, there can be tricky situations when automatic exposure won't make a great photo. Sometimes a "good" automatic exposure from the camera isn't actually the best exposure for your subject, or it isn't the photo you envisioned. To get an exposure that truly expresses your intent in photographing a subject, to bring out a mood or to enhance a composition, there are things you can do to transform a good exposure into the great image you really want.

Check Your LCD

Let me emphasize one thing: the camera's LCD monitor is a huge benefit in getting the right exposure. Professional photographers used to rely on Polaroids to check exposure. They'd take a shot with a Polaroid back (film holder) on their studio camera and then process to check the image for exposure and contrast. But, even then, they couldn't be absolutely sure, because what was seen in the Polaroid was not the final shot.

With the LCD monitor, you can check exposure before, during, and after the real shot! Continue to check as the light changes, because you can see what is happening in the live LCD view. The LCD is not a perfect rendering of what your image

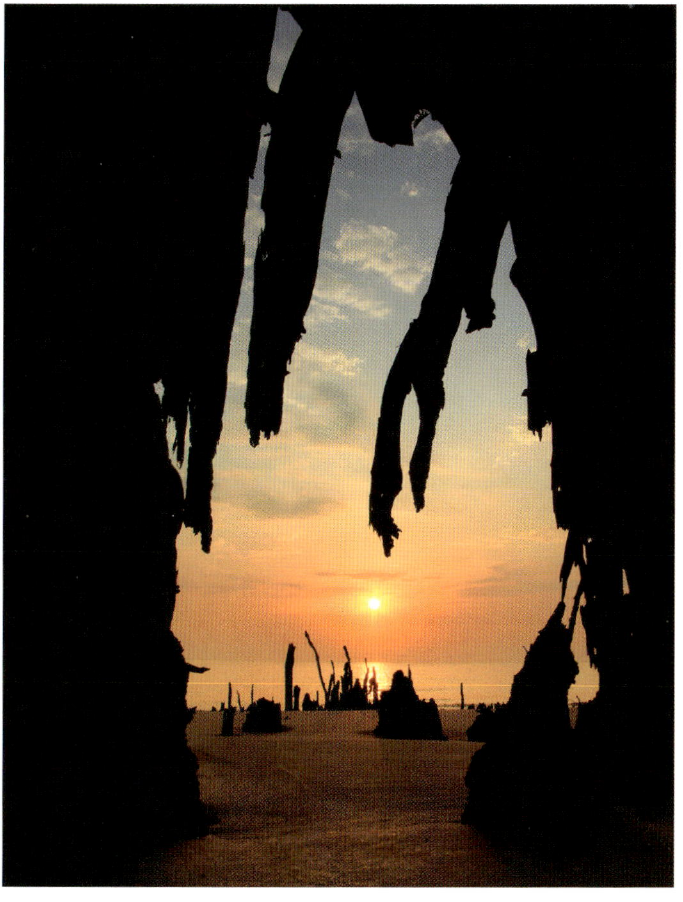

This can be a tricky exposure to make. You want the outer frame to be dark and the sunrise should have rich vibrant colors. Use the LCD to check the effect. Then, adjust exposure and try new shots until the image looks the way you want it to.

The histogram shown in the lower left corner of the photo is a graphic representation of all the tones in this image.

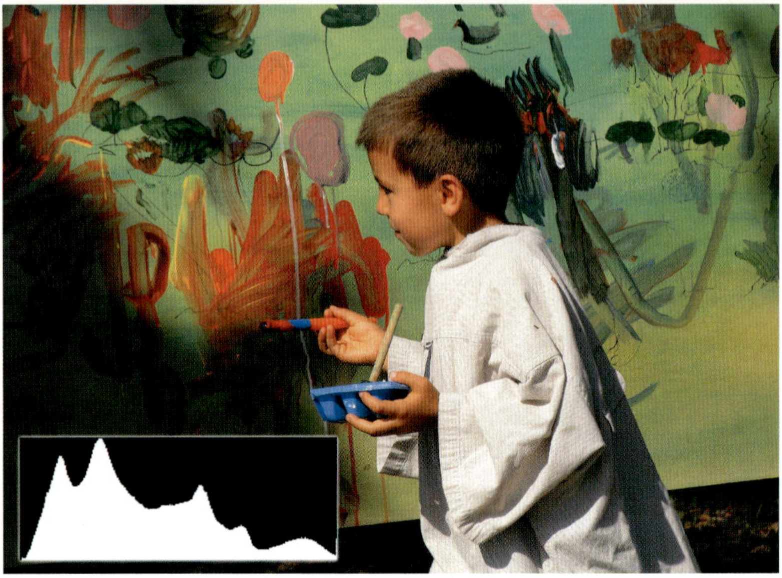

will be, but with practice you can learn to accurately interpret what you see. In addition, since most advanced cameras offer one, I strongly urge you to learn to read a histogram (see page 76), because it provides another way to check exposure. Still, if you choose not to really study exposure or the histogram, the LCD monitor will always give you a good idea of your exposure.

Film vs. Digital Exposure

Film and sensors respond to light differently. Typically, digital cameras act like slide film with highlights (which go pure white quickly with overexposure), but respond more like print film for shadows (which can contain a great deal of detail). Digital cameras are more likely to overexpose highlights than to underexpose shadows. However, even if the same sensor is used (and typically, the same sensor size among different brands indicates the same sensor), there are still variations in the tonal contrasts of the image because of internal processing circuits in the camera. These are different from manufacturer to manufacturer, and from low- to high-priced cameras.

You need to experiment a bit with your camera to see how it responds to light. Be wary of overexposed highlights that need detail (such a bright clouds), and be aware that underexposed shadows can be full of noise. Check your camera's metering system to be sure you have an exposure that keeps detail in the highlights and avoids making shadows too bright.

This may mean compromises, as the real world often has more detail in the dark and light areas of a scene than the camera is capable of capturing. When a digital image has washed-out highlights, no amount of work in Photoshop will bring them back. And, although a very dark image may have detail that can be enhanced, it may lack important color information and show unwanted sensor noise.

Think about your subject and the scene. Are the highlights or shadows most important? In cases of extreme lighting conditions, expose to get the best detail where it matters most for the success of the photo. A bit of overexposed hair when someone is backlit may be fine. Or a completely black shadow may just make the scene more dramatic.

Understanding Metering

If you understand how metering systems work, from the very basics of the sensor's response to light to how the camera's entire system reads and interprets this information, you may be better able to interpret and adjust your camera for the best exposures. Many photographers believe that the camera meter is designed to choose the perfect exposure level. The meter sensor only reads how much light is hitting it from the scene. It is calibrated to give an exposure that will make the scene it sees middle gray—a reasonable choice for many photos because, often, there are a lot of midtones in a scene.

A simple meter can't really tell if the scene is filled with light, midtone, or dark objects, yet if the light is the same on any of them, the exposure should be identical. Unfortunately, the meter will in fact give different exposures, making light objects too dark, and dark objects too light. To compensate, camera manufacturers have developed some rather sophisticated systems for metering that include quite a bit of computing power. (Typically, more expensive cameras have more advanced systems.) These systems usually only work with automatic settings so they cannot be directly compared to the way manual exposures are metered, even with the same camera.

Most cameras have metering systems that utilize multiple sensing points across the entire image area. The camera reads the light at these points and then compares them with rather sophisticated algorithms. It does this very smartly, trying to come up with an exposure that works for the range of light values present in a scene. These multi-point metering systems are called Matrix, Honeycomb, Evaluative, and other names. Each manufacturer's design has its own unique characteristics and strengths.

Differences among cameras include the number of points available for evaluating an exposure (higher-end cameras typically have more), and the proprietary algorithms used by the camera itself to process exposure information. In the last few years, subject distance has been added to the equation. The metering system also takes into account information about the focus distance. Although there are variations among cameras in different situations, there are guidelines to getting the most from your camera's metering system.

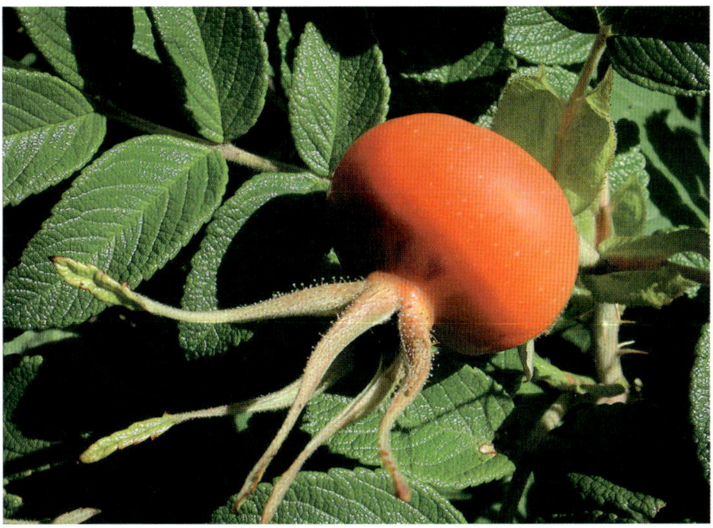

Most digital cameras take exposure readings from multiple points across the scene and compare them to create a good exposure.

Exposure Modes

Every advanced digital camera on the market offers multiple exposure modes that work with the camera's metering system to give you a good exposure. These modes feature approaches to exposure that meet varied needs, but you don't have to use them all. Few photographers do. You will get an equally good exposure with any of these modes, since they all use the complete metering system of the camera to calculate equal exposures for the scene, but they are different in that they offer varied interpretations of shutter speed and f/stop.

Program Mode (P)

Even though the camera is making the basic decisions, the standard Program mode can often be adjusted on a per exposure basis. You can usually shift the shutter speed or aperture slightly and the camera will compensate. Plus, you can use exposure compensation as needed. This is a mode for a photographer who needs to shoot varied scenes quickly, without a lot of thought. The camera will choose reasonable combinations of shutter speed and aperture for the conditions. Street and travel photographers sometimes find this mode useful, as it works without much attention from the photographer.

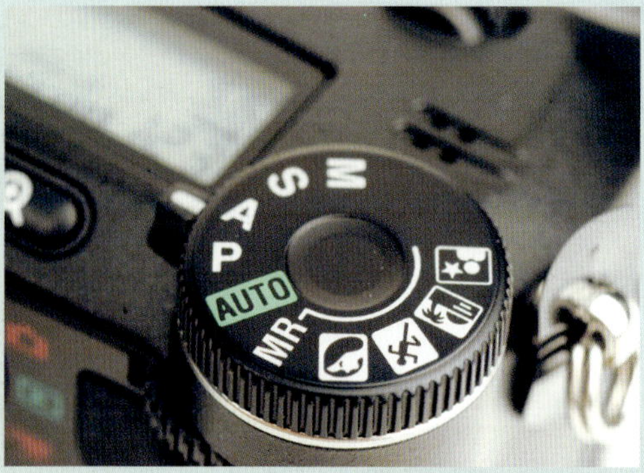

Many cameras use a dial to set the various exposure modes. This camera offers Manual exposure (M), Shutter-Priority (S), Aperture-Priority (A), and Program (P), as well as Full Auto and a selection of four Picture Control modes.

The Autoexposure Modes

- **Program (P)**—The camera sets both the aperture and shutter speed for you.

- **Shutter-Priority (S or Tv)**—You select the shutter speed and the camera sets the aperture. This allows you to control how action is rendered in your photographs.

- **Aperture-Priority (A or Av)**—You set the aperture (lens opening) and the camera chooses the shutter speed. This gives you control over depth of field.

If your camera features all these autoexposure modes, try them out using the ideas that follow. Find a mode that you feel suits you. You may find a particular mode works best for you, one that feels just perfect. Make it your "default" mode, the one you use most of the time. For example, I select Aperture-Priority most of the time, Manual sometimes, Program rarely, and Shutter-Priority almost never. This fits my way of shooting. There is no arbitrary right or wrong choice, only a choice that meets your needs.

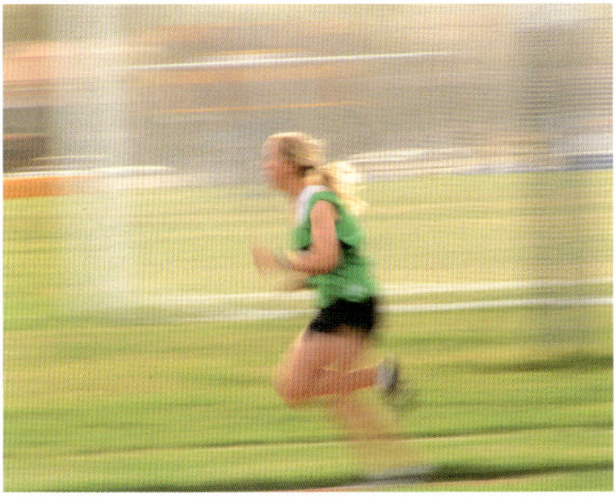

Shutter speed controls how motion is depicted in a photograph. If you need a specific shutter speed to create a blur effect or to freeze movement, Shutter-Priority mode is ideal.

Shutter-Priority Mode (S or Tv)

Shutter-Priority is an important mode when you must have a specific shutter speed for rendering movement, or when you want to get the maximum depth of field possible at a shutter speed appropriate for handholding the camera. The latter may seem a little odd since aperture, not shutter speed, controls depth of field, but it works! For example, you may know that if you zoom your camera's lens to its maximum telephoto setting, the shutter speed must be 1/125 second (or faster) to ensure sharp images when handholding the camera. If you use Program or Aperture-Priority mode, you can't be certain from shot to shot that the camera will set 1/125 as the shutter speed. If you arbitrarily choose a high shutter speed, the camera will use a larger f/stop, and depth of field will be shallow. When you are handholding the camera and know that 1/125 works well, then use Shutter-Priority mode and set that shutter speed. The camera will always set the smallest f/stop for that shutter speed, so you'll always have the smallest f/stop possible for the conditions.

Aperture-Priority Mode (A or Av)

In Aperture-Priority mode, you can select an aperture for specific depth-of-field effects (from deep to shallow) and gain the right shutter speed automatically. You can also guarantee the fastest shutter speeds possible, which is one reason why many pros (and especially sports shooters) like this mode. The fast shutter speed with A (or Av) seems a bit counter-intuitive. This is how it works: When you set a wide lens opening, the camera will always need to choose a high shutter speed to compensate (of course "high" is relative since lighting conditions affect actual exposure). Choose the widest opening (the smallest number for the lens) and the camera must choose the fastest shutter speed possible for the conditions. By leaving the camera set to this f/stop, you guarantee the highest possible action-stopping speed.

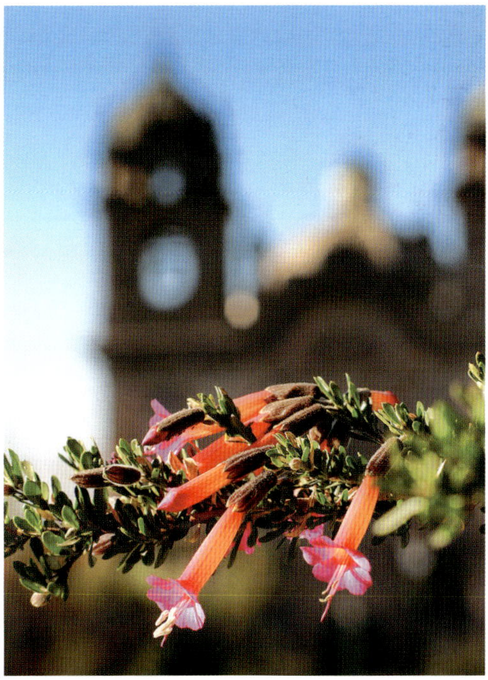

Depth of field is controlled with f/stop settings, making Aperture-Priority mode a great choice for selective focus effects.

Full Auto and Picture Control Modes

Many cameras offer a Full Auto mode (sometimes called Green mode) that really restricts your ability to change the controls. This is a great mode for when you let someone else use your camera. It isn't very useful for the more experienced photographer, because it rarely allows exposure compensation or any other adjustments.

Also, most of the advanced compact zoom cameras include special modes, sometimes called Picture Control, or Subject, modes. These additional autoexposure modes set the camera controls to favor certain subject types. These are designed for specific shooting situations, such as portraits, landscapes, etc. On compact digital cameras, these settings usually control more than exposure, including flash, focus, and white balance.

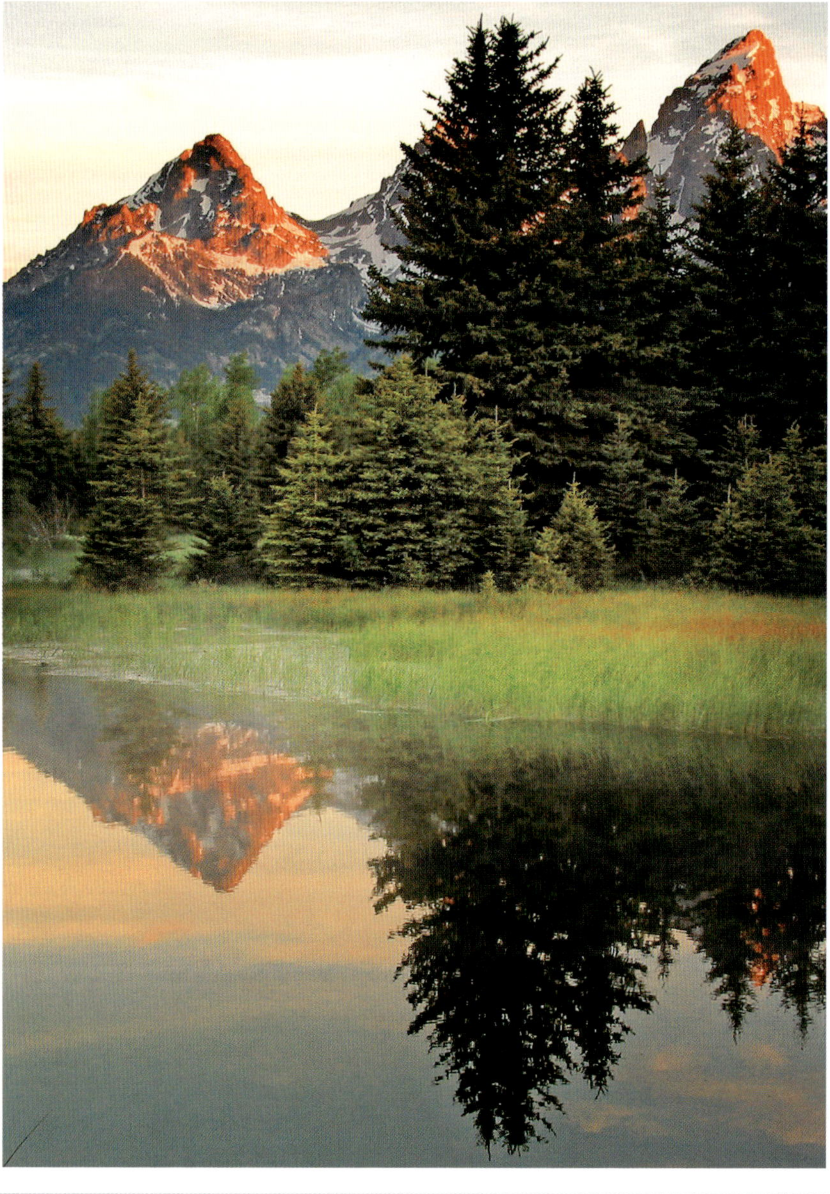

Having the best possible exposure is always preferable, even if you intend to process an image later in the computer, as with this image, which is a composite of two different photos.

• **Portrait**—This mode favors wide apertures and longer focal lengths, for shallow depth of field that accentuates the subject.

• **Landscape**—Designed for scenic photography, this mode favors small apertures and longer focal lengths for maximum depth of field.

• **Action or Sports**—In this mode, high shutter speeds are favored to stop action.

• **Night**—This mode is helpful for long exposures without flash.

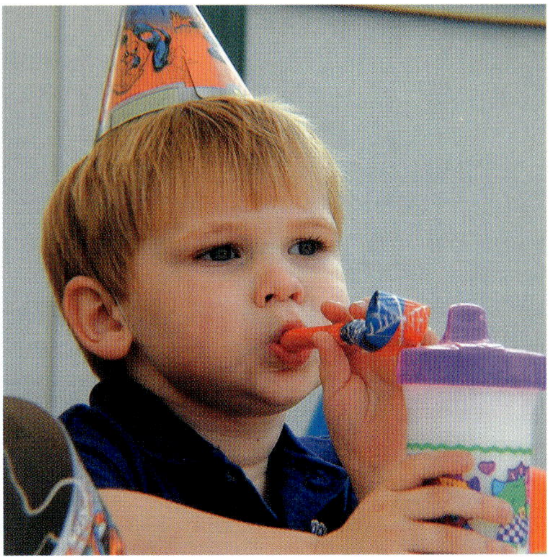

Portrait mode simplifies the choices you have to make. The camera will choose settings that complement close shots of people.

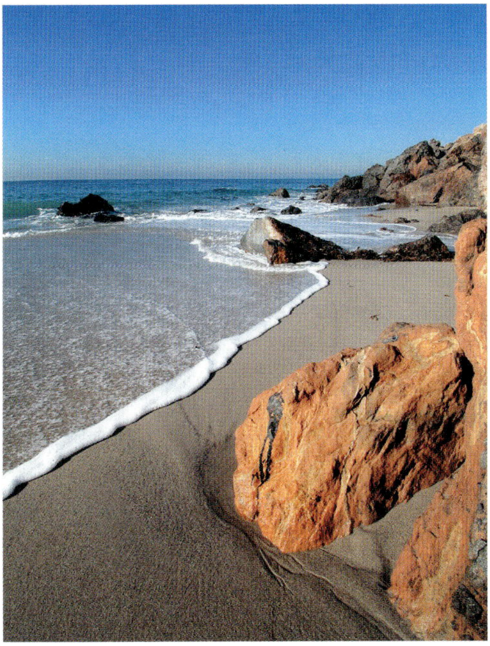

Depth-of-field is usually desirable for scenic shots—Landscape mode ensures a small f/stop will be used for that purpose.

• **Night Flash**—This mode balances flash with the background exposure and is actually useful for more than night photography (try it on people on a gloomy, cloudy day, for example).

• **Close-Up**—To minimize the effects of camera movement during the exposure, a moderate aperture is set to balance a faster shutter speed for close-focus work.

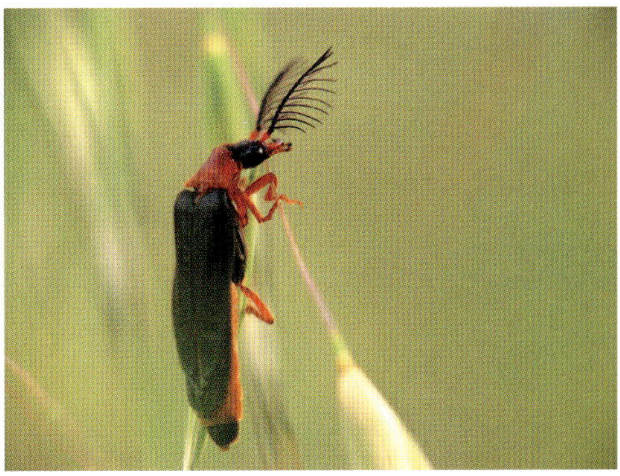

The Close-up mode will favor a higher shutter speed and wider lens opening to prevent blur due to camera movement when handholding up close.

Manual Exposure Mode

Manual exposure is still important but, to make the most of it, you really need to spend some time experimenting so that you understand how it works on your camera: especially since it does not include the sophisticated calculation involved in the multi-point autoexposure systems. Thanks to digital technology, though, you can learn some of the basics very quickly since you can see the results instantly.

Why Use Manual Exposure?

Manual exposure is especially useful in tricky lighting conditions or when shooting side-by-side images to digitally construct a panoramic photo. The sequential photos must match so they can be joined into a panoramic photo in the computer. Manual exposure is also useful for problem flash exposures, when you are trying to match flash with existing light.

A good example of this is when you're shooting indoors near windows. The light on the subject doesn't change, but as you move around, the brightness of the background can change (e.g. as you move to include wall or window). Although exposure should remain constant on the subject, autoexposure will usually fail to do that in these lighting conditions.

Autoexposure will frequently change the exposure as these multiple images are shot, creating problems when you try to use them in some combination (when the images should match). Manual exposure lets you set exposure that will not change from image to image.

Flash that balances the ambient light can be a very effective technique that takes away some of the harshness of direct flash and makes it look more natural. In Manual (or M) mode you freely choose both shutter speed and aperture. The aperture affects the brightness of the flash and the

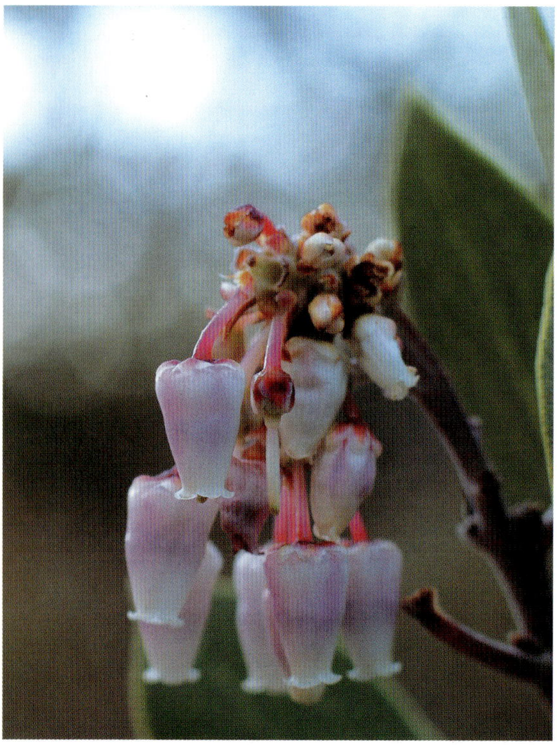

An exposure like this one can be tricky. The bright background could have fooled the meter into underexposing the photo. Using Manual exposure allowed the photographer to override the meter reading and open the aperture.

shutter speed setting controls the ambient light exposure. The digital camera lets you experiment and immediately see what you can get by making these adjustments.

Some compact cameras offer several metering system options for Manual mode, like center-weighted and spot-metering. These are also sometimes available for other modes. (There is no standard, so check your camera's manual.)

Center-weighted systems favor the metering sensors in the center of the image area, then decrease in sensitivity toward the outside of the frame. It is probably the manual exposure system most commonly found in cameras. You can take advantage of this by setting an exposure and pointing your camera to center on the key light of the scene. Then recompose so that it is no longer in the middle.

Spot metering is another useful manual exposure metering technology where a tiny spot in the image area is used for checking exposure. True spot metering is the ability to meter a "spot" that is just a few percentage points of a scene. This is not very common in cameras. Most digital cameras that have this feature typically use something called partial metering, where the metering is centered in a small area of the center of the viewfinder (often about 8-10%). If you zoom to a telephoto focal length, this becomes a true spot meter.

Spot metering is ideal when you have problems getting a reading off a subject where the surrounding areas have varied lighting. (Manual exposure is especially useful during a theatrical show with spotlights.) Metering the overall scene would give an exposure that's over-influenced by the darkness around the lights. A spot meter reading could zero right in on the key parts of the scene in the spot light. Since the metering area is so restricted, spot metering does take some practice to use it effectively.

Truthfully, the digital camera sort of makes metering techniques somewhat obsolete today. Using the LCD for both live viewing and image review, you can easily adjust an exposure to make it work well for the subject and scene, regardless of the type of metering used.

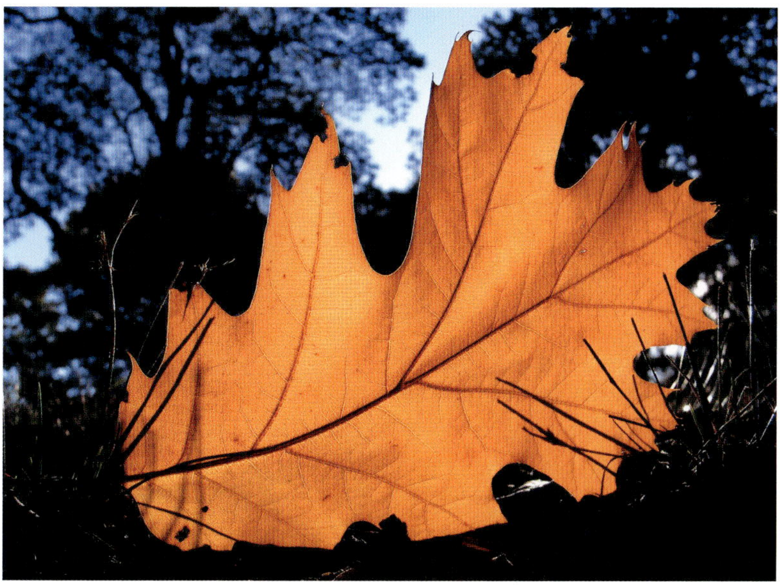

A good exposure makes the photo show off its subject in the way you want it to look.

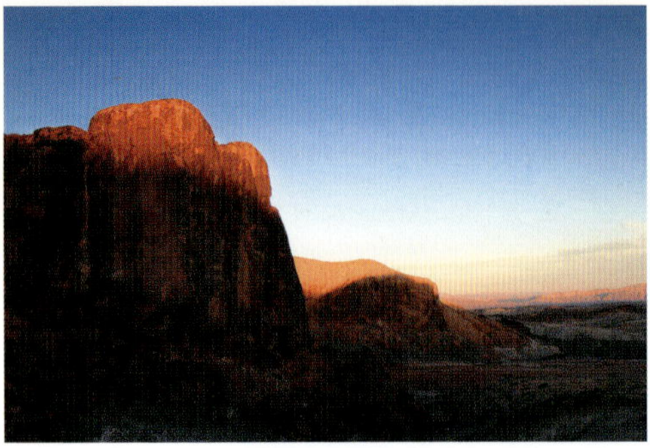

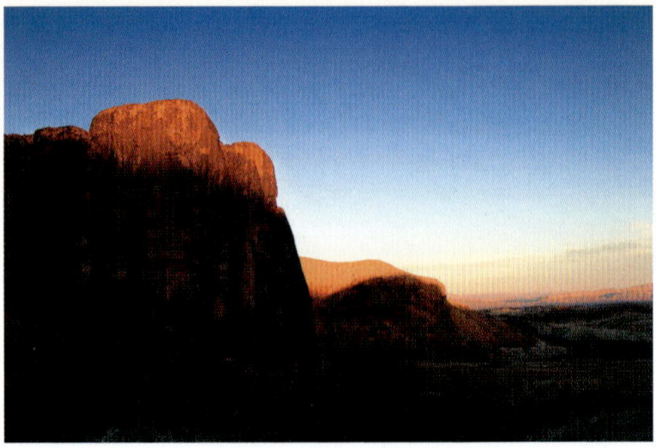

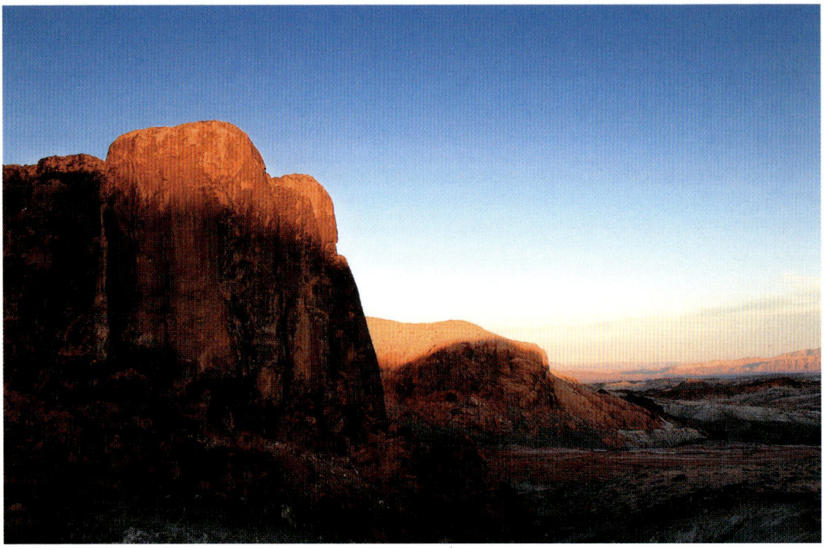

Autoexposure bracketing takes a series of photos with incremental changes in exposure. The variations are subtle but they make a difference in the look of the final photograph.

Automatic Exposure Bracketing (AEB)

Automatic exposure bracketing (AEB) is offered on many, but not all, compact cameras. It is not a necessity, but it can be a useful function whenever exposure is critical and/or subject contrast is unusual. This feature can be used with Program, Shutter-Priority, Aperture-Priority, and sometimes Manual mode. The camera's exposure bracketing system automatically changes exposures for a series of three photos, which deviate by a set range from the metered value. Usually, these settings can be adjusted in one of the camera menus.

Exposure Compensation

For most photographic situations, the camera's smart metering system offers excellent exposure. Problems occur when the scene is mostly very dark or very light, when there is extreme contrast in the scenes, or when a very bright light (like the sun) shines into the lens, especially when it is near an AF focusing point. Once you understand how your meter reacts to light, you can use the exposure compensation feature of your camera to make a quick adjustment and continue to shoot automatically. Exposure compensation is an important tool that allows you to increase or decrease the camera's autoexposure in

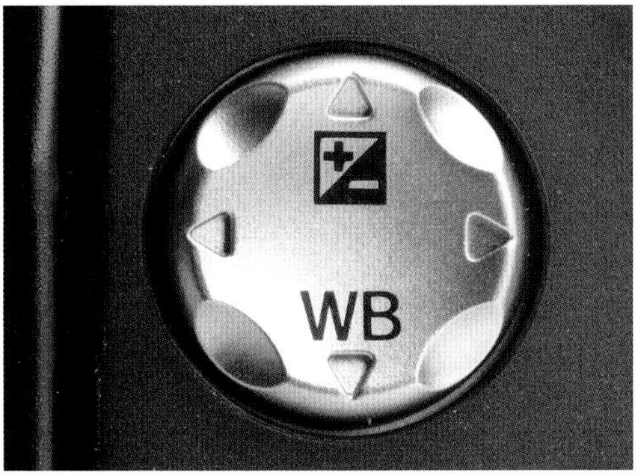

The square divided on the diagonal with a plus and a minus symbol is the icon most commonly used on the exposure compensation button

small steps (usually in 1/3 or 1/2 stop increments—some cameras let you choose the interval, some only offer one choice).

Exposure Lock

Another way to quickly compensate for problem scenes is to use the camera's exposure lock. Most digital cameras will lock exposure settings when you depress the shutter release slightly (usually about halfway). Some advanced cameras even have an exposure lock button. Combined with the live LCD, the exposure lock lets you quickly find the right exposure for the scene. For example, suppose you were shooting a sunrise, but a large part of the scene had a darkly silhouetted rock. In addition, the camera focused on the rock. That large dark area connected to the focus point would likely throw the meter off, making the camera pick an exposure too influenced by it, resulting in the sunrise starting to lose color (from too much exposure). Since you can see this happening in the LCD, you can move the camera so it sees more sky and less rock, and lock the exposure when you see the color in the sky improve. Then, reframe the picture so the rock is the big, dramatic part of the composition you wanted in the first place, but it is not controlling the exposure.

Beyond "Good" Exposure

All this may be well and good, but if automatic systems are so good today, why not just set the camera to Full Auto and be done with it? You could certainly do that, but then you might also miss exposure on important subjects or scenes, and wind up with a lot of work fixing the image in the computer. The big issue for the photographer is not just getting a "good" exposure, but how to get the best exposure for the subject and scene. This can be extremely subjective, depending on a subject's colors, textures, and tones. Some photographers want to stick to arbitrary "rules" of exposure, because they aren't confident in their ability to subjectively judge an image. Let's look at what the best exposure might be for a digital camera.

First, it should be one that gives you the best image data for your purpose. If you want to make a great print, you need to have the appropriate exposure data for highlights and shadows that can be edited in the computer. If you want to make a print directly from camera to printer, you need to know what bias the printer has (e.g., it makes prints lighter or darker than the version on the LCD).

Second, consider the requirements of the subject. A big mistake made by many amateurs is accepting the existing exposure for the scene without thinking about what that exposure does to the subject in terms of rendering it realistically or creatively. A dramatic but dark mountain might look weak and washed out with basic exposure because the dark areas are just too light. Similarly a bright beach might look dim and less than sunny with a basic meter reading. You need to interpret your exposures, and here again, the LCD comes through with a technological advantage.

Using the LCD and the Histogram

As I've stated many times, one of the truly great advantages of digital cameras is their ability to let you review exposure on the LCD. You can see the image right after you've shot the photo (if the camera is set for Review display) and determine what the highlights and shadows look like.

So, what can the LCD do for you? It can quickly tell you if a scene is so contrasty that you cannot capture all the detail there. It will show you if the subject has been captured appropriately: Are the dark trees dark and white buildings bright? It helps you decide if the photograph looks the way you want. If you enlarge the image, you can usually see if needed detail exists in highlights or shadows.

There will be situations when the little LCD monitor isn't as good as you'd like for evaluating exposure. That's when the histogram is used, and while expected on advanced compact cameras, it is surprising how often it shows up on lower-priced cameras. The histogram is a graph that tells you about the exposure levels in your shot. If your camera includes this feature, it becomes the best evaluation of exposure that you have.

For film photographers, the histogram's techy graph-look can initially be confusing or even intimidating. My suggestion is to give it a try! With a little practice, the histogram is actually fairly easy to understand. You really don't need to know any math to read it. At its basic level, it is simply a graphic representation of the number of pixels with specific brightness values from dark (on the left) to bright (on the right).

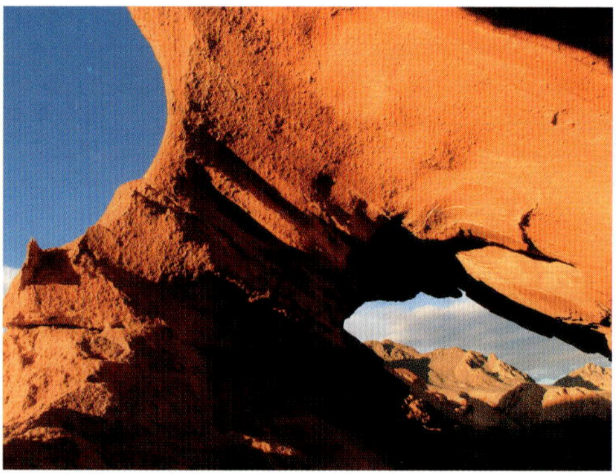

The live LCD monitor lets you preview exposure and composition. After you've taken the shot, you can zoom in on the image to check its sharpness and use the histogram to confirm exposure.

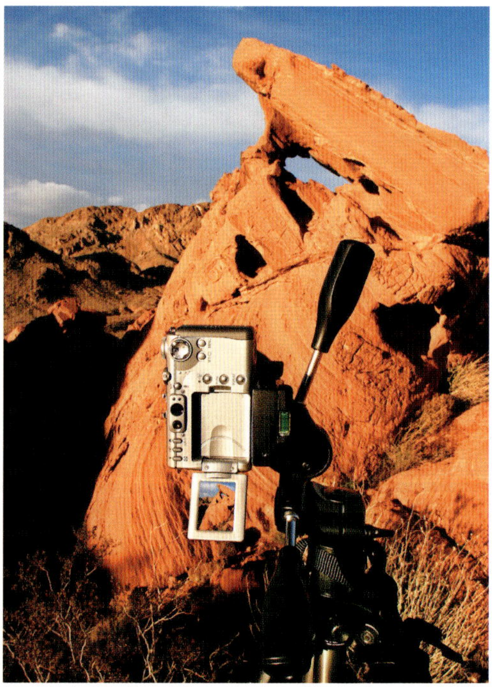

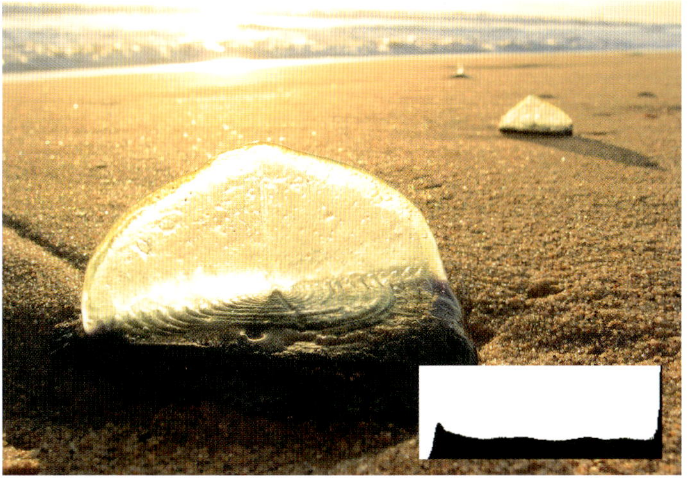

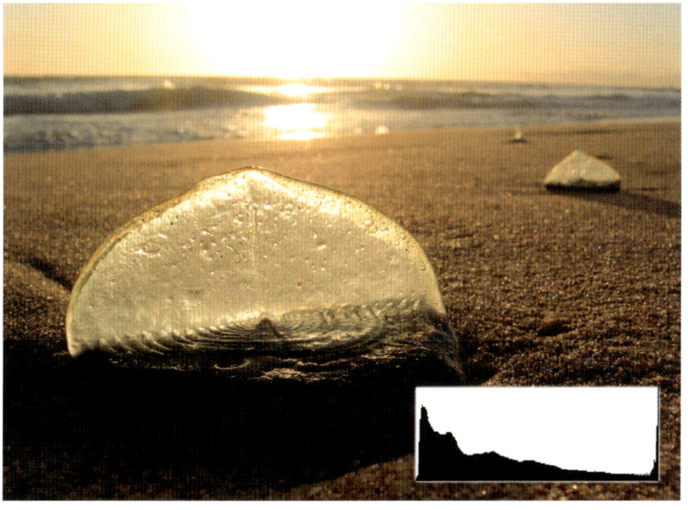

Learning to interpret a histogram can help you better evaluate photos in the LCD monitor. In the top photo, detail is lost in the bright areas. You can see that in the histogram because it is "clipped" off at the right. The bottom photo shows a better exposure with a larger proportion of the darker tones at the left.

How to Interpret the Histogram

The key to reading the histogram is to see what is happening at the left and right sides of the graph. An exposure of an average scene that gives good image data will show a histogram with the graph above the bottom line from left to right, without an imbalance of brightness values on one side or the other. Understand that this is true for a scene that has a full range of brightness. Not every scene will have values that balance completely from left to right. Dark or bright scenes will favor one side or the other.

One thing is critical: The range of tones for important brightness areas of a photograph should finish before the end of the graph at one side or the other. In other words, they should not be abruptly cut-off at either side: detail is important there. Whenever the histogram stops like a cliff instead of a slope at the sides, it means the exposure is "clipping" detail.

This is where you can run into trouble with your exposure. Any values to the right of a clipped right side are gone, washed out, and overexposed without detail. If they weren't captured at this point, you can never get them back. Some live LCDs will display an overexposure alert in the image itself by blinking the tones in these areas. Any values to the left of a chopped left side are also gone without detail. They can only be seen as black, as no data has been captured for them. If detail is important for dark (left) or bright (right) parts of the photo, you need to adjust exposure to bring the slope of the histogram back into the graph.

How the detail in the histogram is arranged can also help you evaluate your exposure. If you're photographing a bright scene, the histogram should show most of the values to the right, where bright values should be in a histogram. Since bright subjects can be easily underexposed, those values may sit to the left half of the histogram. This is the wrong place for them, which may mean problems for you when adjusting the image later in the computer. For dark scenes the story is similar. These tend to be metered with too much exposure and may sit too much on the right side of the graph, the bright side, instead of where they belong, at the left. The graphed values should reflect the scene. So a bright scene should have much of the graph on the right side, while a dark scene should have the graph favoring the left.

A great benefit of the LCD monitor and the histogram is that you can shoot on automatic and use all the computing power and advanced metering systems that you paid for. All you have to do is check exposures on occasion and you never have to be surprised by exposure problems again.

Long Digital Exposures

Very long exposures have been a challenge for digital cameras at any level, including digital SLRs. The problem is in the technology available today. As exposure lengthens in time, noise increases from the sensor. In addition, tiny signal amplifiers associated with sensors will begin to heat up with long exposures, often adversely affecting the image. These effects are most noticeable with small sensors. For this reason, many small cameras do not include a Bulb mode, which keeps a shutter open as long as you hold down the shutter release. Some cameras do let you get longer

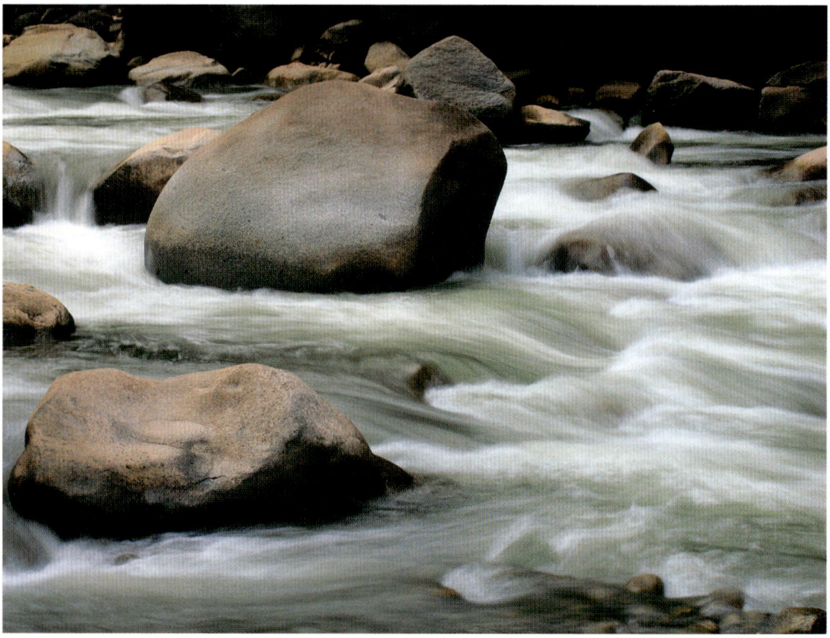

Put the camera on a tripod and use a long exposure to turn flowing water into a blur.

exposures up to 15–30 seconds automatically. However, as your times increase into the minutes range, you will find that the image deteriorates in most digital cameras. This should change in the future.

The long-exposure noise reduction function on most advanced compact digital cameras will help produce great results up to about 15–30 seconds, the longest timed shutter speed on most of these cameras. To go longer, you need to use the Bulb setting if it is available and hold the shutter release down for the time desired. Don't expect great results, however, beyond the manufacturers limitations of shutter speed, but sometimes it is worth a try. You won't waste anything except a little time!

Combining Exposures

A great challenge for photographers is capturing the range of tones we can see versus the fewer tones that film or a sensor can handle. This has always been a major limitation of the technology of photography. Many, many dramatic photographs of scenes, such as brightly sun-drenched clouds in a scene with dark pine trees, look nothing like the real scene that appeared before the photographer's eyes. Compared to what our eyes and brain can process, the ability of most films and digital cameras to capture everything in such a scene is extremely limited.

To deal with this problem, Gustave Le Gray developed a way of taking two photographs of a scene, such as one exposed for the landscape and one for sky, then combining them into a single photograph. This is not a digital technique—Le Gray lived over 150 years ago and developed this technique in the 1850s! He did it in the darkroom. This was done back at the very beginning of photography, when photographers strived to get the most from the limitations of the evolving medium.

Today, in the digital world, this is still an elegant way of handling a scene with extreme tonal differences. You make one exposure that is optimized for the bright areas and a second exposure for the shadows. You then combine the two shots into a final image in the computer, using the good exposure of bright areas from one photo and the good exposure of shadows from the other. It is even possible to combine more than two exposures for big variations in tones in a scene. Still, the basic technique is the same.

Here is where a digital camera really shines! As long as you are careful not to move the camera, both photos will line up exactly. There is no film to slightly shift position in the camera or scanner to make lining up difficult later. The worst that usually happens is a slight movement of the camera as you change exposure.

How to Combine Two Exposures in One Photo

1. Put your camera on a tripod and take all exposures with the same composition and framing. (Handheld shots will be hard to match.)

2. Meter the bright and dark areas. Remember these exposures because once you start the next steps, you cannot reposition the camera.

3. Make an exposure based on the bright areas of the scene.

4. Without moving the camera, make a second exposure for the dark areas.

You can make these two exposures by using the exposure compensation adjustment, too. Try a shot with the compensation on the plus side, then one on the minus side. Another option is to use auto exposure bracketing if your camera has it.

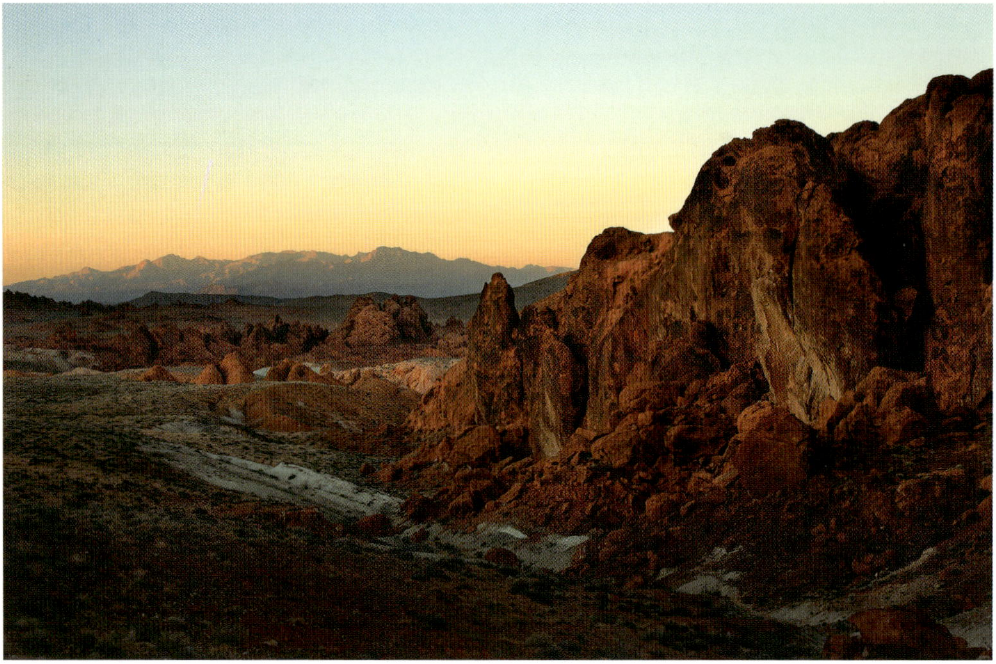

This image was made by combining the two images on the right. This composite image is a better representation of the real scene than is possible to capture with a single exposure (either film or digital). For this shot, the lighter image was placed over the dark version, then the light sky and background were removed

The camera then changes the exposure for you automatically as you shoot three photos: one at the meter reading, and two variations in exposure (usually above and below the meter's choice for exposure).

Using a layers-based image-processing program, you will make basic adjustments to the pair of photos (color, levels, etc.). Then, line up the two photos (one on top of the other) in separate layers. I like to put the shadow exposure on top of the highlight exposure. Then remove the washed-out highlights of the shadow exposure, which will let the good highlight exposure show through from below. If your program includes it, a layer mask will give a lot of control over the removal process. Otherwise, you can use the eraser tool or the selection tool to delete the poorly exposed areas. Most programs will even let you undo mistakes to bring back things if you erase too much of the image.

Next, fix the edges between the two photos. This is where technique is so important. With practice you can make edges blend quite nicely. Try using soft brushes in your layer mask. Soft eraser tools on programs without a layer mask can help, although they often require a lot of "doing and undoing" to get it right. Adjust the opacity/transparency of the top layer until the detail looks right to you. (Changing the opacity can also help line up the images.)

The bottom line is that this double-exposure technique works, and it delivers an image that you can control without being limited by film technology. You gain a wonderful color and tonal range that can be closer to what your eye actually saw in the scene. How bright the shadows should be is very subjective, so just make your final adjustments based on what is appealing to you, as well as what you want to communicate about the scene.

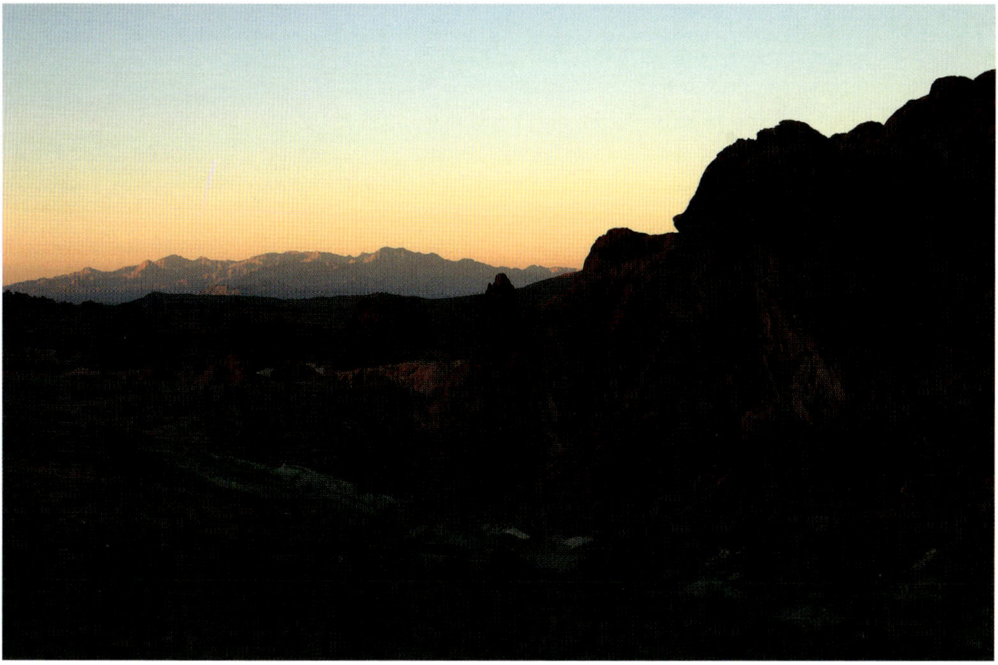

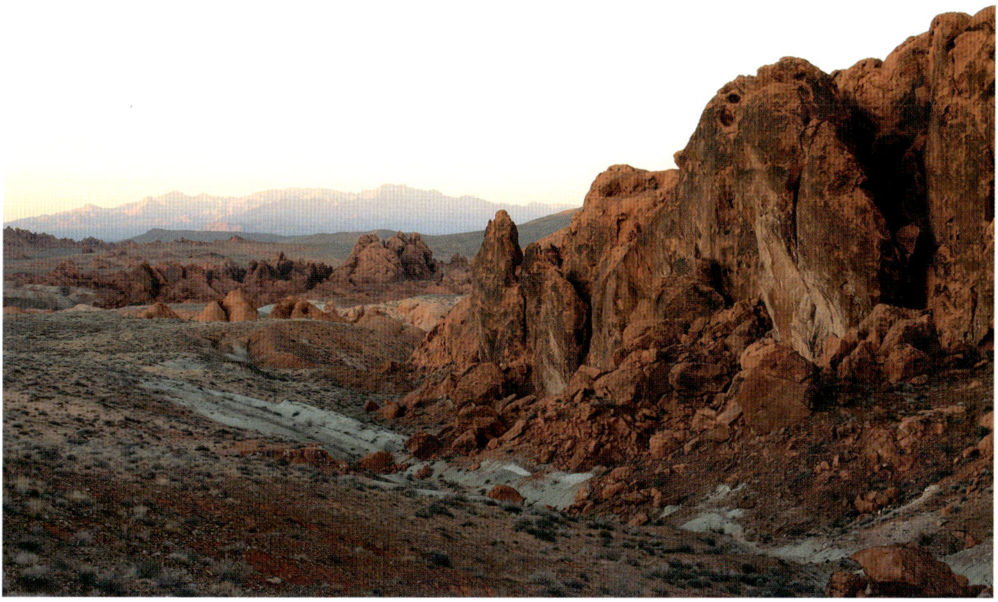

These two images are straight from the camera. The darker image was exposed to capture the sky. The lighter image shows all the detail in the rocky foreground. When combined in the computer (see the photo on the left), I effectively increased the exposure range.

white balance

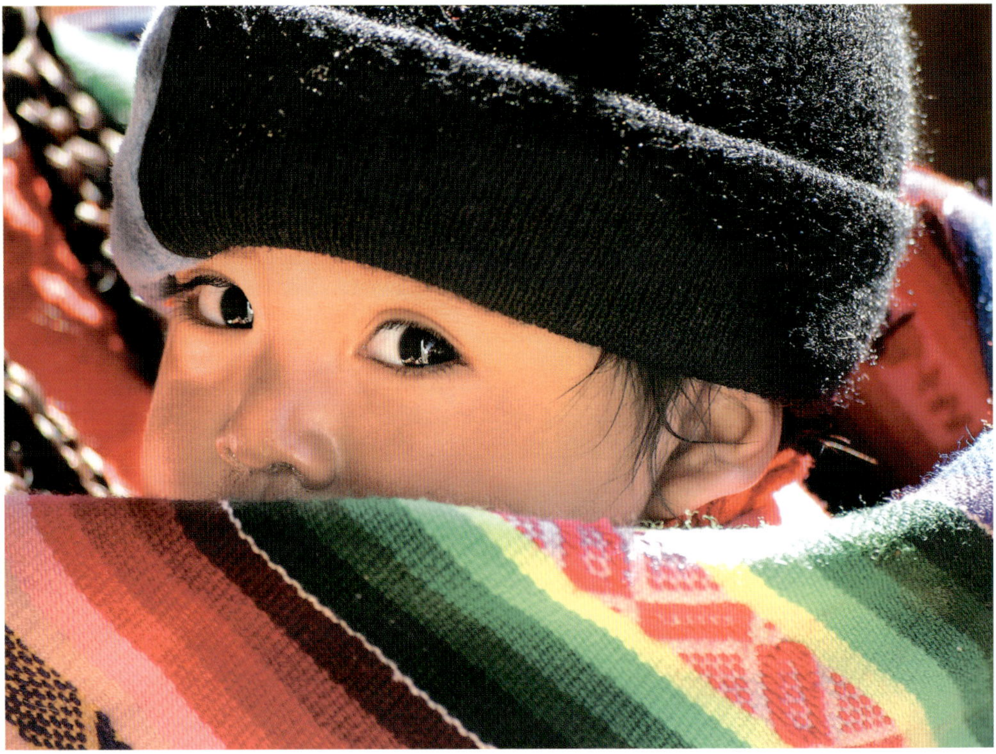

Learning to control white balance can greatly improve the color of your photos.

A totally new control for most photographers, white balance is an important tool to understand and use. I believe it is such a key tool of any digital camera that it is vital that you get to know it. It is both a corrective and creative tool of value to every photographer. While it does add complexity to taking pictures, it really does not take long to learn how to use it well. Once you see the benefits of white balance, you will be glad that you have mastered its use.

The Color of Light

To understand white balance you need to know a little about the color of light. Our eye-to-brain connection makes most normal light look neutral so that colors stay consistent. A white will look white to us whether it is in the shade, in the sun, or indoors under fluorescent lights. Yet those three lighting types have very different colors of light which are measured by something called color temperature. With most light-sensitive recording devices (film, video camcorders, digital cameras), various types of lighting will render colors differently. This is why a scene or subject often looks green when photographed on film under fluorescent lights.

Without getting deeply into physics, let's lay out the basics. Color temperature is a standard that measures the color of light based on how a theoretical black body emits light when heated. It is expressed in Kelvin (or K)—a basic unit of thermodynamic measurement. (Technically it has no "degrees," but you will often see it expressed as degrees K.) It is the reverse of our weather temperatures, where high = hot and low = cold. In the Kelvin system, low numbers such as 3,000K are warmer colors, and high numbers like 10,000K are colder colors.

Incandescent lights tend to be between 2000–3800K, while sunlight at noon is near 5000K, and light from the open sky is at 10,000K or higher. With daylight film, the noon sunlight would appear neutral (because the film is balanced for that color temperature), and the open sky light would be bluish. Fluorescent lights are a little different since they have what is called an incomplete spectrum, so any color temperature for them is a bit of a compromise. Depending on the type of fluorescent bulb, the light that film and sensors see is somewhere between incandescent and sunlight.

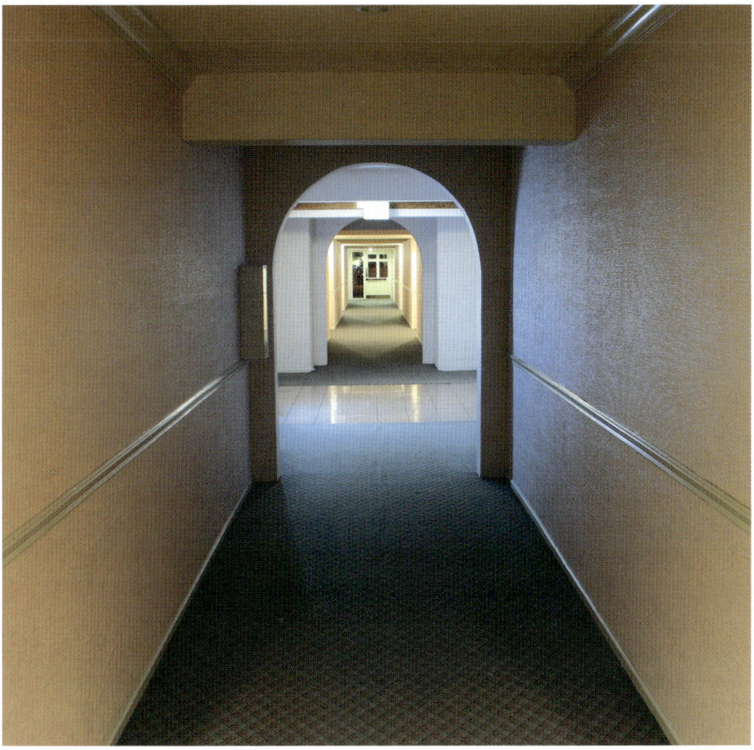

You can see how light has many colors in this photo of the view down a hallway. It is lit by daylight, fluorescent lights, incandescent lights, and reflected light.

What is White Balance?

While new to still photographers, white balance has long been a key part of video. With the arrival of the portable color news camera in the 1970s, videographers began white balancing their images. These video shooters had no automatic white balance and had to point their camera at something white and tell the camera to make that white a neutral white—with no color cast to it.

White balance on digital cameras today is far more sophisticated, but works on the same principle—making whites and other neutral colors neutral, without color cast. When photographers first start shooting with a digital camera, they often have no idea that they can change white balance settings. To be fair, until recently, many manufacturers buried white balance. Many photographers just figured the cameras didn't have it, yet nearly all digital cameras offer some control over white balance. Some cameras allow you to get to it from a single button push, but others have it hidden in menus that require a bit of juggling with dials and buttons. No matter where white balance is, it is definitely worth the effort to find and use! In fact, white balance is as important as the exposure controls if you want to get the most from your digital photography.

How the Camera Adjusts White Balance

To achieve white balance control, the camera looks at the white and neutral colors of a scene, either automatically or with your help, and makes them appear neutral in that light (regardless of the source and its K temperature). It usually makes the scene look more like what it does to the eye than film does.

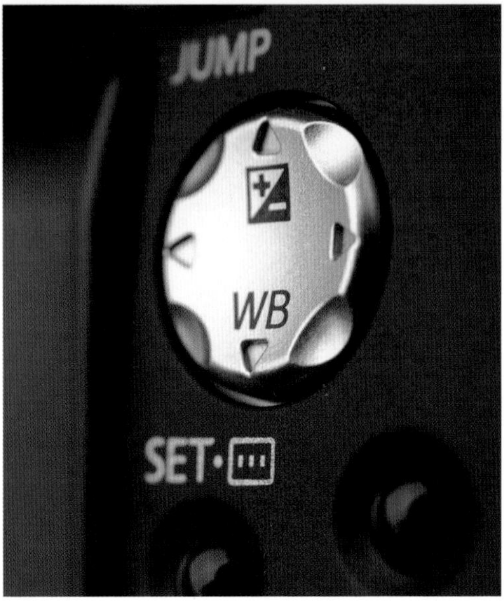

On many digital cameras, finding and setting the white balance is easy—the control is usually marked with the letters WB.

It is obviously a corrective tool in that you can be sure the colors are right for a scene (such as making whites look correct regardless of light, whether fluorescent indoors or sun at midday). But it can go too far, making the warm light of a sunset, for example, technically "correct" yet lacking the warmth we expect in a photograph of a sunset.

White balance is also a creative tool. You can change the response of the camera so that the light is warmer or cooler than the camera wants it to be based on its "agenda" of making all light neutral. In this way, you can have a sunset photograph that looks more like you expect sunsets to look. Also, you can adjust the color of a scene, so that it gives you the look you might expect—making a friendly family scene look warm, or a snowy winter day look even colder.

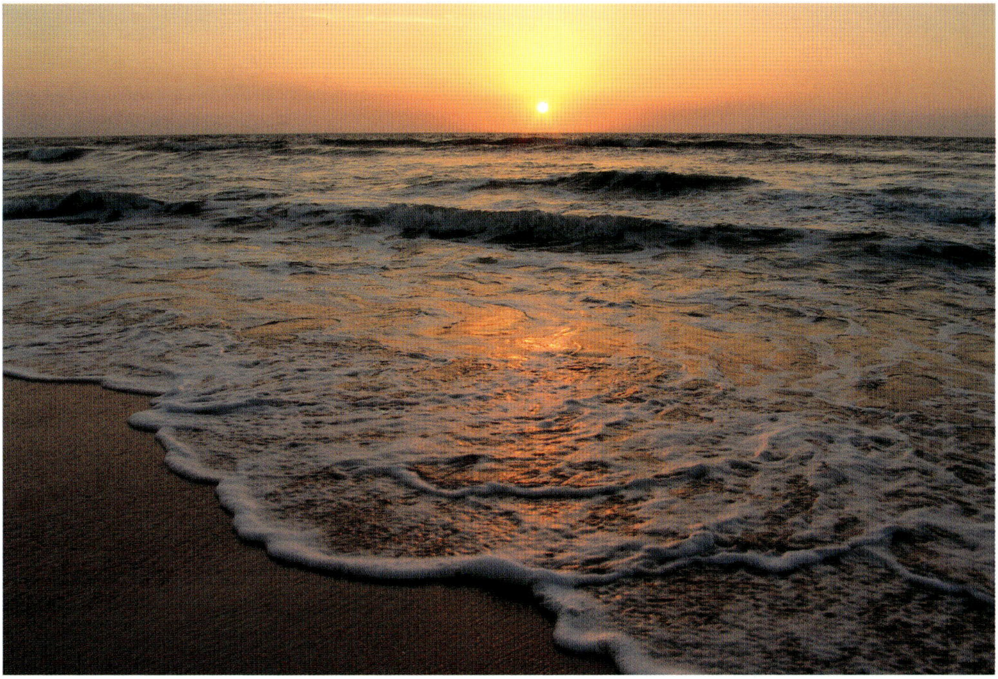

White balance can be used as a corrective tool. The Cloudy WB setting, for example, warms up the light in a sunset. As a result, the photo looks more like the actual scene.

Why You Should Adjust White Balance as You Shoot

It is true that you can make color adjustments in the computer, and if your camera lets you shoot RAW images, you can totally change white balance after the fact. There are some very significant reasons not to do that, however.

• **Better review photos**—If the white balance is good, you are evaluating photos on the LCD for composition and exposure—without being distracted by color casts.

• **Better craft**—Photography is a craft. Paying attention to details such as exposure, action-stopping shutter speed, depth of field, and focal length, is part of the process that enriches the photo and the photo experience. White balance selection is a new part of that process.

• **Higher quality**—Adjustments made later, in the computer, have the potential of affecting the actual pixels in the photo and reducing image quality.

• **Connection with the scene**—If you do adjustments later in the computer, you are no longer at your location, so any adjustments have less immediate connection with what is "right" (either objectively or creatively) for the scene.

• **Less work**—A photo that has the proper white balance from the start requires less work later. Even with RAW files this is an advantage, as you won't need to agonize over color corrections in the computer.

Caution: *RAW files offer such a large degree of adjustment that the range of choices can sometimes be overwhelming and even counter-productive.*

Automatic White Balance

While automatic white balance is useful for shooting quickly in changing light conditions, I rarely select Auto as my standard. I only choose it when it is appropriate—it becomes simply another choice in the white balance menu. The Auto setting often gives inconsistent results simply because it is an automatic function dealing with the real world of color and light. If you use it and take two photos at opposite ends of your zoom range, for example, you may find the wide-angle shot shows a different color balance than the telephoto. This is because there is so much variation in the scene as it is taken in by the two lens settings.

Another example of a white balance problem is when you photograph at sunrise and sunset. We are used to photographing at these times (and seeing images of them) with daylight-balanced film, which makes them warmer than what we actually see with the eye. For years, nature photographers have used films and filters designed to produce more intense colors. If you shoot with Auto white balance, the digital camera will usually try to remove some of that warm color, as it doesn't know what you expect from the scene. It just sees what seems to be a lot of very warm light that needs to be corrected. In this instance, you are better off choosing one of the presets.

All digital cameras come with a package of predetermined, preset white balance settings. These are very useful because you can try to match the conditions to the preset's name—Sun, Shade, Cloudy, Fluorescent, etc. This is especially useful if you need to take a photo indoors under fluorescent lights. The lighting can be tricky to balance. Using the Fluorescent setting, the colors will clean up quite well. Some cameras come with many different presets, even including multiple fluorescent choices.

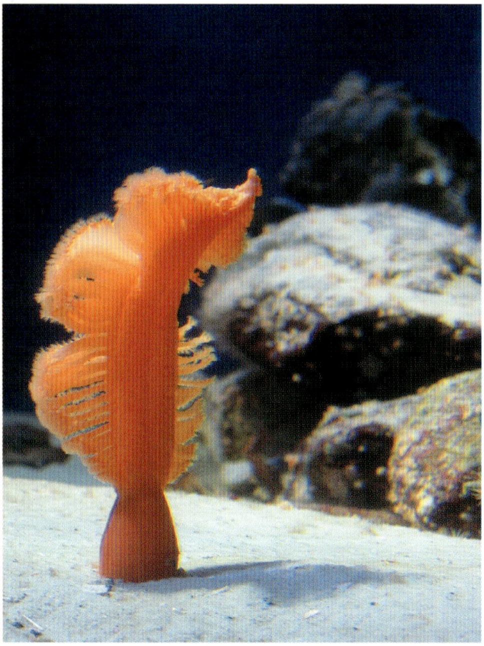

Auto white balance

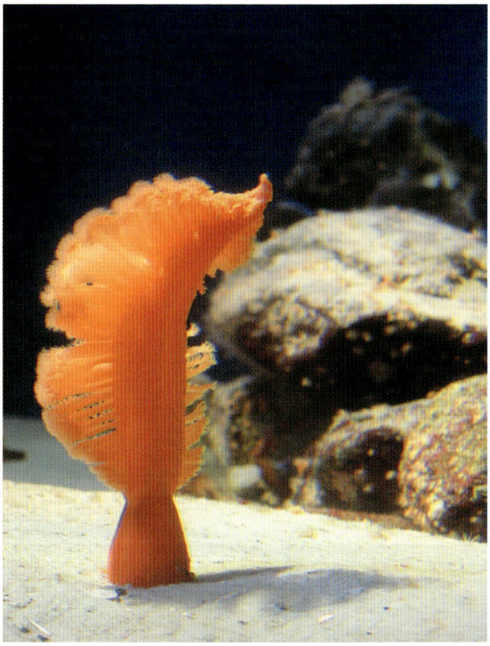

Cloudy white balance preset

The first critical issue in choosing which white balance setting to use is to consider matching the preset to the light it was designed to measure. This does several important things for the photographer:

- Colors look natural.
- Neutral tones stay neutral (or at least reasonably neutral).
- Photos have consistent white balance in a given lighting condition.

With a preset in a specific lighting condition, all photos will have the same color balance and do not change color from shot to shot. When shooting with Auto white balance, you can get variation in color as the camera tries to compensate for different objects in the frame, even though the light has not changed. It can be very frustrating to cope with variation of the color in photographs due to the unpredictability of Auto white balance.

Getting the Most from the Presets

To get the most from white balance, you need to think beyond the preset's specific name. Using the Flash white balance setting for most outdoor photos is like adding a warming filter to the scene—an effect I like. Unfortunately, there are no precise "standard" specifications or definitions of manufacturers' white balance settings, so this may or may not work for you. You may find that your camera does a nicer job using the Shade or Cloudy settings.

I believe that it is really worth experimenting with white balance settings. Try the different preset settings on the same subject to see what they do and think how you might use them beyond their specific names. The really neat thing about doing experiments like this with a digital camera is that you waste no film, and you don't even have to take notes! The picture's metadata (see page 90) will tell you nifty

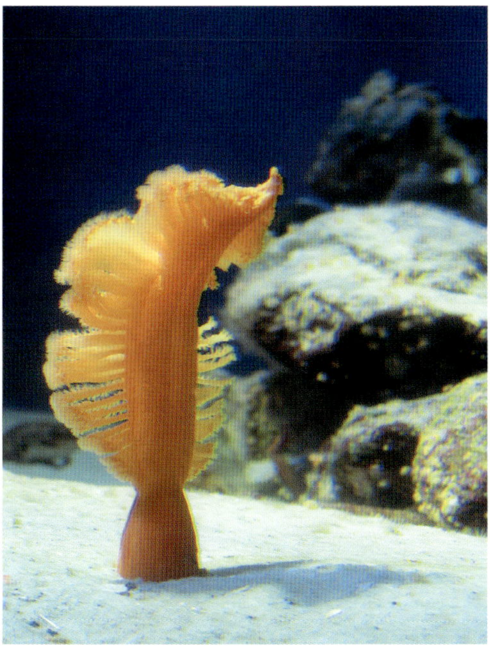

Fluorescent white balance preset

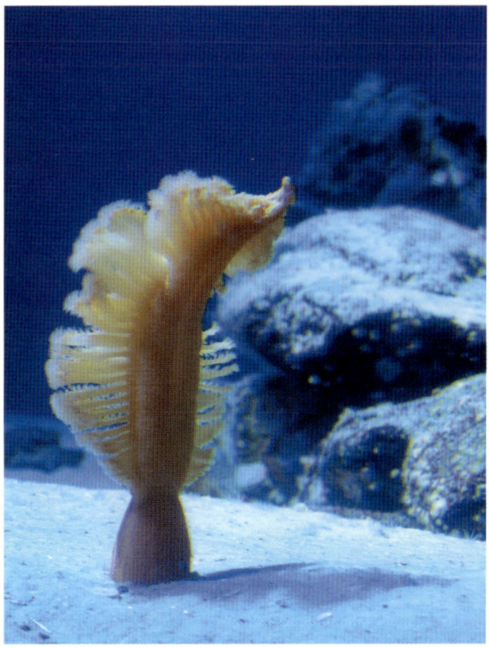

Incandescent white balance preset

things like the white balance that was used for the shot. There is a button on most cameras that you push to see basic data about a photo on the LCD. It is often labeled "Display" or "Info." You can also read complete metadata in many browser and image processing programs.

Although you can't completely evaluate the effects of the preset white balance settings until you download the images to your computer, your camera's LCD can help you roughly judge the different settings on a particular scene. It is true that the little monitor on the camera isn't that accurate for judging all colors, but still, it gives you a very good idea of what the colors are doing in a given situation.

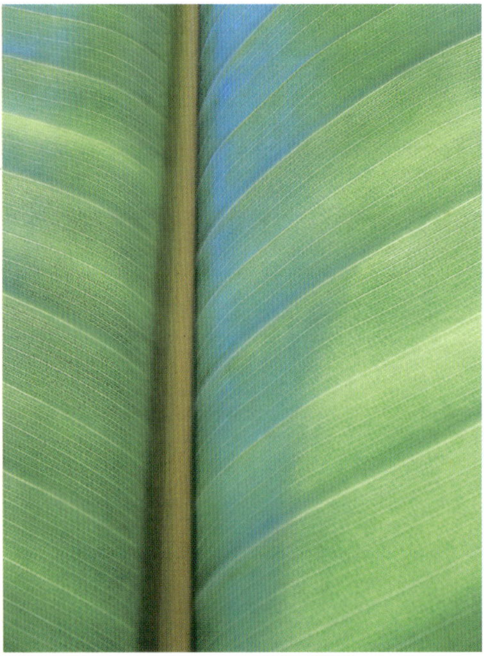

Daylight balance keeps the leaf a brilliant green, but also shows the blue reflection of the sky.

Custom or Manual White Balance

Another level of white balance control is the custom (or manual) setting, available on all advanced compact digital cameras, but sometimes missing from less expensive cameras. Custom settings can be very helpful when you need to precisely match a given lighting condition. The camera will help you pick an exact white balance for the light color, which becomes very natural—with no color casts from the light.

To do this, point your camera at something white or gray (it does not have to be in focus) and follow the procedure for color balancing. Typically, you center a box or other outlined area over the neutral target and push the appropriate button (there is

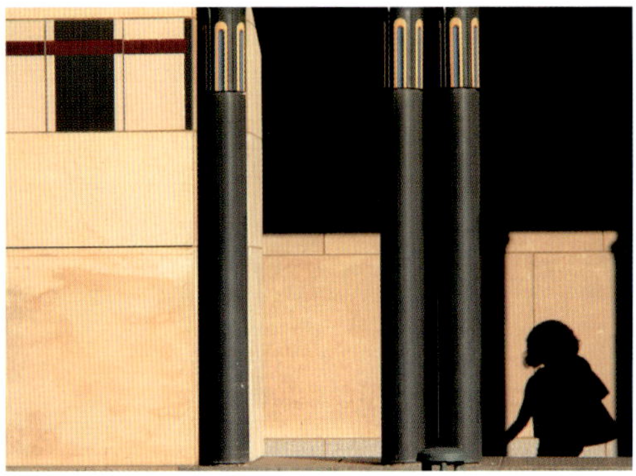

Cloudy white balance warms this sunlit shot.

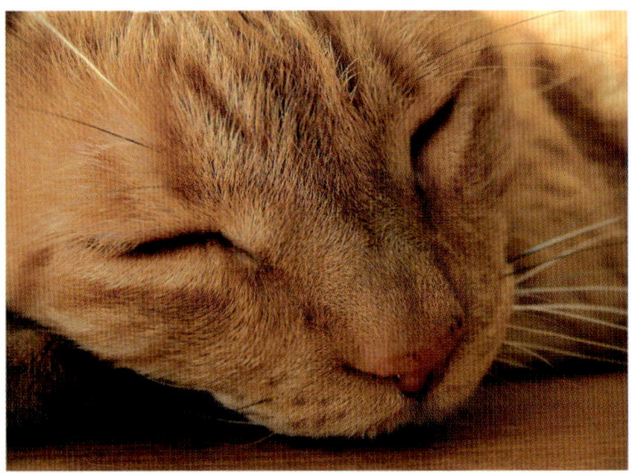

Incandescent white balance makes a neutral-toned photo of an indoor cat.

no standard way to do this—even different camera models from the same manufacturer do it differently, so you need to check your camera's manual). The camera analyzes the specific white or gray tone and adjusts the color so that it is truly neutral.

This technique is useful for a variety of purposes. One is simply to deal with unique lighting situations (more common indoors) when you need to get a neutral light. This can give quite remarkable results in tough situations with industrial fluorescents. (It can't make yellow sodium vapor lights and similar lights neutral, since those lights only have a limited range of color in the light.) The camera will make the white or gray object as neutral as possible so you can shoot without filters and get results close to what the eye sees.

You can also use custom settings creatively by white balancing on something that isn't white or gray. You use a paper with a pale color tint to it and the camera will remove that color and make the paper appear pale gray. This will make the photo look like you shot it through a filter of a color opposite to the pale color you used for "balancing." A good example of this is using a light blue card for white balancing. The camera warms up the photo because blue is removed. With the right shade of blue you can get some very pleasing warm tones when photographing people's faces. You can try all sorts of colors for a whole range of interesting effects. For example, color balancing on a pale red-magenta paint chip would be like having a green enhancing filter, because overall, greens will be boosted.

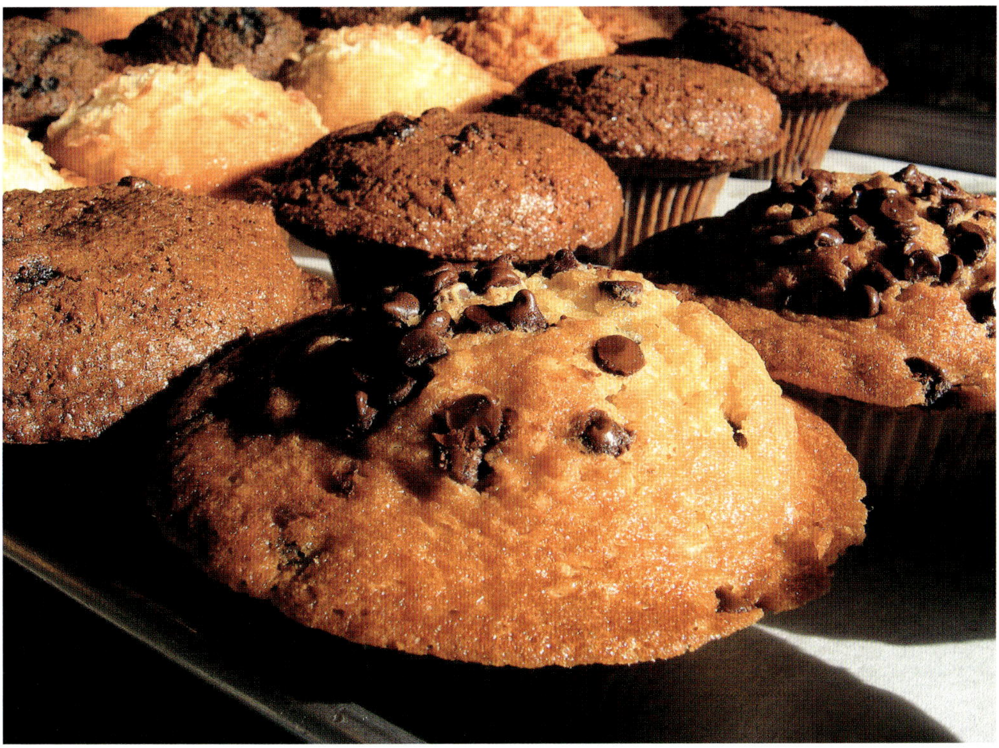

Daylight white balance was the right setting to use for warm, morning sunlight.

An Instant Enhancing Filter

Creative use of white balance works just like an enhancing filter, but it enhances everything in the photo, so check the image in the LCD to make sure you get the effect you want.

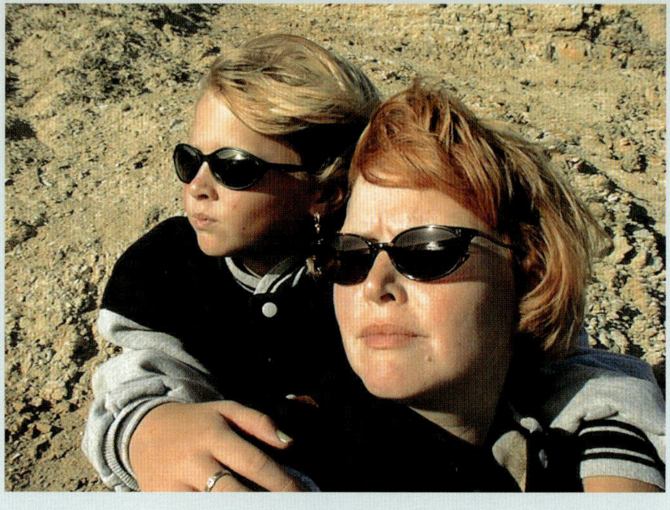

RAW Files and White Balance

Finally, shooting in RAW influences color balance choices. RAW files give you the ability to go back and change your original white balance choice. This does help compensate for automatic inconsistencies, but requires more processing work. This, however, will mean you can get much more consistency with multiple images. However, this should never be an excuse for not setting white balance as best you can.

About Metadata

A great way of learning about photography is to shoot a lot of experiments and record your settings so that you can compare it to the results later. But actually doing that is tedious. With a digital camera, that's all changed. The camera does it for you. This is a basic part of even the most elementary digital cameras.

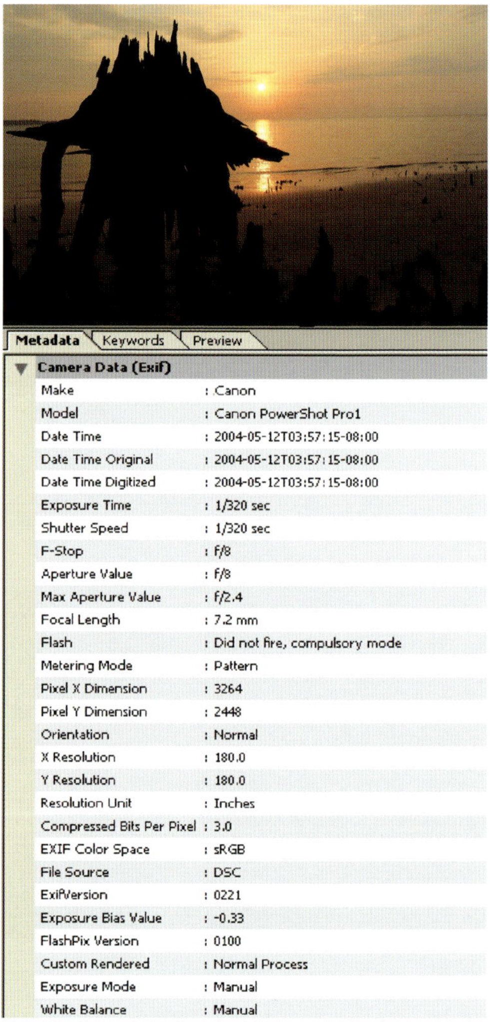

Metadata | Keywords | Preview

Camera Data (Exif)	
Make	: Canon
Model	: Canon PowerShot Pro1
Date Time	: 2004-05-12T03:57:15-08:00
Date Time Original	: 2004-05-12T03:57:15-08:00
Date Time Digitized	: 2004-05-12T03:57:15-08:00
Exposure Time	: 1/320 sec
Shutter Speed	: 1/320 sec
F-Stop	: f/8
Aperture Value	: f/8
Max Aperture Value	: f/2.4
Focal Length	: 7.2 mm
Flash	: Did not fire, compulsory mode
Metering Mode	: Pattern
Pixel X Dimension	: 3264
Pixel Y Dimension	: 2448
Orientation	: Normal
X Resolution	: 180.0
Y Resolution	: 180.0
Resolution Unit	: Inches
Compressed Bits Per Pixel	: 3.0
EXIF Color Space	: sRGB
File Source	: DSC
ExifVersion	: 0221
Exposure Bias Value	: -0.33
FlashPix Version	: 0100
Custom Rendered	: Normal Process
Exposure Mode	: Manual
White Balance	: Manual

Metadata provides a wealth of information about the image. It is recorded by the camera when the picture is taken.

A special set of detailed information about each photo you take is automatically recorded by the camera with the image file. This is called metadata ("data about data") because it is information about the data that makes up an image file. You'll also hear about EXIF data—that is a specific set of metadata.

How to Use the Metadata

The metadata from your camera will include such things as shutter speed, f/stop, focal length, white balance, ISO setting, flash usage, and much more, although the specifics depends on your camera model (you won't find any information on this in the manual or on the manufacturer's web site—you really have to shoot photos and check the data). There is also information in most camera's metadata that is useful mainly to computer engineers. But the basic photographic parameters are there and ready for your use.

You can access metadata in several ways. On most digital cameras, when you play back an image, you can change the display to read the histogram and key information about exposure—shutter speed, aperture, and ISO—immediately.

Computer Access to Metadata

Many computer programs can access the image metadata. Adobe Photoshop and Photoshop Elements include it in the browser function. Browsers, such as ACDSee from ACDSystems and MediaPro from iView, will display it, and RAW conversion software will show it, as well. In addition, browser programs often let you make index prints that include data like shutter speed and f/stop with the photo. Directory Opus (www.gpsoft.com), a Windows XP Explorer replacement, includes easy access to this information. Programs vary as to how much metadata is included and how it's displayed, but they all have the key photographic information.

memory cards and workflow

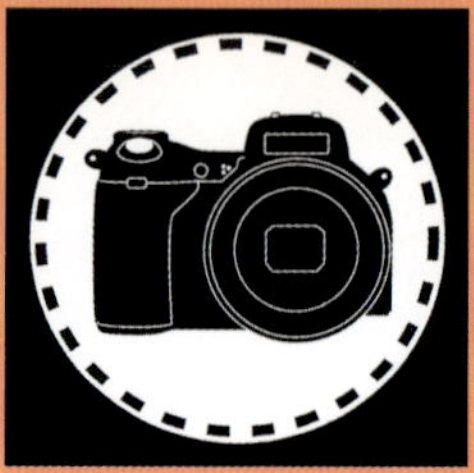

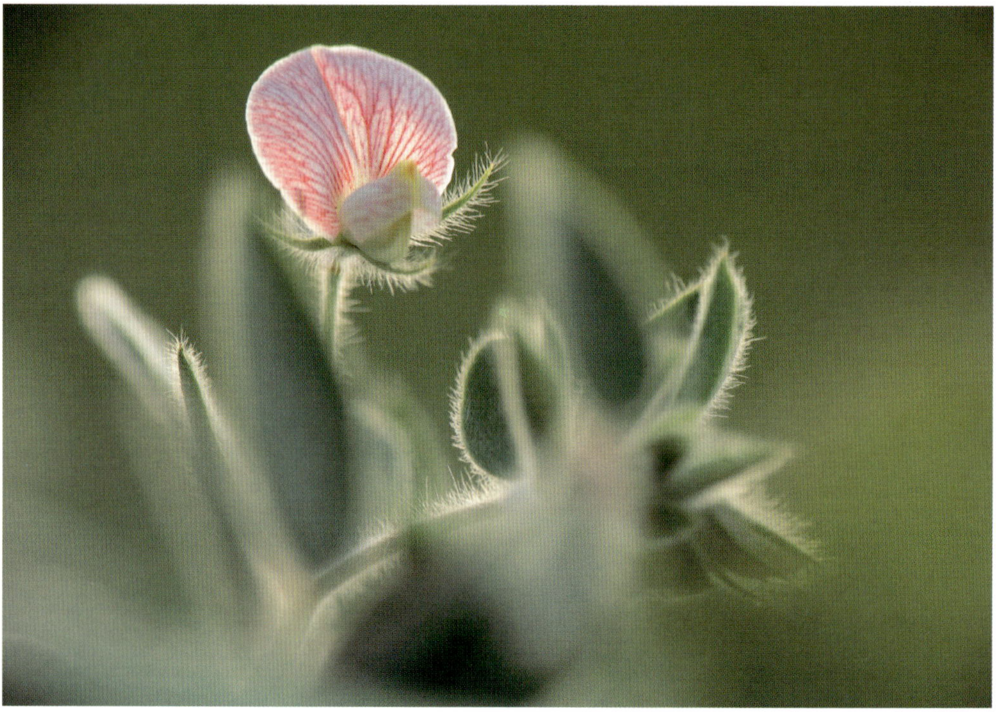

Memory cards are sometimes called "digital film" since they record images and can be removed from a camera like traditional film. There is a big difference, however, because film is light sensitive. Therefore film acts like the sensor and the memory card combined.

Still, thinking of a memory card as digital film is helpful, since it is a way to remove images from your camera and take them for processing to produce prints. It is worth knowing a little about memory cards in order to get the most from them.

Types of Memory Cards

Memory cards come in a variety of sizes and shapes. Almost all memory cards use solid-state memory—there are no moving parts. The only exception is the Hitachi Microdrive (formerly IBM), based on a miniature hard drive. While most digital SLRs use CompactFlash (or CF) cards, compact digital cameras use all sorts of card types, including CF cards, SD cards, xD cards, and Memory Sticks. (SmartMedia is an older card type that is still available but not used much in cameras today.)

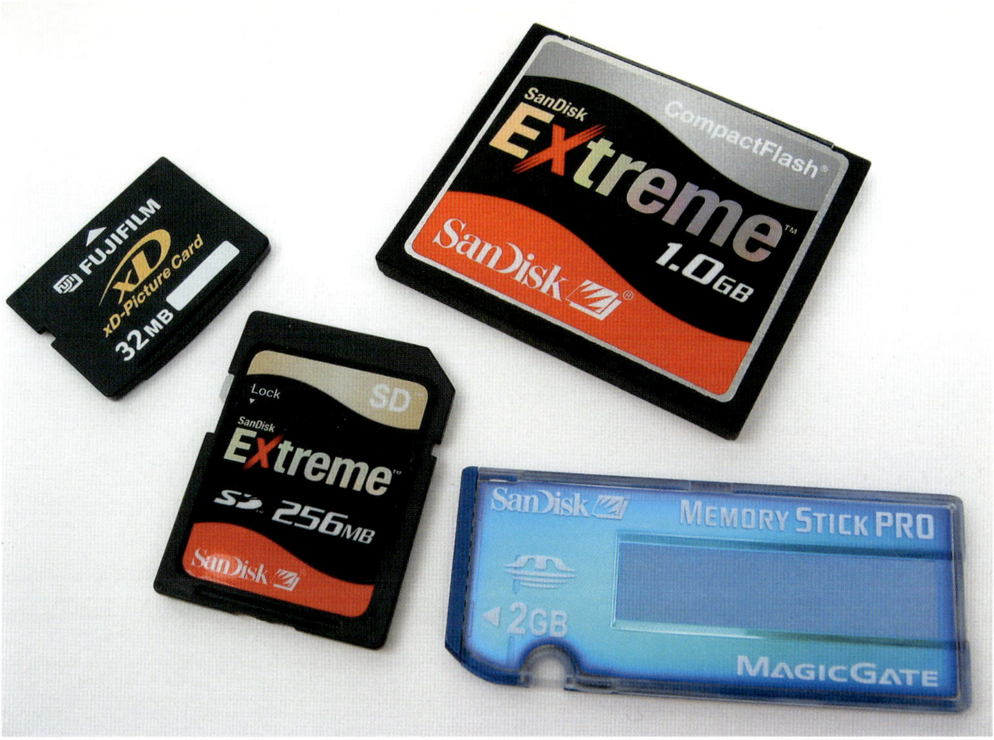

A high-capacity memory card should be one of your first purchases to go with your digital camera. They come in a variety of shapes and sizes to fit different cameras.

Many of the most advanced digital cameras use CF cards just like their big brothers, the digital SLRs. CF memory cards are solid, reliable memory cards about the size of a matchbook. They come in two versions—Type I and Type II. Most cameras that use CF cards accept both, though today, the most common is Type I (the biggest need for a Type II card is for the largest memory capacities). There is little that can damage this type of memory card. If you drop one in the mud or sand, clean it and plug it back in. I have even run them through the wash with no ill effect, though heat from the dryer can damage them. I learned that from experience. Now, I am careful to never put these cards casually in my pocket. Instead I always put them in a case that is designed for carrying memory cards of all types.

There are even some "extreme" types of cards that are designed for the severest conditions, particularly heat, because heat can cause problems for electronics. These cards will actually continue to perform in hot conditions that could cause problems with the camera itself.

Microdrives look like a CF card of the thicker, Type II model, but they are a different type of device. They are actually tiny hard drives. They offer increased storage at lower prices, but they are also much more sensitive to damage than CF cards. Since they have little spinning disks inside, they can be damaged if dropped, and water will ruin them. I would not recommend them for any type of photography that requires the card to be changed frequently, increasing the possibility of damage.

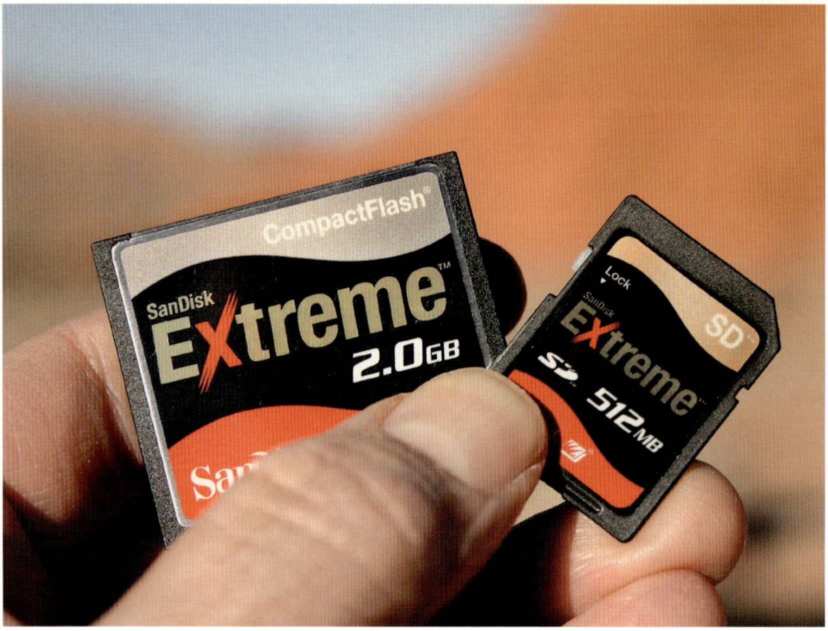

CompactFlash cards are very common, but the smallest cameras often use the smaller SD cards.

Many of the smallest digital cameras use SD and xD cards. These are very small cards not much bigger than your thumbnail and much smaller than CF cards (xD cards are the smallest). They allow manufacturers to make cameras more compact. Since the CF card is so entrenched with larger cameras, there is the misconception that these little cards are somehow inferior and less "professional" than CF cards. That isn't true. There is no difference in image or card quality among any of these cards. CF cards just came first. SD and xD cards are newer technology and often offer faster speeds, even better than the best of CF cards today.

Memory Sticks are a unique type of proprietary memory card that Sony uses for its cameras. These look like a stick of gum and offer no advantages over the other cards except, of course, if you have a Sony camera that only takes such cards.

You have little choice in the type of card your camera can use. Nearly all require different mounting mechanisms and circuitry on-board the camera—a few offer dual card systems. I have heard stories of salespeople at large retail stores who do not understand the differences among these cards and have told customers that a camera using one card type or another offers better quality photos because of the card. This is total nonsense. A memory card has absolutely no effect on image quality; it is simply a storage device.

Memory Card Speed

Memory card manufacturers promote higher and higher card speeds. This is essentially how fast the card can write data to memory. You'll see all sorts of speed references, but they can be very misleading. Each speed noted with CF cards simply refers back to the original card speed (which was 1x). Even the fastest CF cards with the highest speed specifications are slower than SD and xD cards. Plus, card speed actually has very little effect on the camera speed of compact digital cameras.

The main thing that a fast memory card affects is shooting speed with high-speed digital SLRs—how many photographs you can shoot at any one time before the camera has to stop and wait for its buffer to clear. At the time of this writing, no small digital camera has circuits that can take advantage of high-speed memory cards. However, digital gear is constantly evolving, so it is possible that this will be important in the future.

Memory Card Capacity

The good news is that memory cards today are relatively inexpensive. It wasn't too many years ago that a 64 MB card cost many hundreds of dollars. That size card doesn't hold many images and is now considered very small. Unfortunately, in order to keep camera prices low, manufacturers pack very small cards that won't hold many photos with their digital cameras.

So what size card do you need? It depends on how you like to shoot. Consider that for a 4-megapixel camera, a high-quality JPEG file is about 2 MB, while an 8-megapixel camera will give a high-quality JPEG file of about 3.5 MB. RAW files are typically about 2–3 times that of the high-quality JPEG. You can see that RAW files mean a lot fewer images saved per memory card. You can obviously get by with much less memory when shooting high-quality JPEG. When you consider that a memory card can be used again and again, the per-picture cost is very low. With memory cards, there should never be an excuse for "running out of film."

If you want to use one of the really large, multi-gigabyte cards, make sure your camera can handle it. While most advanced cameras purchased in the last couple of years will support these large capacity cards, older cameras cannot support cards larger than 2 GB, and less expensive cameras often won't either.

You will also need to consider how to buy and use your memory cards. Do you buy one big card and just shoot with it until it is full? Or would a number of smaller cards better meet your needs? There is no simple answer to this. It is more a personal preference as to how you would like to work. One big card is certainly more economical, but then multiple smaller cards give you backup and downloading can be done more conveniently.

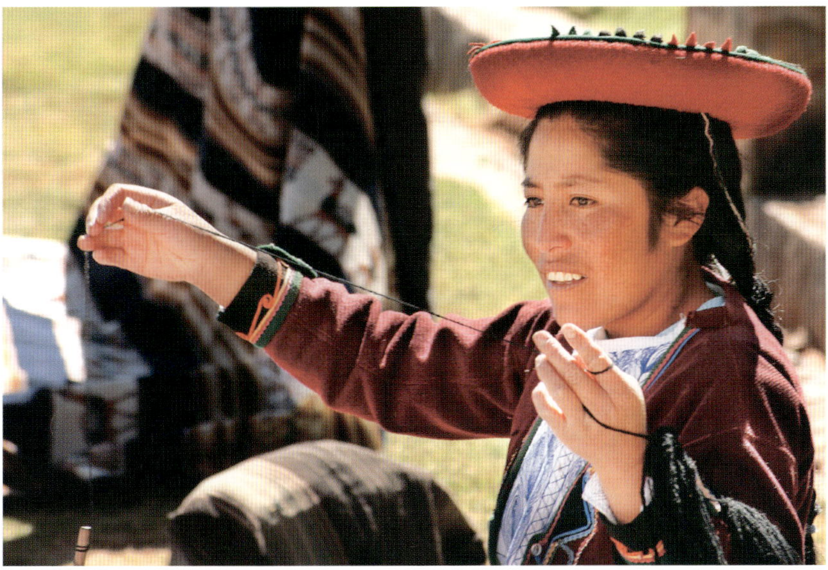

If you're going to be traveling with your camera, consider investing in several large capacity memory cards.

Card Capacity Chart

This chart shows approximately how many photos fit on a particular sized card.

File Type	Card Size				
	64MB	128 MB	256 MB	512 MB	1 GB
4 MP, JPEG	32	64	128	256	500
4 MP, RAW	12	24	50	102	200
8 MP, JPEG	18	36	73	146	286
8 MP, RAW	7	14	28	57	111

The numbers in the chart above aren't an exact indicator of how much capacity you need in a card. You will be able to shoot much more if you erase junk as you go. In addition, since JPEG is a variable compression technology, the numbers are an estimate. If you shot a lot of people in a studio against a solid background, you would find the files compressed smaller than pictures of landscapes (though both are the same quality). JPEG cannot compress a highly detailed image as well as something with solid color.

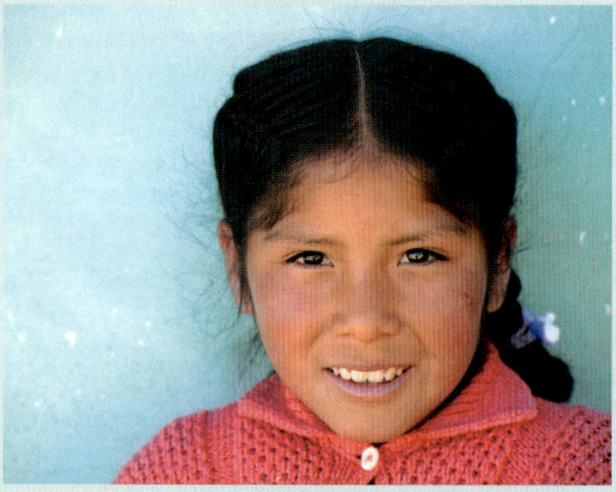

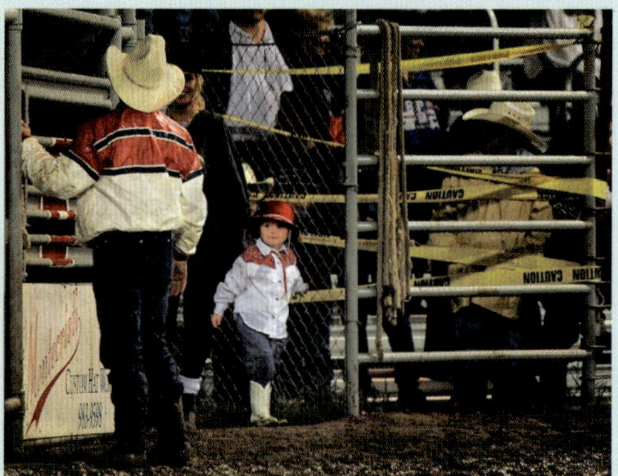

Because JPEG is a variable compression, there is some variation in the file size created. Images with large, smooth areas of solid color can be compressed more than very detailed scenes, and therefore result in a slightly smaller file size.

Downloading Images from Memory Cards

Once you have your photos stored on a memory card, you will need to download and store them elsewhere. While you can print directly from your card or camera, after a while, you won't be able to shoot any new images because the card will be full. Typically, you want to download the photos off the card so they can be used in other applications and to clear your card for reuse.

There are three main ways to download your memory card and its images: access through the camera, removing the card from the camera for downloading on its own, and taking the card to a photo-processing lab. Each method has its advantages and disadvantages.

Downloading From the Camera

Nearly all digital cameras offer the ability to transfer images from card to computer (or other storage device) with a direct connection from camera to computer. This usually involves some sort of cable (typically a USB connection), although infrared and other wireless technologies may be seen in all digital cameras in the future. The type of camera connection cannot be changed, because it is built into the camera.

You don't need to remove the card from the camera and you don't need any additional devices. When you download from the camera, you simply hook one end of the cord to a port on the computer and the other end to the camera. When you turn on the camera, computers with the latest operating systems will usually recognize it and help you make the transfer. If not, you'll have to add the camera's software.

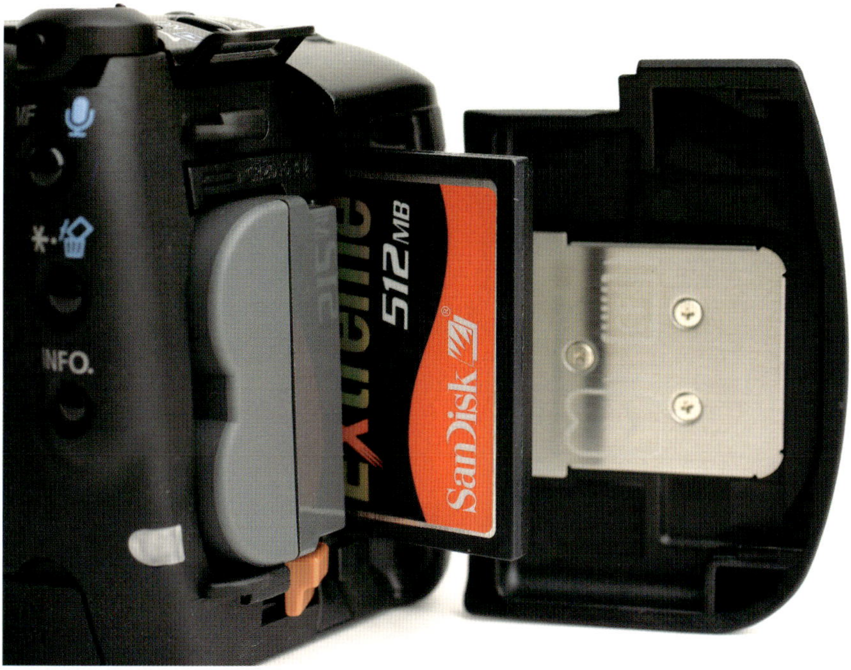

Always turn your camera off before changing cards or removing the card for downloading.

Depending on what imaging programs you have on your computer (and the camera's software), you'll often find a program to help you move photos onto the hard drive. At this point the digital image files are being copied from one place to another.

Hint: Pay careful attention to where the files are saved when you download them to your computer. Too often the files end up somewhere on the hard drive—but where? If it is not clear, the program will usually tell you in Options, Preferences, or Tools.

Card Readers

I strongly recommend a card reader for downloading. This is the fastest and simplest method. A card reader is a small, stand-alone device that plugs into the computer (USB or FireWire), and it has a slot for your camera's memory card. Many of these readers come with capabilities of reading different card types. This can be a real benefit if you have more than one camera and they use different cards. Otherwise you will probably just want the simple, less expensive unit that only reads the type of card your camera uses.

The card reader is easy to use and very affordable. In a way, it makes your camera act like the traditional film camera. You simply take your "digital film" out of the camera and put it into the slot for "processing." The computer will recognize the card as a new drive (on some older operating systems you may need to install a driver for the card reader, which will be on software that comes with the unit).

The card reader now allows you to work with the image files. If you are not familiar with how computers deal with files, transferring images may take some learning. But if you have even basic computer skills, you will find that this reader now allows you to work with the image files just as you would any other files—like selecting all the photos on the card and copying them to a new folder on your hard drive.

Finally, I would strongly suggest a FireWire reader. While more expensive (and requiring a FireWire port on the computer), it is a great convenience because it downloads files so quickly. This can be quite important if you have big cards filled with images.

Laptops with FireWire and USB connections work in the same way. Some even have slots specifically for memory cards (usually the common CF card) for direct transfer. Most Windows laptops also have PC card slots (the old PCMCIA slots) and you can get memory card adapters that fit into these slots. Transfer of images from these slots can also be very, very fast.

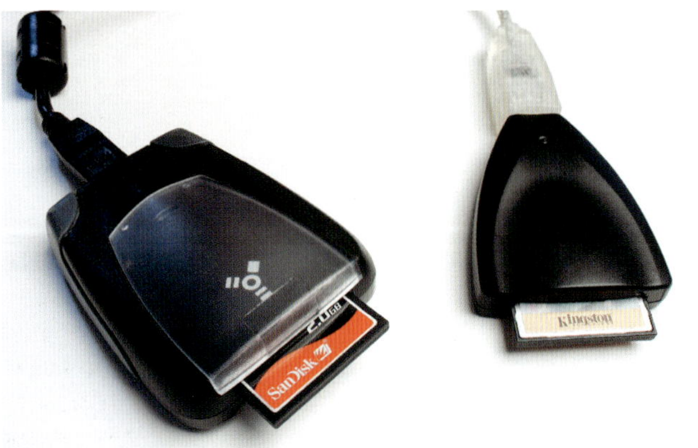

Card readers come with either FireWire (left) or USB (right) connectivity. If you have FireWire on your computer, look for that type of card reader, as it is very fast.

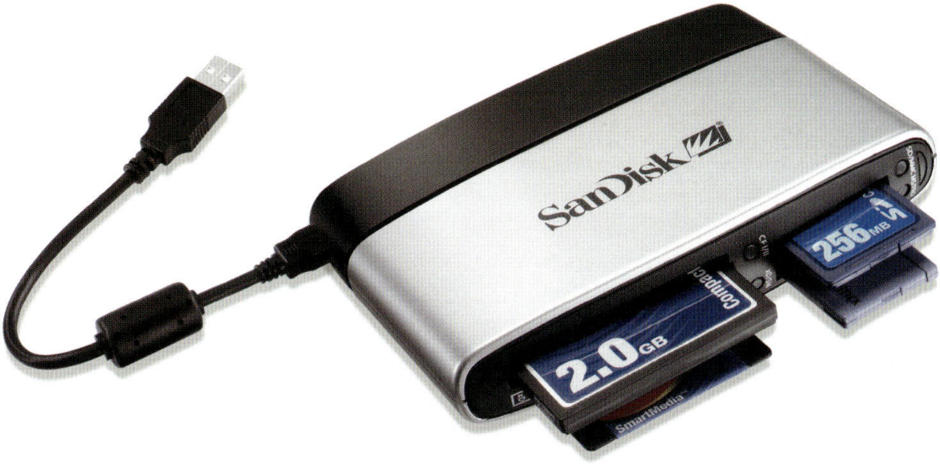

Most photographers prefer to use a card reader to download images to the computer. Card readers are readily available, relatively inexpensive, and are faster to use than the camera's connection cord. For a little more money, you can get a multi-card reader with slots for different card types. If you own digital cameras that take different cards or think you'll be buying another digital camera, this can be a good option.

Working with a Card Reader

- Set up a folder on your computer ahead of time so you know where to put the images.
- Card readers are faster than downloading with a connected camera.
- No special camera software is needed.
- It is always connected, so you are not struggling with the clutter of unused cables.
- It uses little space on the desktop.
- You don't have to have the camera on the desktop, where it can be accidentally knocked off the desk.
- If you don't have FireWire speed on your camera, you can get it in a card reader.

Taking Your Card to a Lab

Many photo enthusiasts are finding another way of transfer quite attractive—using a lab. Take your memory card to the minilab where you, or the lab, download the images and make prints. It's just like dropping off film. Often, labs have self-service kiosks that allow you to do digital photo printing directly, plus download to a disk. Many digital cameras even have a DPOF feature (Digital Print Order Format) that allows you to select in camera which shots your processor will print. These prints are made on photo papers just like traditional film prints.

The major benefit of using a lab is that you can take advantage of a digital camera without using or owning a computer. By going to a lab, you can get those prints done fast and easy. Most photographers—whether pros or amateurs—will take casual images that only require quick prints for friends and family.

Clearing the Card

You've downloaded your images. Now what's best way to erase images off of a memory card—camera or computer? It's just data, right? So why not use the computer to erase the card after downloading images? Some photographers do this, and there is even software that seems to recommend it. Minilab operators may offer to do it for you. However, before making this decision, you should know what erasing and reformatting a card actually does.

Erasing the Card

When a memory card is erased, no image files are actually destroyed or removed from the memory. (This is true for all computer files when erased, which is why there are security issues in sensitive government locations.) Erasing removes only location/identification data that tells the computer where the file is located. Once this location/identification data is removed, new photos can overwrite the old image files. After new photos are saved over the old images, the original photos are "lost."

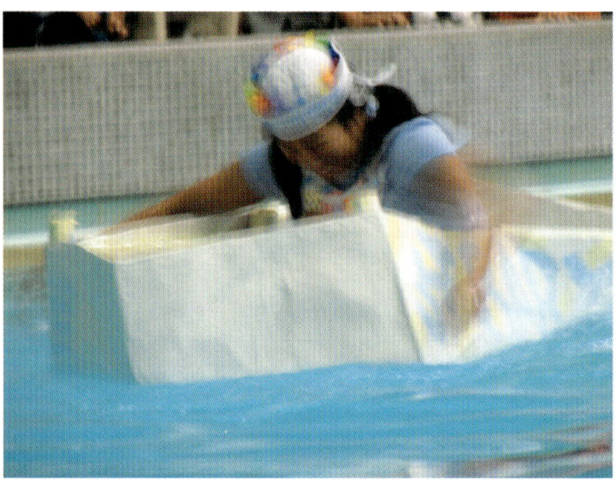

If you didn't delete the blurred photos immediately after shooting, use the camera to erase all the images from the memory card after you've downloaded the images you want to keep.

Reformatting the Card

When formatting, the camera or computer completely rebuilds the directory structure of the card (which tells any device reading the card how to find the data). This results in the "erasure" of the photos by removing the links to the actual data.

All of the technical gurus I have talked to recommend using the camera for erasing and reformatting of the card. Formatting your card in the camera lowers the risk of corrupting or accidentally changing the file system of the card.

Caution: *It is actually possible that formatting a card with FAT32 or NTFS (computer formats) could make the card unusable in the camera. This can usually be fixed by reformatting with the camera.*

My friend and digital expert, Tim Grey, has an interesting take on this, "Reformatting in the camera causes the card to be re-initialized, helping to avoid possible problems with the FAT [File Allocation Table—the directory] data becoming corrupted over time." He adds, "I don't like to erase the card until I am actually ready to use it. This then serves as a last-resort backup for the images as long as they are sitting on the card. I then have to make a conscious decision to remove them rather than casually delete them at the computer."

What if you have more than one brand of camera? Generally speaking, erasing or formatting in different cameras has little effect on the card. It may throw off the picture count for the card.

It is a good idea to reformat your card every month or so if you are a casual shooter, perhaps every week or two for high-volume photographers. Some photographers like to reformat every time they put a card back into the camera. There is nothing wrong with that and no harm will come to the card.

Field Storage

When you are shooting, cards do fill up. Eventually you will want to download images while shooting to empty your card to take more photos. For me, a more important reason is backup. With traditional photography, if you lost or damaged the film, your photos were gone forever. With digital, you can back up all of your digital images with exact copies and rarely lose photos. I tend to back up photos every day that I am shooting—whether I am using up cards or not.

You could keep a lot of memory cards with you (they are becoming quite reasonably priced), or buy some very big cards instead of backing up, but I think it is very important to take advantage of the backup ability of digital. Since you can, why not back up your files—especially with photos that are very important to you?

Downloading to Your Laptop

Small laptop computers and dedicated handheld digital storage devices are also good storage solutions. Personally, I prefer a small laptop with a built-in CD burner—many pros like this choice. Even photographers in the toughest conditions will find rugged laptops on the market designed to take abuse in the field—and still weigh no more than a couple of pounds. A laptop allows you to download images to its hard drive, review them on the bigger screen of the computer, edit as needed, and then make a backup copy on CD. Short of someone stepping on them, CDs are pretty durable and they can be a good way to ensure you have your images.

Downloading to a Handheld Storage Device

Most portable storage devices are battery-powered laptop hard drives with a built-in card reader (some even include a small LCD screen to allow you to see images). You simply plug in your memory card and the images are transferred quickly to the hard drive. For sheer size advantages, they can't be beat. They easily fit into a gadget bag so they can always be with you. However, since they are hard drives, you do have to be careful not to drop them.

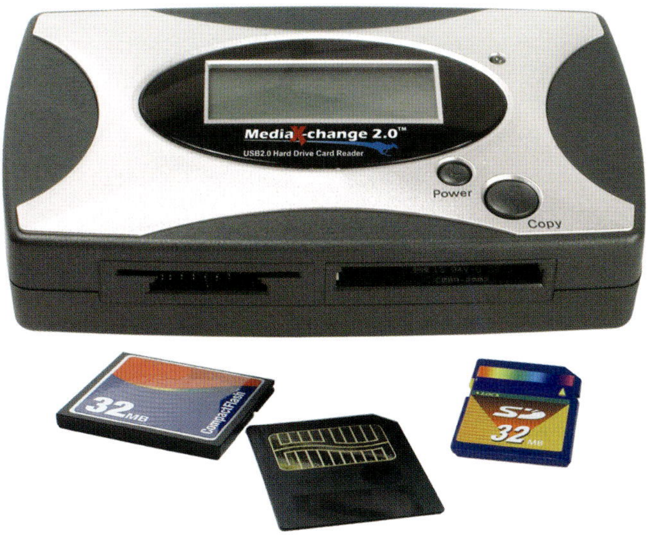

A portable storage device can be a great alternative to buying a laptop computer.

Stand-Alone CD Burners

A number of stand-alone CD burners are now available, and we may see similar DVD-burners soon. These allow you to download a memory card directly to CD, skipping the computer altogether. An advantage of a CD is that you can make multiple copies. This can be very important for really critical work. Some photographers like to use 512 MB or 640 MB memory cards because they fit directly onto a CD. If you have memory cards that will hold more images than the capacity of a CD, be sure that any stand-alone burner you get can do "disk-spanning," which means it will take image files from a large memory card and automatically distribute them over several disks.

Protecting Your Images

No matter how you download your pictures, you will have image data files that need to be protected. This is a really critical part of the digital age. You want to be sure that you can get your photos when you need them and that nothing terrible happens to them. Now, I can't offer you anything that would protect your digital photos from a disaster such as fire, although digital safeguards can actually help here, too, if you keep very important duplicate files in different locations. I know of photographers who actually keep duplicate files of important images in bank vaults. It makes sense if you make your living from these images.

A small portable hard drive that attaches to your computer can be a very useful backup tool that allows you to make complete copies of your files on a device that can be moved from computer to computer. These drives offer a lot of gigabyte storage space, making a huge number of images instantly available. They also come with both USB and FireWire connections for ease of use and speed. Their disadvantage is that they are moving magnetic media—damaged by dropping—and the data fades with age.

Caution: *Data on magnetic media fades with time. Most manufacturers will only recommend 8–10 years for their media. While there is no doubt that this is a conservative number (many people are able to access magnetic data longer than that), remember that enough problems occur in this time frame that it is worth looking to back up images in non-magnetic ways.*

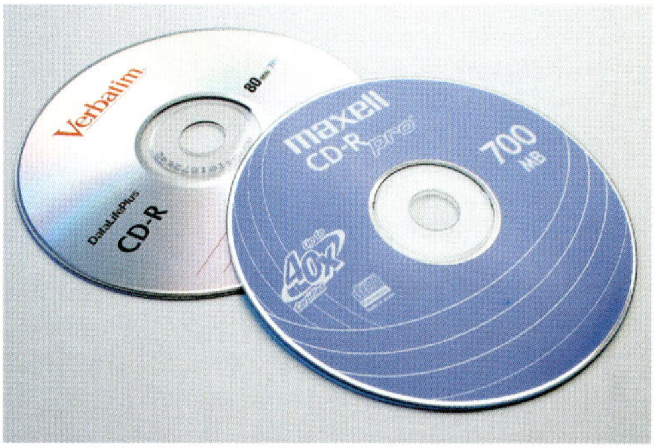

CDs are an excellent way of storing and protecting your photos, so use quality, name-brand media. For best results, look for the words long-life or archival.

CDs

The recordable CD (CD-R) is an excellent backup medium, as is the DVD. These optical storage media have a life of 50–100 years depending on their quality. Cheap CDs are fine for short-term storage (or backup), but if you want your photos to last, look for disks with distinct claims for archival or long life. These disks are very stable in their data saving capacity. You do need to protect the top of the disk from damage (this is the side with a mirror that reflects the device's laser), which may include writing on the CD with markers specially designed for CDs.

Most computers today have CD-R/RW drives, and CD-writing software has become drag-and-drop simple. The CD has become a common way of storing and transporting images for photographers.

I have intentionally not mentioned rewriteable CDs (CD-RW). While you can use them to transfer any type of file from one computer to another, or for temporary storage, they should never be used for image backup and safe storage. CD-RWs are designed to be erased and reused, which means the medium is meant to change! No photographer wants to rely on a storage medium that can be changed.

After photographing with a digital camera, I almost always immediately copy all my unmodified files to CD. They become like my film archival negatives. I can always go back to them. I then keep this CD in a safe place and make duplicates of any very important work.

DVDs

DVD is rapidly becoming another very important optical storage medium. Since DVD drives read CDs as well, you may end up using CDs for basic backup. The advantage of DVD is storage space, but you don't always need or want several gigabytes of storage. Less-expensive CDs may help you keep your files better organized than a single DVD because you can categorize the images on each CD. Yet, when you need the added storage, DVD is great. In the future, all disk storage will become increasingly DVD, however, there are still some compatibility issues that have to be resolved before DVD can be considered the best storage method. For now, CD is more universal.

With a CD you can get up to approximately 700 MB of data on one disk (this has a slight variation depending on the disk). DVDs, on the other hand, are rated at 4.7 gigabytes but, for a variety of filing and technical reasons, you cannot record that amount of image files on one. You actually get a little more than 4 GB of usable storage—still quite a lot. Currently, a single DVD will hold the equivalent of nearly six filled CDs.

As digital cameras increase in megapixels (and RAW capture becomes more commonly used), you will go through a lot of storage space. A big vacation could easily fill up a CD. As you use Layers when working on photos in the computer, you can get individual files reaching 100 MB or more. A DVD gives you a lot more flexibility in storing these.

One unfortunate part about recordable DVDs is that the manufacturers have not agreed on one single standard. There are competing formats, although DVD-R and DVD+R are probably the most important for photographers. All DVD formats other than DVD-RW work well for image backup and storage. (The same thoughts about CD-RW apply to DVD-RW.)

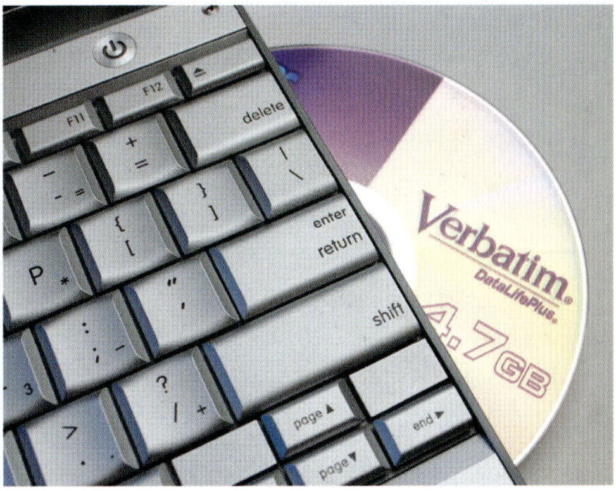

Many new desktop and laptop computers include a DVD player/burner. If you have lots of large image files to backup, DVD might be the best optical storage medium option.

Simplified Digital Workflow

Photography is still photography when shooting digital. However, there are enough different things involved that it is worth looking at the overall process. The simplified process here can be used as a checklist to see how you can make your own photography more effective and efficient. Try the ideas, use what works for you, modify the rest to find your own ideal way of working.

Before You Shoot

1. **Check batteries**—Be sure you have enough and that they are charged.

2. **Format your memory cards**—Get them ready for shooting and be sure you don't have anything on them from earlier photo sessions that needs to be saved.

3. **Do test shots**—If you have any new gear, try it out before you have something important to photograph.

4. **Prep your camera bag**—Be sure you have everything you need.

During Shooting

1. **Exposure mode**—Cameras vary in how modes are set; some are easy to accidentally bump into new modes. Get into the habit of checking to see that you are in the right mode.

2. **White balance**—Get into the habit of choosing white balance for the shooting situation. Use your LCD as a reminder and check that the colors are right.

3. **Review**—Check your review settings to be sure that the LCD stays on long enough so that you have time to review images.

4. **Protect and erase**—Know how to protect key images. Most cameras let you protect the photos you want to save, then if you erase all the images on the card (not format), you save the protected shots.

Transfer Images

1. **Create a destination folder**—Set up a destination folder that will hold your images.

2. **Connect to your computer**—Put the memory card into the card reader.

3. **Access the image files**—Drag and drop them into the destination folder you identified in step 1.

4. **Do a visual check**—Confirm that your photos are all on the hard drive with a browser program.

5. **Back up**—Save your image files to a CD or DVD.

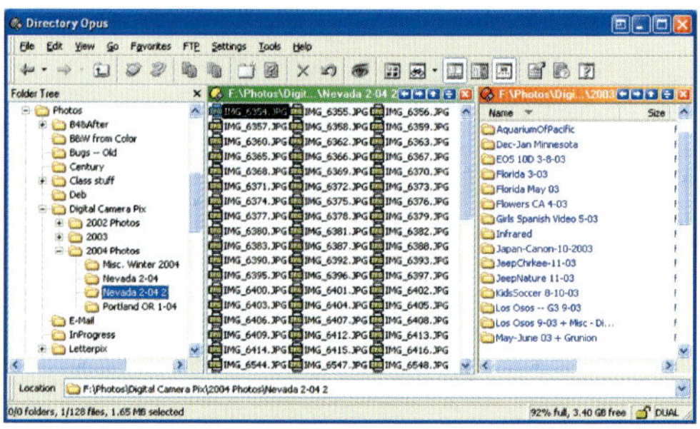

Set up a destination folder for images on your computer. When you download photos—either from the camera or with a card reader—put them into the folder. Then you won't waste time searching your hard drive.

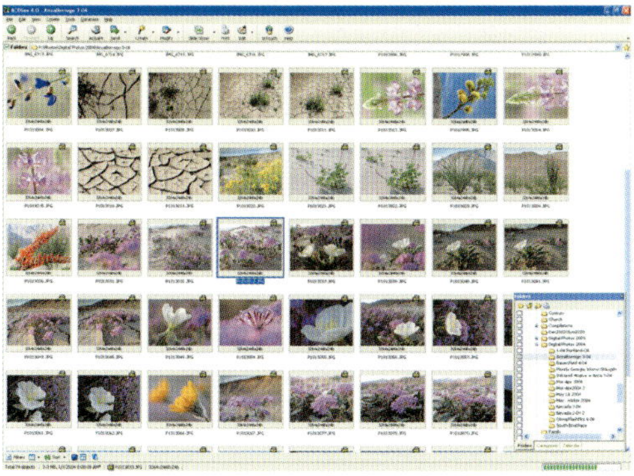

Browser programs, like ACDSee, show thumbnails of all the images on a disk or in a folder. By viewing images this way, you can easily edit your shots, sort them into categories and folders, and see trends or themes in your shooting style.

Browse Images

1. **Browse your photos**—This helps you determine what works, and what doesn't. Look for trends in shooting that you might be unconsciously developing (ACDSee and iView Media are examples of browser programs).

2. **Organize photos**—Copy and move photos to subject-specific folders. This allows you to set up different folders on the hard drive that are labeled with names specific to your photography: "Los Osos August 05," for example.

Processing Images

1. **Select the images you want to process**—Image browsing programs can be very helpful for this.

2. **Use "Save As"**—Once an original file (whether JPEG or RAW) is opened, do a "Save As" to a TIFF or native image-processing software file (such as Photoshop's PSD) before making alterations. This protects the original.

***Caution:** Never use JPEG as a working file format.*

3. **Rotate and crop**—Rotate the image to the position in which you intend it to be viewed and crop out any unwanted picture space.

4. **Check overall brightness and color**—Is the photo too bright or too dark? What colors are problems?

5. **Check the details**—Look at individual areas in a photograph to see where small parts should be adjusted separately from the whole image

6. **Isolate areas for processing**—Use selection tools and Layers to isolate parts of the photo so that they can be adjusted separately

7. **Flatten layered files**—Save your layered master in case you want to rework the image, then flatten the image and "Save As" for specific use.

Hint: Reserve sharpening for this stage.

8. **Save layered files and flattened files separately**—Layered files let you go back and make adjustments, while the flattened files are better for printing and other applications.

accessories and flash

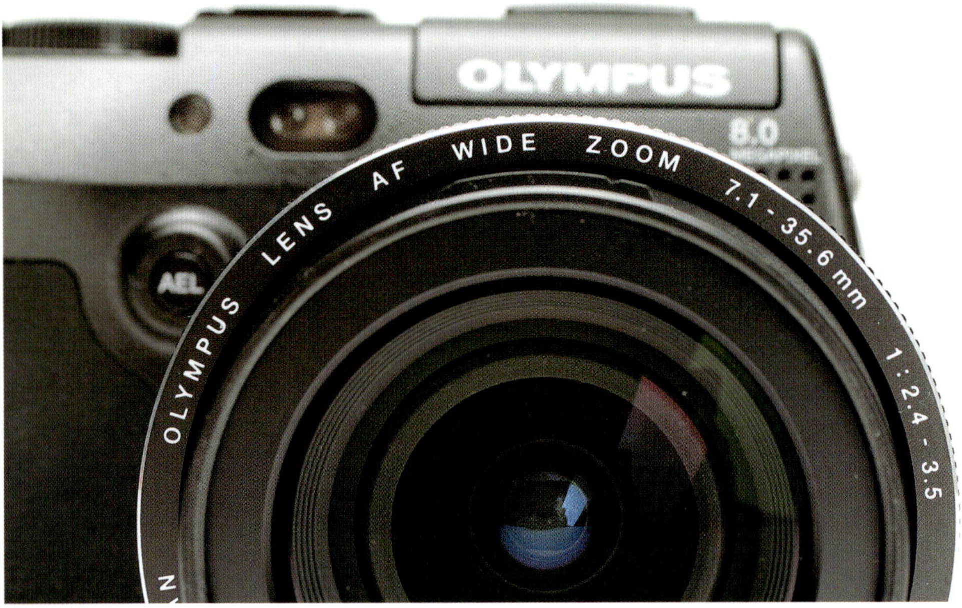

Lenses

One advantage of a digital SLR is that you can choose from a whole range of lens focal lengths in order to increase your photographic possibilities. However, with small compact digital cameras, you can't interchange the base lens. In many situations, this is not a serious problem, since the attached lens will cover the most used focal lengths. In addition, you can buy high-quality accessory lenses for many cameras that will allow you to shoot at telephoto and wide-angle focal lengths.

We will use an important convention to talk about lenses with digital cameras: 35mm equivalents. Sensors on digital zoom cameras are very small, and the lenses (along with focal lengths) are also small, as explained earlier. This puts an interesting spin on focal lengths. While many cameras do show actual focal length on the lens, this doesn't tell you much. A lens' focal length is meaningless without a reference to the image area, or frame size, within the camera. Different digital cameras will have different imaging areas, which makes any comparison of focal lengths between two cameras a real challenge unless there is some common point of reference. This is the 35mm equivalent, which tells us what view the lens would offer if it were on a 35mm camera.

Lens Speed

Before we go further with lenses we need to look at lens speed. This is one topic that isn't always well understood and can cause some major problems for a photographer. Lens speed refers to the maximum f/stop—the widest aperture—of a lens. This determines the maximum amount of light that a lens lets into the camera. This is the number that is always given when referring to a lens and its focal length. For example, a digital camera with a 35-105mm (35mm equivalent) f/2.8 would be a zoom lens with a maximum aperture of f/2.8. The wider the aperture, the smaller the f/number and the faster the lens. An f/2.8 lens is twice as fast as an f/4 lens; it lets in twice as much light.

A faster lens lets you use faster shutter speeds (or lets the camera select these speeds). This helps when you need to shoot action, obviously, but it also helps when the light gets low. That's when every little bit of faster shutter speed can help, and you get that with wide apertures.

This gets tricky, though, with the little zooms on many small digital cameras. These zooms typically have variable maximum apertures so a 28-90mm (35mm equivalent) lens might have an aperture of f/2.8–4. This means that the lens has a speed of f/2.8 at 28mm, but it drops to f/4 at 90mm. In-between focal lengths have in-between f/stops. The reason lenses are made this way is size. A variable aperture lens can be made a lot smaller than a constant, or fixed, aperture zoom lens. This can be a huge advantage for compact cameras. However, it is something to watch, as it can mean you have an aperture/shutter speed combination for lower light levels (such as 1/60 second at f/2.8) that can be handheld, but this shifts to a hard-to-handhold 1/30 at f/4 for the telephoto setting.

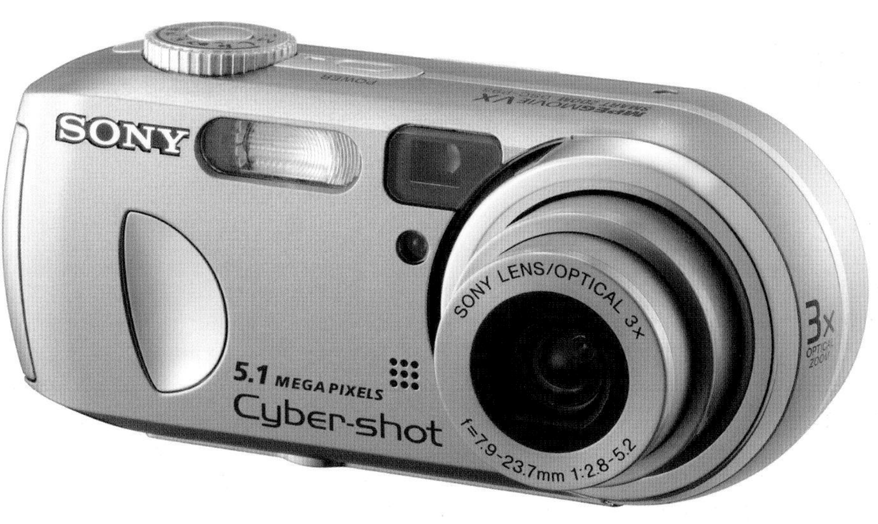

Listed on the camera's zoom lens is the actual focal length (7.9-23.7mm) and the maximum aperture (1:2.8–5.2). (Technically, the f/number is a ratio and manufacturers often write it this way.) This camera has a variable maximum aperture. At 7.9mm it is f/2.8, at 23.7mm it is f/5.2.

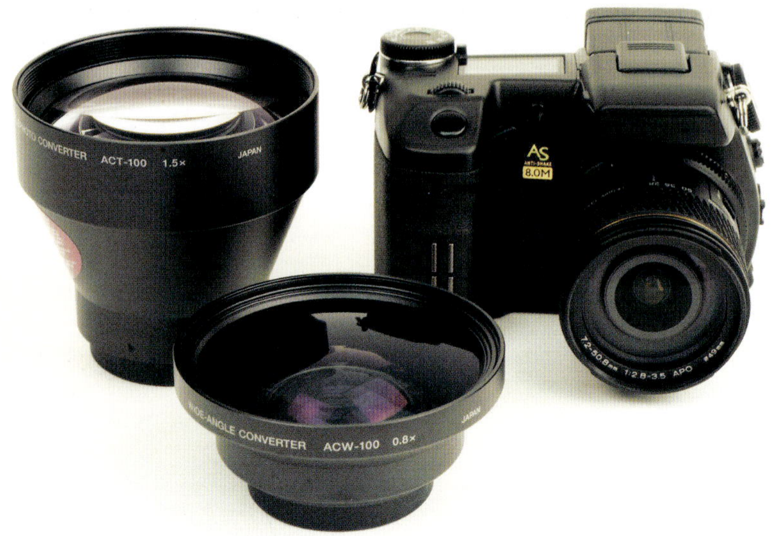

Adding accessory lenses to your digital zoom camera can significantly expand your photography options, yet their cost is low and they are easy to carry.

Beyond the Zoom

The zooms on compact digital cameras keep getting better in quality and focal length range. On top-of-the-line cameras, these lenses can rival anything you can buy for a digital SLR in quality, but even on the least expensive cameras, the lenses can be quite good. While most cameras will have focal lengths confined to a limited range because of size restraints (long focal lengths cannot go on the smallest cameras), there are some EVF-cameras (SLR-inspired) that offer lenses that go from wide to long telephoto (as much as 300-400mm—35mm equivalents) without an added accessory lens.

Still, most cameras will have a range that may not be as wide as you want and may fall short of the long telephoto focal lengths needed to photograph wildlife or sports. This is not necessarily a problem. Most advanced digital cameras offer accessory lenses that increase the amount of wide-angle and magnify the telephoto end. There are also some independent manufacturers who offer similar lenses.

These accessory lenses can be very, very good. Because they aren't terribly expensive, some photographers think they can't possibly be very good. Consider this—these accessory lenses have nothing except the glass. There are no complicated focusing mechanisms, no autofocus motors, no lens apertures, no controlling mechanisms for any of this, no electronics—nothing except glass, lens barrel, and mount. In addition, the whole package is not very big compared to a 35mm lens, so this all adds up to a lower cost to make and sell such lenses.

The best ones are usually those made by the manufacturer specifically for the camera, for the obvious reason that the accessory lens can be matched to the characteristics of the underlying lens. Any accessory lens can only be as good as the underlying zoom and how well the two match. This is why independent accessory lens manufacturers have a hard time with this type of lens. You might find that the same lens works great on one camera and awful on another. You have to read as many reviews as you can find and try them out.

I have even found that lenses from different manufacturers will work quite well on another brand, but this cannot be predicted without experimentation since the lenses were not made for each other. It can be worth trying, though, since you might not have the focal length you want otherwise. When the Canon PowerShot Pro 1 came out, for example, I wanted to get a wider-angle than the 28mm equivalent, but there was no wide lens available. I tried many different wide adapters, but most had vignetting problems until I tried one of the Olympus accessory lenses originally made for the E-10 and E-20. This is a great reason to patronize your local camera store, as they can let you try these things out at the store to see what works for you.

Besides focal length changes, accessory lenses can help with close-ups, too (which I'll cover in detail a little later). They make your camera's zoom into a macro zoom. I am not talking about cheap close-up lenses or filters, but about highly corrected, achromatic, multi-element, close-up lenses. While most digital cameras do have close-up settings built-in, this typically is limited at the telephoto settings. These close-up lenses let you use all focal lengths at macro distances for great close-ups.

Accessory lenses attach to the camera in two basic ways: they screw into the filter ring, or screw into a special lens adapter. Either way works and you usually don't have a choice of one or the other. The special lens adapter does tend to give a stronger attachment to the camera, however. In addition, on some camera models, this adapter bayonets to the camera, so if you buy an adapter for each accessory lens, you can then bayonet the lens quickly on and off of the camera.

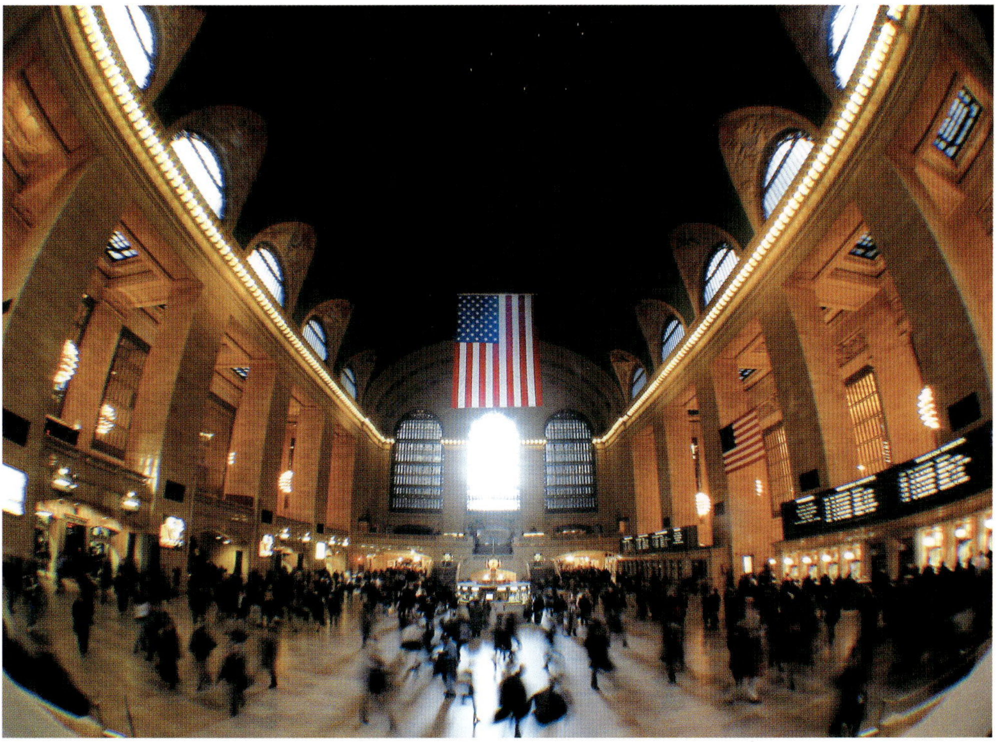

Add a super wide-angle accessory lens to your digital zoom camera and expand your camera's capabilities.

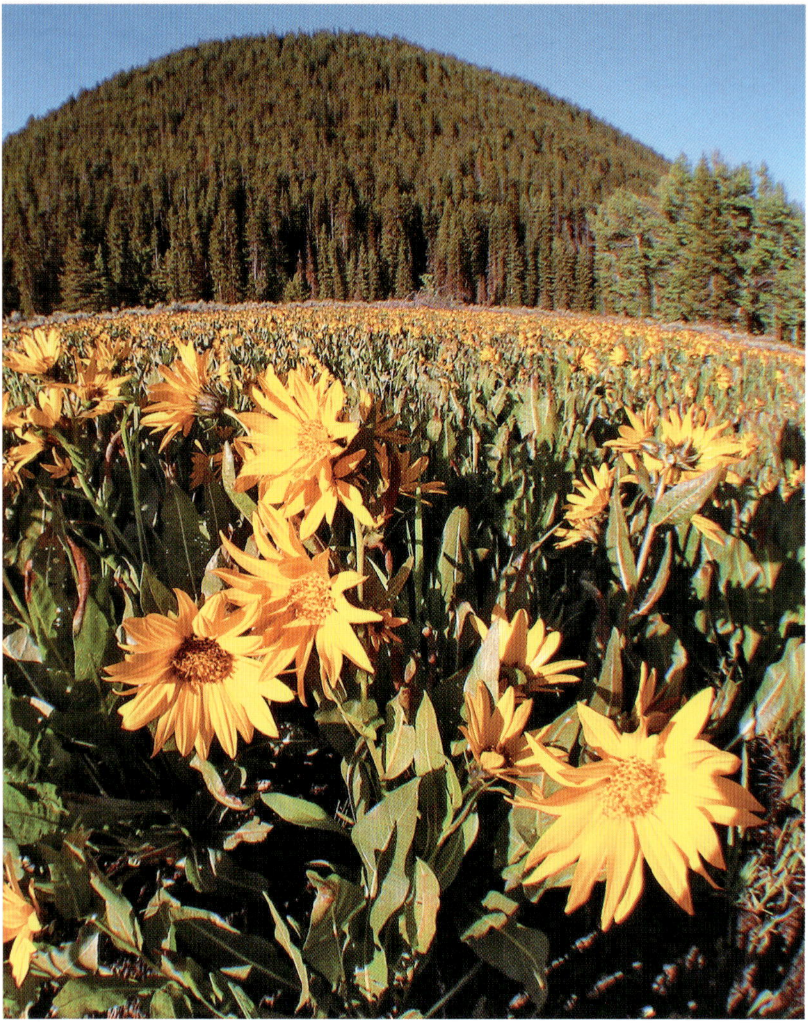

To add drama, use a wide-angle lens, get in close to an object in the foreground, and use a small aperture for extensive depth of field. Using an ultra wide-angle lens creates the "curved earth" illusion.

Wide-Angle Focal Lengths

Wide-angle is one of the fundamental focal length categories for the photographer. Wide-angle lenses have the ability to take in more of a scene from left to right and top to bottom. The difference between a wide-angle and any other lens is somewhat arbitrary and is based on a focal length's relationship to a "normal" lens for a given format. In 35mm, that normal lens is approximately 50mm (which is related to the diagonal of the format). The wide-angle is then any focal length that is shorter. All following references to focal length will be based on 35mm film camera equivalents because the variation in sensor size on small cameras makes any comparisons based on real focal lengths confusing and difficult.

The 35mm focal length used to be very popular with photojournalists. It is wider than normal, but not so wide as to call attention to itself. This focal length, or something similar, such as 38-39mm, is very common for small digital camera zooms. This is not as wide as many photographers like, and this limitation on wide-angle shooting is a common complaint about small digital cameras. Wide-angle accessory lenses do help.

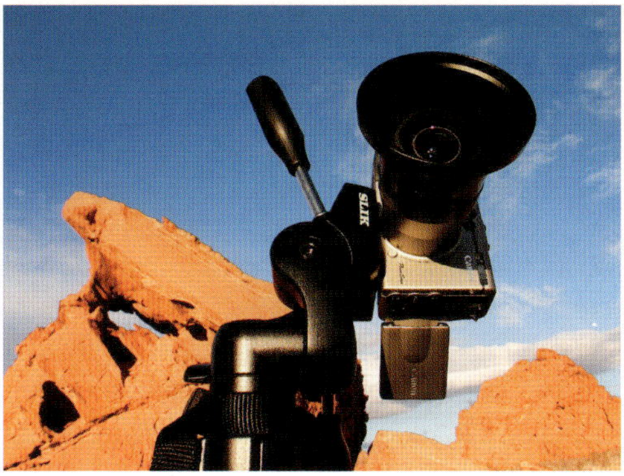

Don't think you are limited by the camera's focal length range. There are accessory wide-angle, ultra wide-angle, and even fish-eye lenses

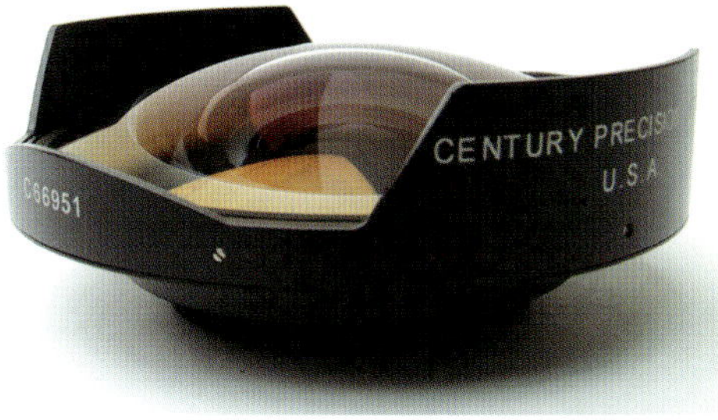

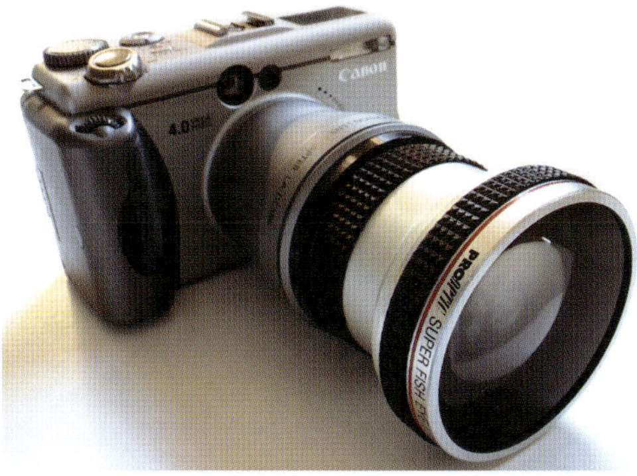

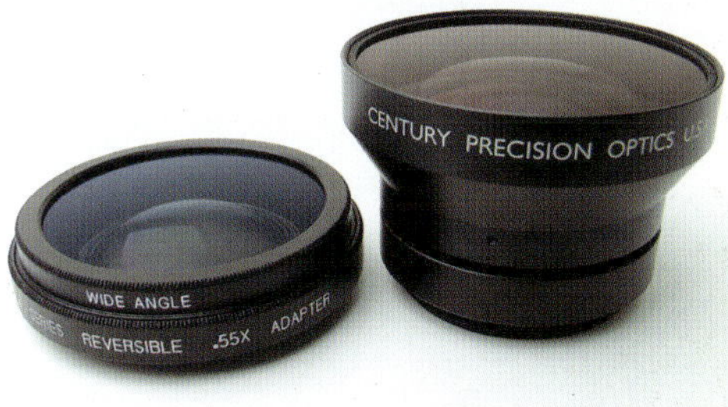

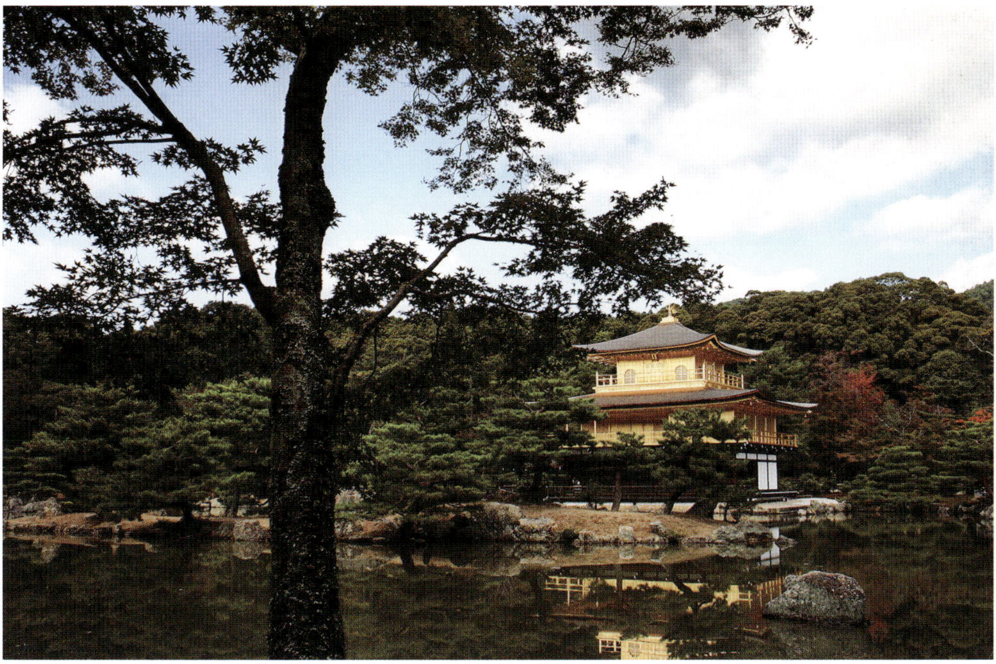

The lens on a digital zoom camera offers you the ability to precisely compose your photographs.

Traditionally, the most popular wide-angle focal length has been 28mm. This is wide enough to really make a change in what you see of the scene. The 28mm focal length is becoming more common with compact digital cameras. Wider focal lengths are rarely seen in compact zoom digital cameras.

Telephoto Focal Lengths

Telephoto focal lengths are just the opposite of wide-angles with their ability to zero in on a scene. They have a very narrow angle of view, magnifying a scene in the viewfinder and on the sensor. They also allow the photographer to stand at an unobtrusive distance from the subject and still get a reasonably-sized image of that subject. Telephoto lenses are any focal length that is longer than normal and they are also referred to as "long lenses."

The 80-90mm focal length is a moderate range that used to be very popular with photojournalists. It is slightly longer than normal, yet not so much of a telephoto as to call attention to itself. This focal length is also very common in the small zooms on digital cameras. Many camera zooms have something like 35-80mm or 35-105mm as their focal length ranges. These are good portrait lenses for showing a bit of the body as well as face. The longer 105mm allows the photographer to be a good distance from the subject and creates a pleasant facial perspective.

Hint: Wider angles tend to distort our perceptions of a face.

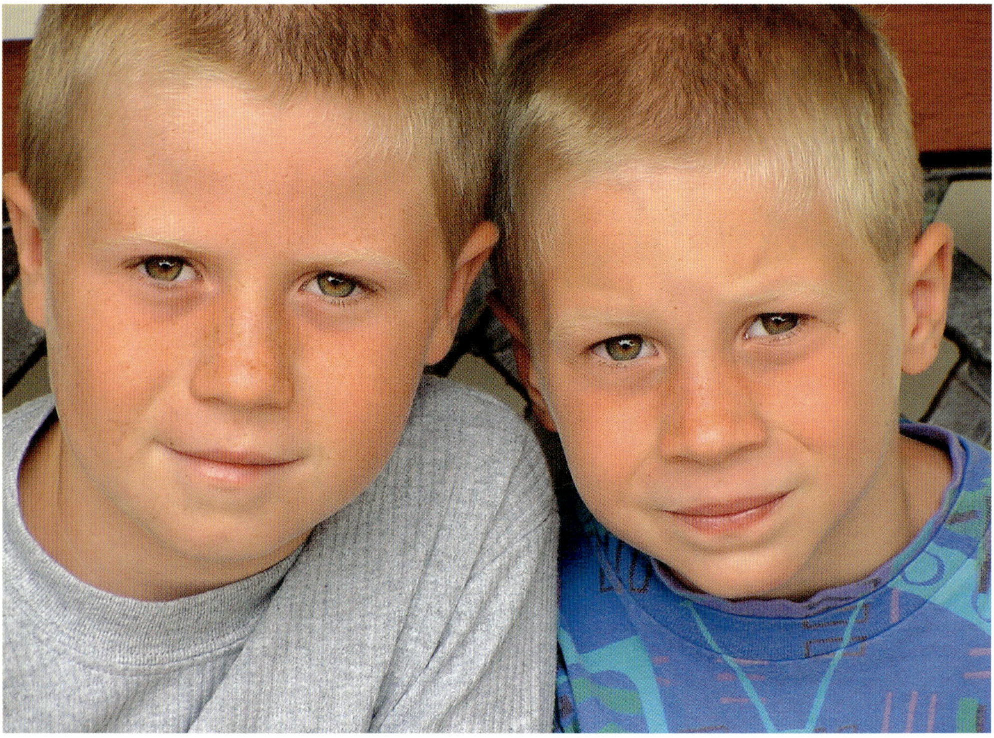

Use your camera's longest focal length setting or add an accessory telephoto lens for portraits. You can stand at a comfortable distance from your subject and still fill the frame.

Some zoom cameras have focal lengths extending up to 200mm in the telephoto range. This represents a good telephoto distance. This is long enough to allow you to photograph subjects that are not right next to you, but lenses of this focal length are still reasonable in size and cost.

The 300-500mm range of focal lengths offers a lot of magnification. Compared to a 50mm lens, they offer 6–10x the power. This is why wildlife photographers and sports photographers prefer these focal lengths. A few digital cameras offer these focal lengths as possibilities, especially with added telephoto accessory lenses.

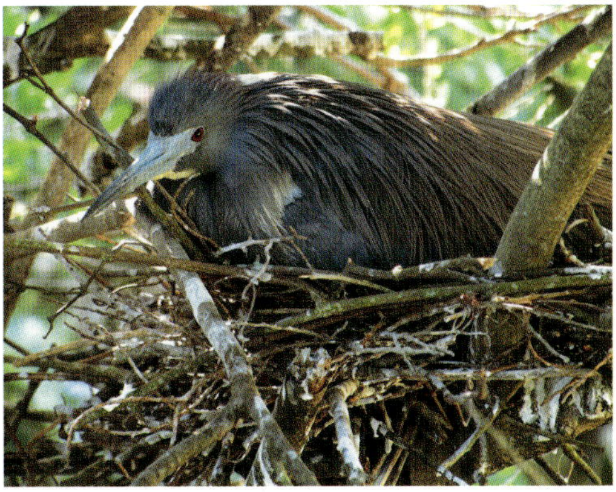

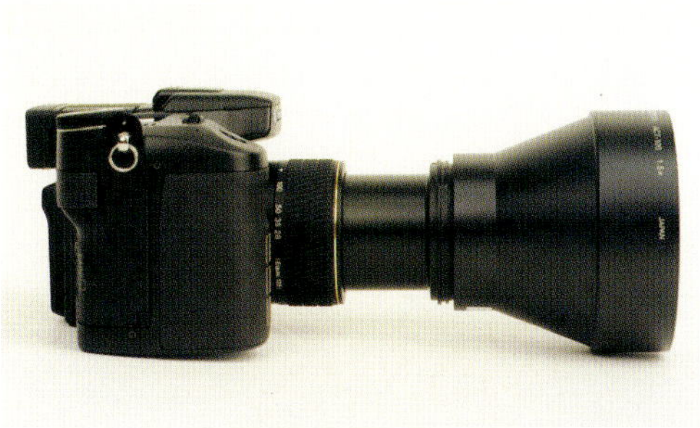

Above: Telephoto lenses of 300-500mm are necessary for photographing wildlife. You can maintain a shooting distance that is safe for both you and the animal.

Left: Accessory telephoto lenses are fairly bulky. You may need a tripod to ensure that there is no image blur due to camera shake.

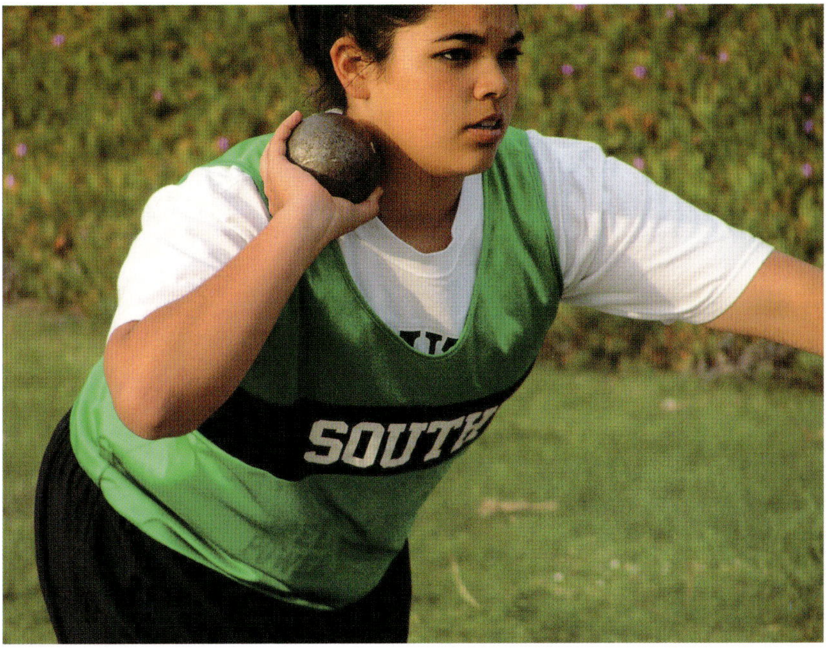

At sporting events, stand back at a reasonable distance and capture that look of concentration on the athlete's face by using a telephoto lens.

Getting in Close

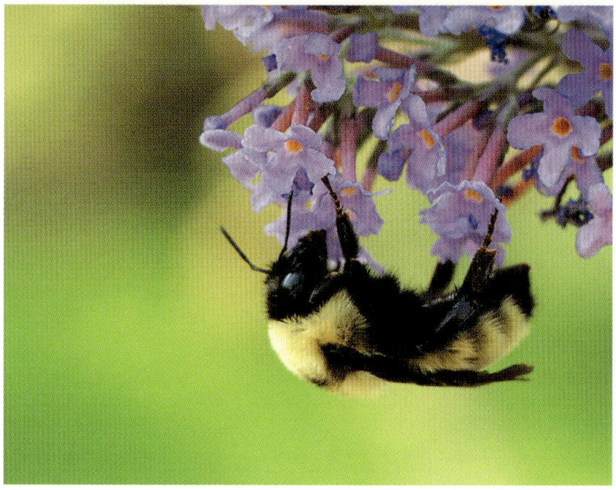

Close-up photography is a fun part of using a digital camera. Since you can always focus through the taking lens by using the LCD (or EVF), whatever you see in the LCD for a close-up will be captured by the sensor. While many photographers think they need an SLR and a "macro lens" for close-ups, there are excellent ways to focus close with a digital zoom camera.

Close-Up Mode

Almost every compact digital camera on the market today has a Close-up mode. This is represented by a little flower icon and is usually accessed by a button. This can give quite remarkable results. Some cameras let you focus as close as an inch without any additional accessories.

This offers some remarkable possibilities, since you are always "ready" to take close-ups. I have found amazing little details in all sorts of places that were possible only because I had a camera that so easily could do a close-up. It also helps that this is a digital camera feature, since you can adjust white balance for nearly any condition, plus you can see the results immediately for confirmation of your composition.

Usually, the close-up setting works mainly (and sometimes only) with the wide-angle part of your zoom. This can offer some interesting perspectives. You will see more of the background, plus you'll get more depth of field. It does offer some challenges, as well. You have to be physically closer to the subject when using wide-angle focal lengths at close settings. This can be a problem with skittish subjects, such as butterflies, or in low-angled light where you can't get a clear angle on the subject without blocking some of that light. You also can't get the selective focus and shortened perspective effects that telephoto focal lengths produce.

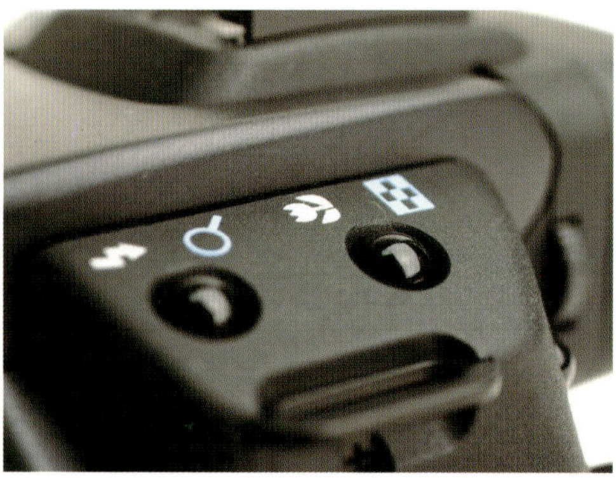

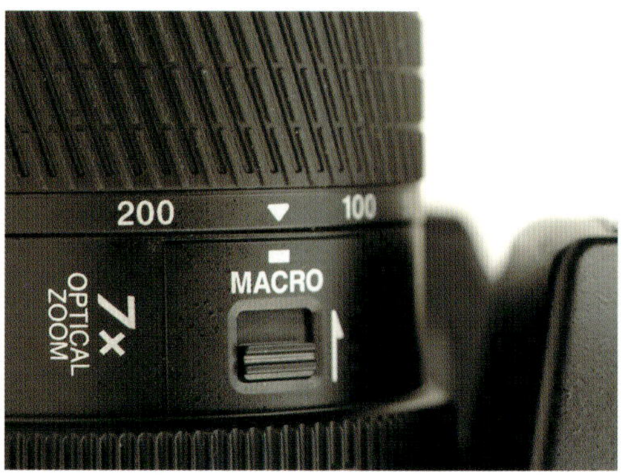

Close-up mode (indicated by a flower icon) may be accessed with a button or there may be a sliding switch (marked MACRO) on the camera lens.

Accessory Macro Lenses

The way around the limitations of the built-in close-up function is to use supplementary close-up lenses (sometimes called close-up filters) that screw on to the front of the lens. The inexpensive multi-lens packages can be useful for beginners, but the quality is marginal at best. I really can't recommend them. A better choice would be an achromatic close-up lens. Century Optics, Canon, Hoya, and Nikon all make them, although I have found the Century Optics "diopter lenses" offer the best range, as well as consistently outstanding results.

This type of attachment is a two-element glass filter designed to very high sharpness standards. It is screwed onto the front of your lens (or lens adapter) and lets you focus very closely. No exposure adjustment is needed. Final quality does depend on the lens under the filter, and these add-on lenses will only fit camera lenses or adapters with a specific filter size.

The great advantage of these lenses is allowing you to focus closer at all focal lengths. You can really get some remarkable compositions when shooting with the telephoto settings of your zoom. I have even used these add-on lenses in between the camera zoom and an accessory telephoto lens for even more dramatic effects. You don't really need them for shooting with wide-angle accessory lenses since the camera will usually focus quite well up close with them using the built-in settings.

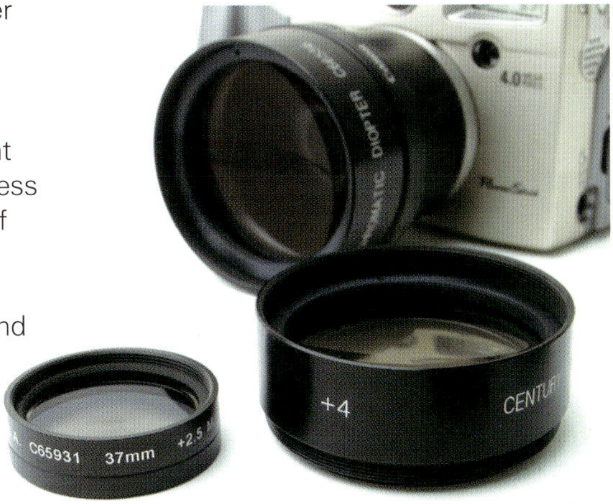

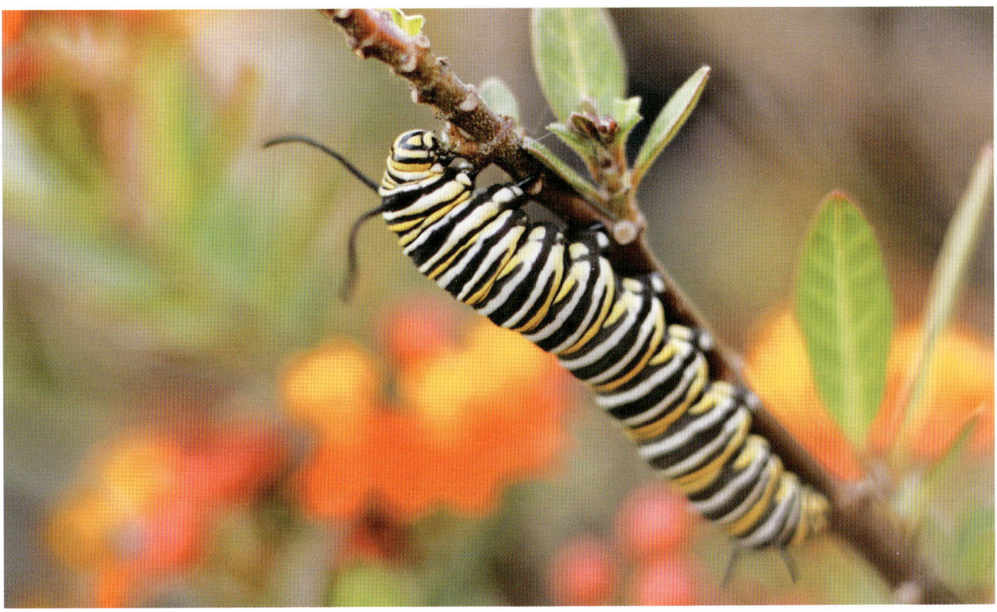

To focus on small subjects that are close to the camera, add an accessory macro lens. These lenses come in different strengths that allow for different focus distances.

Modern Technology and Digital Camera Lenses

Lens manufacturers have managed to do some amazing things with lenses in the last 10–15 years. Computer design, new materials, and new technologies have allowed manufacturers to make better lenses for less money. They've introduced zooms with ranges that were impossible to create even a decade ago. Let's look at some important lens advances that influence the quality and convenience of digital photography today.

Special Glass

Lens manufacturers have used special low-dispersion glass to improve the quality of telephoto lenses for 35mm gear for quite a while. However, it is only relatively recently that manufacturing technologies have advanced enough to make this glass available for moderately priced lenses (they used to be very expensive). These glass elements are now a common part of the overall design of zooms on the top-of-the-line advanced compact cameras. Low dispersion glass allows higher correction of lenses, especially telephoto focal lengths. Telephotos are highly susceptible to chromatic aberration—different colors of light focus slightly differently, making the image less sharp and lowering contrast. Lens manufacturers correct this with low dispersion glass.

Aspherical Lenses

This is another technology that has been around a long time but was very expensive. Today, new lens manufacturing technologies allow aspherical designs to be included in very inexpensive lenses. Without them, there is no doubt that low-priced, compact digital cameras with zoom lenses would have to be priced much higher, and the lenses themselves would likely be bigger.

An aspherical element is a uniquely shaped lens. It has a contoured surface that changes the way light goes through the glass. Wide-angle lenses have long been predisposed to spherical aberration. This occurs when light from the center of a lens and from its outer areas focus at different points causing unsharpness, blooming highlights, and other flaws. Aspherical lenses limit this problem and have become a key part of wide-to-telephoto zoom lens designs.

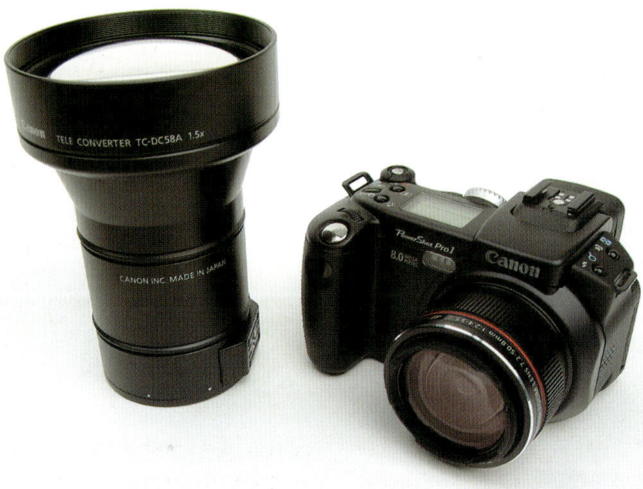

The best lenses use special glass to correct for chromatic aberration, and aspherical elements to control unsharpness and image distortion.

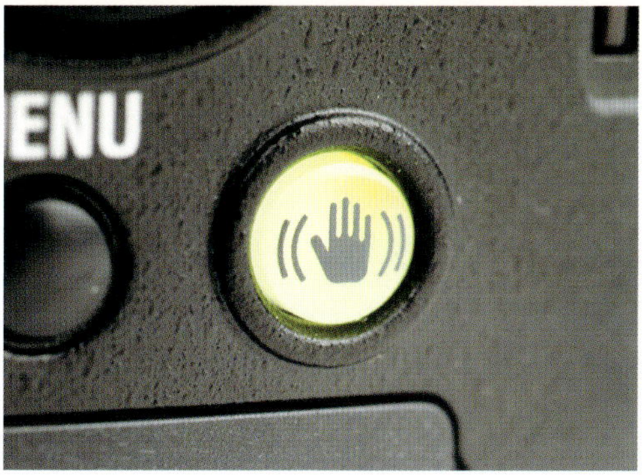

The Minolta Anti-Shake (AS) feature can reduce blur due to camera movement.

Image Stabilization

One factor that has always limited sharpness is the slight camera movement that can occur when the shutter is open during slower shutter speeds. Image stabilization is a technology in certain digital and 35mm SLR lenses that allows the lens to sense movement of the camera and lens, and then compensate for it. A small gimbal-mounted lens group moves to cancel camera shake and allow for much slower shutter speeds when shooting handheld. It is surprising that this technology has not shown up yet in small digital cameras, although it is true that it would make the cameras more expensive and change the lens construction.

Minolta, however, took a unique approach to this challenge, first in the older Dimage A-1, and has continued it in other cameras. This stabilization feature uses a moving image area instead of elements in the lens. The sensor actually vibrates in a way that matches the movement of the camera, seriously reducing camera movement unsharpness. It's called AS, for Anti-Shake. Typically, the average photographer can expect sharp images at shutter speeds that are two to three full stops slower than would otherwise be possible. This can also help photographers who have muscle tremors or other involuntary movements.

Lens Savvy

There are many lens applications that can make big differences in your photography. Of course, with a digital camera, you can check the results of any changes in the use of your focal lengths in the LCD and determine how best to apply the following techniques and variables.

Angle-of-View

Most people select a focal length to use when photographing based on the angle of view of the lens. How wide is the zoom? How much of a telephoto or narrow angle-of-view?

This is certainly important. If you are traveling and expect to be taking pictures in confined spaces, nothing but a wide angle of view will do. If you are photographing a soccer game where the action takes place from near to far, you'll need a zoom lens that provides a whole range of angles of view. With wildlife, a telephoto is critical.

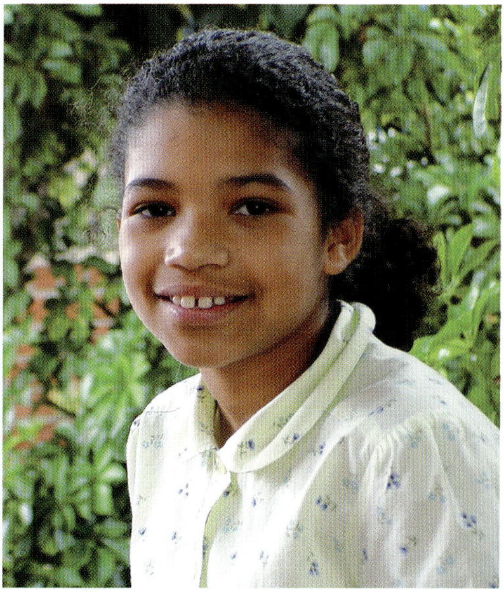

For portraits, use a moderate telephoto lens and set up the camera so it is at eye level with the subject.

This is more than a subject consideration, though. It is easy to be trapped into shooting with one focal length for a particular subject even though your zoom has more possibilities. Everyone shoots the soccer game with the telephoto angle-of-view, when a wide-angle shot might be very appealing—showing off an interesting setting for the game. The wide-angle interior might be the best overall shot, but zooming in with a narrow angle of view can help you capture details.

I think the best way to deal with this is to take the shot first with the focal length that seems best suited for the subject. Then try an extremely different focal length—a telephoto for cropped-in details, a wide-angle to show off the environment. A portrait demonstrates this idea. Take the shot with the moderate telephoto focal length (such as 80-100mm). From the same position, look at what a wide angle-of-view will do for you, and then try a more extreme telephoto, if you can. At this point, don't move—use your focal lengths strictly for how much or how little they will show of the subject.

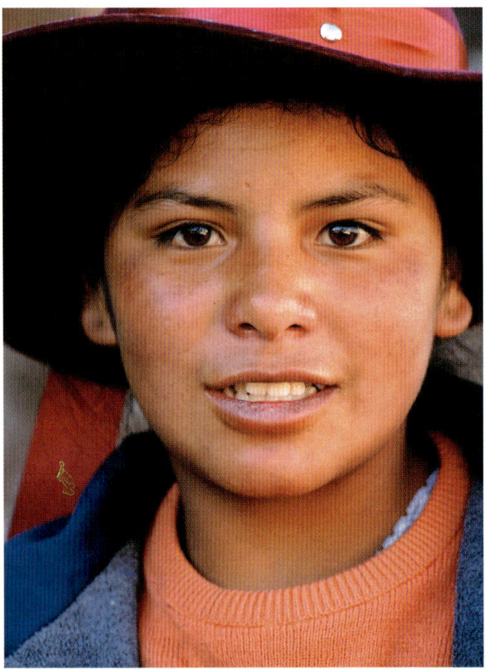

A variant of angle-of-view is magnification. Sometimes, you really do want to think about magnifying a shot—getting a closer shot of a tiger at the zoo or finding an architectural detail in the ceiling of a cathedral. Since you cannot physically move closer to such subjects, the only way to do this is by magnifying the image.

Perspective

Perspective is a major tool for image control and is affected by focal length choice. Heavily used by pros, it is one thing that sets off their images from everyone else's. Perspective is how we see size and depth relationships between objects within a picture. The classic example of this is a series of telephone poles going down the road. The closest one looks much bigger than the rest as a result of perspective. When you are far from the whole group, they all look similar in size for the same reason. If two poles are photographed so that they look similar in size and appear close together, then the perspective is flat. If they are photographed so that the near one looks big and the rear one small (and distance appears between them), the perspective is deep. Knowing how to control this with focal length choice can be a great photographic tool.

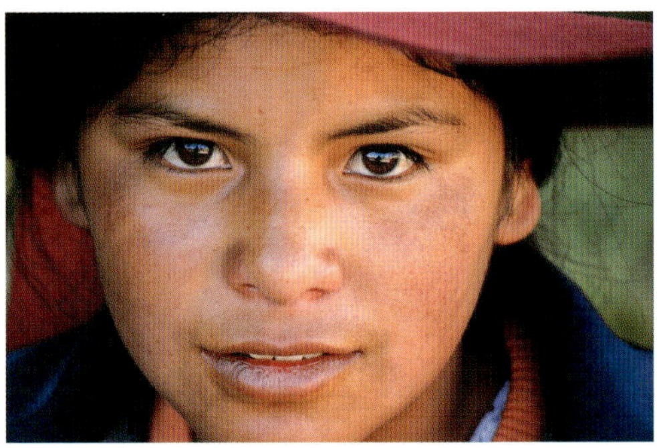

For a portrait, try changing the camera orientation from vertical to horizontal and zooming in for a tight crop. This is one way to accentuate your subject's features and eliminate distracting details.

Simply zooming your lens in and out does not change perspective. Perspective is a function of distance plus focal length. If you photograph a scene with a zoom from the same vantage using both telephoto and wide-angle settings, and then enlarge the center of the wide-angle shot to match the crop of the telephoto, you would discover the perspective is the same!

Let's go back to the telephone poles and take two photographs: one with a wide-angle focal length and one with a telephoto (this can be done with a zoom or with different lenses). The trick is to take both photographs so that the foreground pole is the same size in each. This requires you to move closer with the wide-angle shot because the lens will see more in the scene, making the pole appear small if you don't move in. Or, you will have to back up with the telephoto, otherwise the lens would see a smaller section of the composition and crop a portion of the foreground pole. Change your distance to the subject to keep the front pole relatively the same size in both photos.

Now you'll discover some magic has been performed. While the foreground poles are of equal size—the background poles are different! The wide-angle shot makes the back pole shorter while the telephoto makes it taller (in relation to the first pole). This is a perspective change.

Once you understand how to change perspective by changing focal length and distance, there are many things you can do. One is to play with sizes of subject and background to make your photo stronger in composition, and for creative effect. You could use a wide-angle to put some distance between your subject and background. Make your subject dramatic and big—up close to the lens—while the background appears small. Or, you could use a telephoto to close down the distance between subject and background. Make your local road look like LA at its worst: Get out that telephoto to compress the distance between cars.

These techniques can be used in very practical ways. Suppose you want to take a portrait in front of a dark doorway, but the doorway is too small to really do the job. Back up and use a telephoto focal length to enlarge the door compared to the subject. Next, try having some fun with a person's face. Use a wide-angle lens and get very close. This will make people's faces look odd, with big noses and "deep perspective." This is a lot of fun to do with kids and pets. You can also do things like stretch a car or make a house look longer.

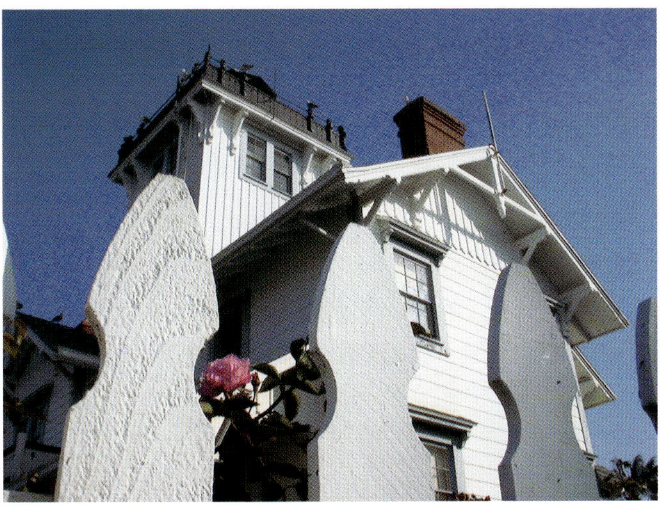

A wide-angle lens will make objects that are close to the camera appear large.

Experiment with Your Focal Lengths

I am a great believer in experimenting with focal lengths. Even though I have been photographing for many years with a variety of cameras and lenses, I still like to play and push the limits of my lenses. Here's a good exercise that will get you into the mode of fully testing your focal lengths' capabilities. Try shooting images using radically different focal lengths. Take one picture with the widest angle setting. Take the next photo at the most zoomed-in telephoto setting. Zoom out for the next photo, zoom in for the following, and so on.

Rather than simply adjusting the zoom, try to make each photo a distinct composition with an arbitrarily chosen focal length. Sure you could "cheat" on this exercise and tweak the focal lengths for the subject but you'll get more out of it if you don't. It works best if you use some extremes—a wide-angle vs. a telephoto, not just one shot a little wider than the other.

Another good exercise is to shoot a series of photos (set a number such as 10 or 20) with one focal length. Try shooting every photo in a series of images with the same wide-angle zoom setting, or with the same telephoto accessory lens. This can be extremely challenging but it will get you to see what that focal length sees.

Whatever you do, have fun! The great thing about digital cameras is that you can't waste film in your experiments and you can just erase your mistakes. So why not give these ideas a try and discover what lenses can really do for you and your photography?

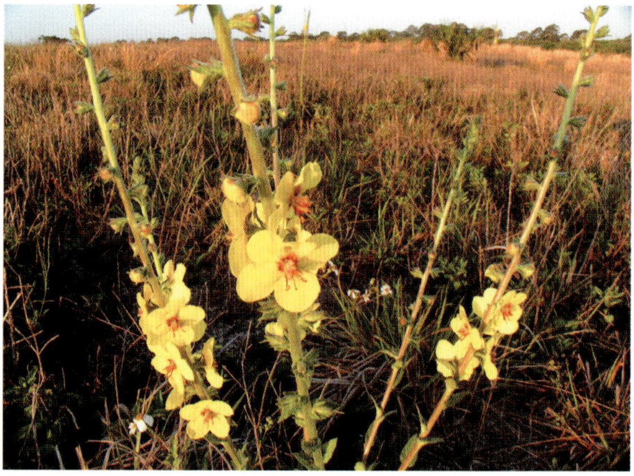

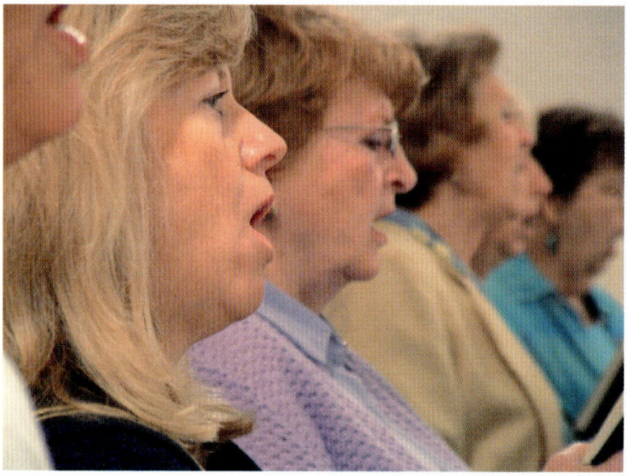

Experiment to learn what your camera can do and to understand the capabilities of your camera's zoom lens. Try taking pictures using your camera's shortest focal length setting (top) and its longest (left).

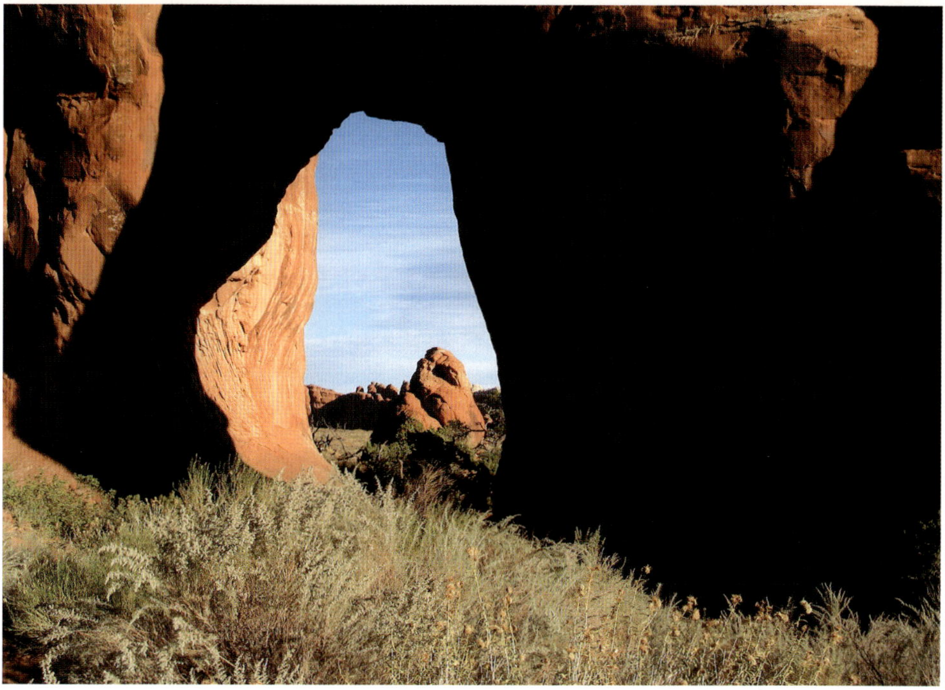

If you want everything in the foreground and background to be in sharp focus, use a wide-angle lens and a small aperture (higher f/number).

Depth of Field

Depth of field is the sharpness in depth from front to back in a photograph. It is what allows you to have both a flower in the foreground of a photograph and the mountains in the background in equally sharp focus. Four things influence depth of field: f/stop, distance to the subject, focal length, and size of the print.

When you need to have a scene appear sharp from close to far, use the wider settings of your zoom, or add a wide-angle accessory lens. If you want to limit sharpness through a selective focus technique (where one point is sharp and everything else is out of focus), try using a telephoto setting, or a telephoto accessory lens with a larger aperture. These are not just techniques to use when photographing big scenes like a landscape or a city street—they apply to photographing everything from close-ups to portraits.

Controlling Depth of Field

• **f/stop**—Small apertures (higher numbers such as f/11) increase depth of field, and large apertures (such as f/4) decrease depth of field.

• **Distance**—The farther you are from the subject, the greater the depth of field. The closer you get, the shallower depth of field becomes. (This makes close-up photography a real challenge at times.)

• **Focal length**—Wide-angle focal lengths give greater apparent depth of field while telephoto focal lengths reduce the depth of field.

• **Print size**—Small prints appear to have more depth of field, and as you make larger prints, differences in sharpness in the photo become more noticeable, so apparent depth of field decreases.

Maximizing Image Sharpness

Many photographers get less sharpness in their images than the camera's sensor is capable of rendering with the lens being used. This is really a shame considering the high quality of lenses on advanced compact digital cameras. These sharpness issues result from a very common problem: the camera moving slightly during the exposure. On a good tripod, this doesn't happen. When you are handholding a camera, it is free to move or "shake," especially with small, lightweight digital cameras. A fast shutter speed will freeze the movement to maintain sharpness, but there is a point at which the shutter speed will not be fast enough and blur will occur.

Many very good photographers don't realize that this problem doesn't simply mean obviously blurry or fuzzy photos. Very slight camera movement while the shutter is open will also decrease contrast in the image—so the scene loses brilliance and snap. It will look okay as a small print, but this softening means your photo will not be as good as it could be. No amount of image-editing will bring it back.

Just because a digital camera is easy to handhold doesn't mean it will automatically produce its best results that way. Unfortunately, a small LCD screen can be very misleading when it comes to sharpness.

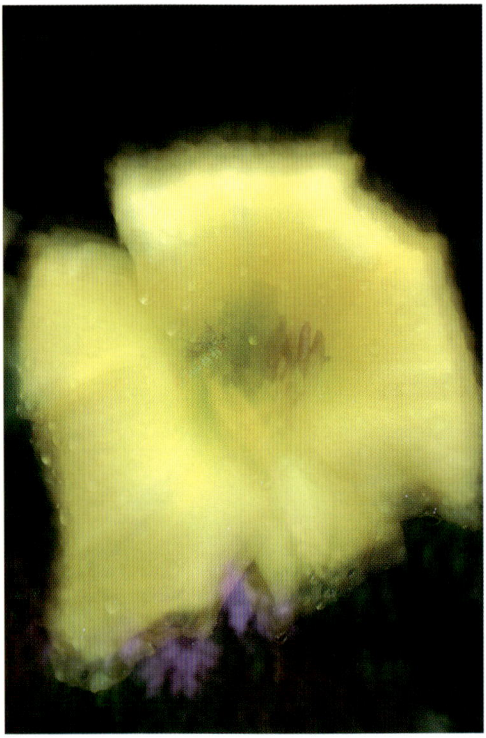

An extreme example of image blur caused by handholding the camera at a very slow shutter speed.

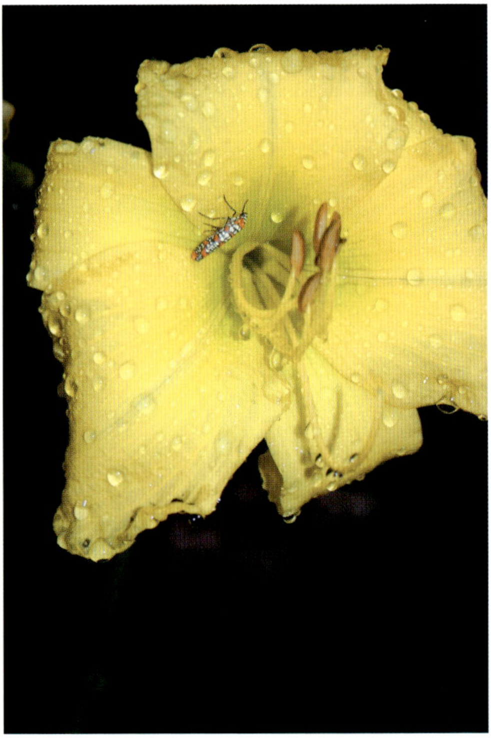

If you can't set a faster shutter speed, use your camera's flash to prevent blur. (© Mimi Netzel)

To accurately judge sharpness, magnify the image (use the magnification feature of your camera). The best way to see how sharply your handholding technique captures an image is to compare the handheld shot to a photograph taken with the camera mounted on a tripod.

In doing some informal tests with colleagues, and in workshops that I teach, I have found that most people using the handheld method start having trouble matching the steadiness of a tripod when the shutter speed drops below 1/125 second for standard focal lengths, and much faster for telephoto settings (even 1/250 second can be too slow for handholding a focal length of 300mm).

The solution when you are handholding? Use fast shutter speeds. Shutter speed can be a problem when photographers shoot totally automatically and assume that the camera is taking care of the right speed. Major challenges occur with variable f/stop zoom lenses. The shutter speed might be okay for the wide-angle setting at f/3.5, but it might not be when the lens is zoomed to telephoto because the lens loses speed (maybe going to f/5.6). Thus, a slower shutter speed will be selected by the camera. This slower shutter speed may be the cause of unsharpness from handholding. Thus, you need to be especially wary of shooting in low light with the telephoto settings of variable aperture zooms.

Here's an old rule of thumb for sharpness that really works: Use a shutter speed for handholding that has the same number as the (35mm equivalent) focal length of your lens or higher—never lower. This means that a 28mm equivalent needs at least a 1/30 second shutter speed, while a 200mm needs 1/200 second. You can see that a 28-200mm zoom lens might be able to be handheld at 1/30 second at 28mm, but, if you zoom out to 200mm, the shutter speed requirement will jump to 1/250.

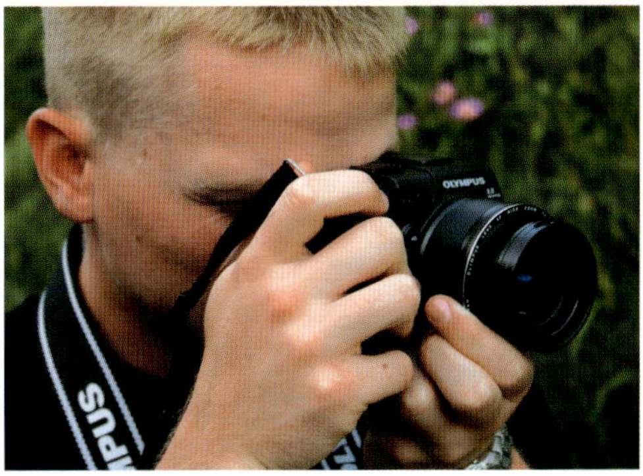

Grip the camera firmly with your right hand, place your index finger on the shutter release and support the camera from underneath with your left hand.

Proper Handholding Technique

Sharp pictures require good handholding technique and you should practice it at all times or you may be disappointed with your image sharpness.

Grip the camera firmly with your right hand, placing your index finger on the shutter release. Many advanced compacts have a grip that facilitate this way of holding the camera. Next, place your left hand palm up to cradle the lens and body. On some cameras, this will even place your fingers so they comfortably reach the lens' zoom and focusing rings. For the smallest cameras, simply grip the left side of the camera firmly. For vertical (or portrait-format) photos, turn the camera so your right hand is on top and the opposite end of the camera is cradled in your left hand. With either format, keep your elbows in—pressed gently against your body—for additional support. Spread your legs slightly in a firm, but comfortable, stance.

Some people think you need to hold your breath when shooting at the slowest shutter speeds. That can actually create less steadiness. The best bet is to breathe out slowly, then just after exhaling, press the shutter firmly with steady pressure.

A tripod is a requirement for photographing in the dappled sunlight of a forest. You want the image to be really sharp with good depth of field. If you set a small aperture, the shutter speed may be too slow for handholding, even with a short focal length setting. Carry a tripod so you won't limit your creative options.

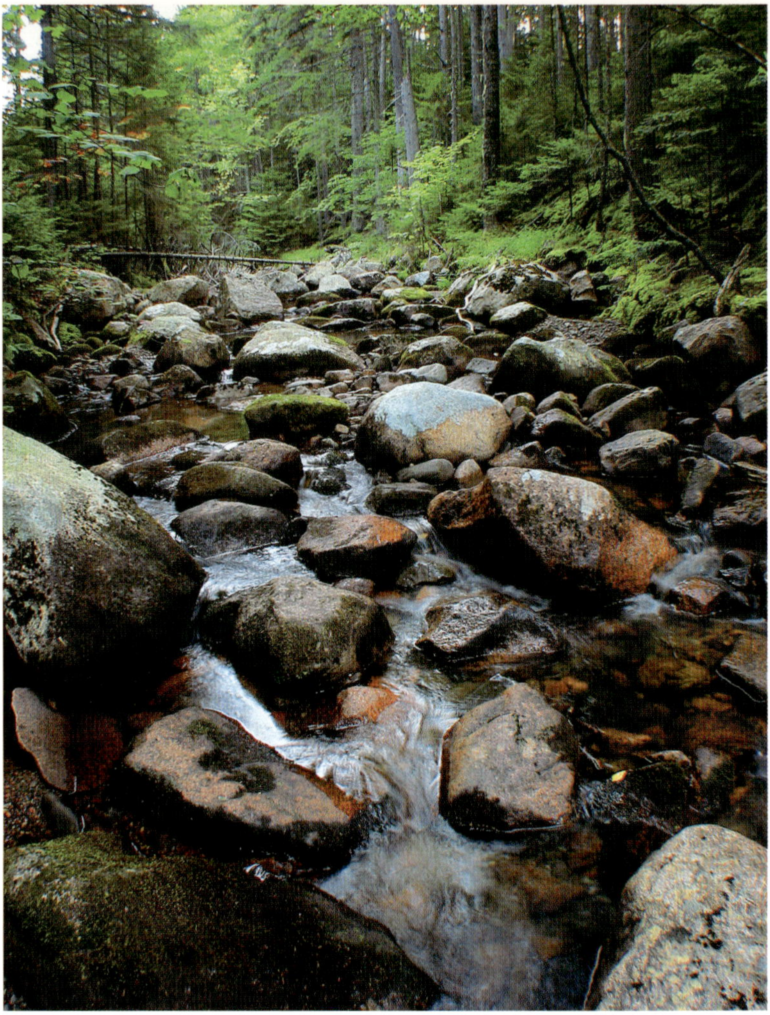

Camera Supports

When light levels drop, or you are using long telephoto or macro lenses, it can really help to use a camera support. Because compact digital cameras are so small and simple to handhold, it is easy to get lulled into the idea that they should be handheld. I once had a student in a field workshop say that she thought it looked odd seeing my little advanced compact on a tripod. Many people get this idea. Yet, if you want to get all the sharpness your "megapixels" and lens are capable of, sooner or later, you must use a tripod.

You can get very handy, compact tripods for small digital cameras that will fit in a carrying bag. These are small, but they can be set up anywhere—on a table, a rock, against a wall, and so forth—and will help a lot. Bean pods are also quite handy little devices that fit in most camera bags. They provide a soft medium that cushions and stabilizes the camera on a hard surface, such as against a railing or fence post. You can even buy a bean pod that includes a tripod screw so the camera can actually be attached to the pod.

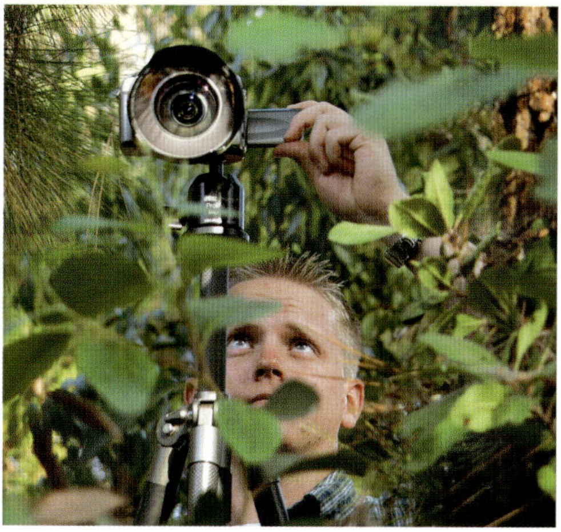

With a tilt or swivel LCD on your camera, you can easily use the monitor with the camera positioned high over your head on a tripod.

Tripods

There is no question that tripods will help you get the most out of your camera and lens, but you need to invest in a good one. A cheap, flimsy tripod can be worse than none at all. And don't look for a tripod with a long center column—they are extremely unsteady. The key to buying a tripod is to be sure it is rigid and sturdy, as a flexible, bouncy tripod will cause problems with camera movement. Set up a tripod to its full height (keep the center post down, though). Lean your weight on it and see how stiff it is. It should not flex much, bounce, or collapse.

Also, see how easily and securely the legs lock. The last thing you want to do is struggle with the legs of a tripod when you are photographing—or have the tripod slowly lean to the side as one leg slips. Be sure the head is secure and easy for you to adjust. There are two common types of tripod heads for still photography: the pan-and-tilt head and the ballhead. The pan-and-tilt head uses multiple handles (or knobs) to lock the various axes of movement of the head. This allows you to adjust side-to-side angles separately from front-to-back. It allows very precisely controlled movement, and the camera can never go off on its own direction. For this reason, many studio photographers prefer it. The disadvantage is that this head takes more work to adjust and it tends to be bulky, with handles sticking out in sometimes awkward places.

The ballhead uses a single control to loosen tension on a ball and socket so the camera can be quickly positioned at any angle. It is much faster tthan the pan-and-tilt head for setting up a camera, and much easier to adjust when the tripod is on uneven ground. These are some of the reasons nature photographers usually prefer ballheads. Their disadvantage is that the camera can go in all directions at once. Thus, it can quickly tilt in an unexpected direction, which can be hazardous to the camera. This also makes it difficult to make very precise adjustments.

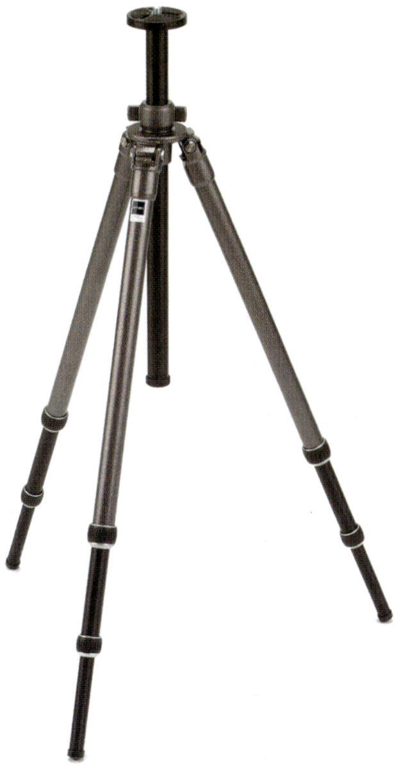

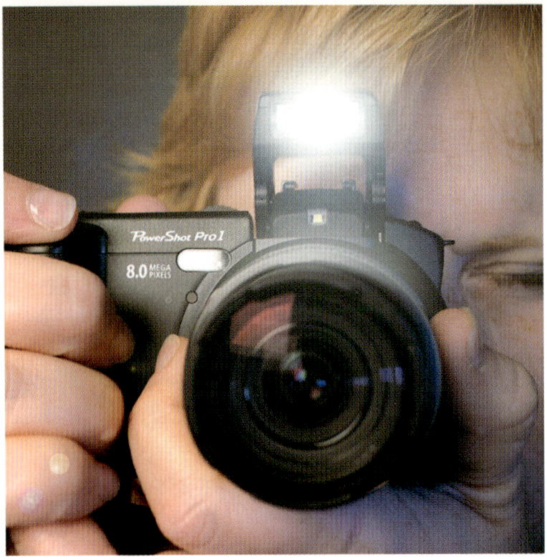

The built-in flash on digital zoom cameras is handy and easy to use. Some are surprisingly powerful, too.

Flash Made Easy

More and more pros have been using flash outside of the studio in recent years. Yet many amateurs—even very good photographers—use flash only sporadically with film cameras. Flash is hard to predict, especially when trying to balance flash with ambient (or existing) light. Even with the best automated systems you could never be totally sure you got what you wanted until you saw the photos. And, too often, the results just weren't satisfying.

With digital photography, this has changed dramatically. Flash units are built into nearly all compact digital cameras (quite handy) and you can add an accessory flash unit to any digital camera with a hotshoe. Both manufacturers' and independents' (camera-brand specific) units work with all the bells-and-whistles you'd expect in a modern flash unit. (If you are not sure if a unit will work with your camera, check with your photographic dealer.)

You may be surprised at how much you can do with your compact digital camera. You have a secret weapon compared to the days of film: Take a picture and check it! Film photographers (especially those in the studio) would often shoot test Polaroids to check flash exposure and balance. You no longer have to do that. Your digital camera gives you the actual image on the LCD.

Balancing flash and ambient light was often a big challenge. Most of us don't have enough experience to automatically guess the right settings to balance these lights perfectly. Now, so what! Take that picture with the settings the camera gives you and check it immediately. Reviewing the image on the LCD will give you a good idea of what the flash is doing.

Basic Flash Exposure

Digital cameras use a flash exposure system that is very similar to the basic metering system. Both are through-the-lens systems, so they only measure what the lens is seeing of your subject. Multi-segment metering systems (using distance calculations) look at the light from the flash coming back from the subject and use sophisticated computer technology to select a good exposure for you. Most film cameras have similar capabilities. It is amazing that cameras today have more computer processing power than big business computers typically had thirty years ago.

A significant change in autoflash metering from film to digital is that digital cameras do not typically measure the flash coming onto the sensor at the time of exposure (film cameras will measure the actual light hitting the film). So the camera will send off a burst of light called a preflash an instant before the flash exposure actually occurs. The preflash allows the camera to determine the exposure. This happens so fast that most people don't notice. For the actual exposure, the flash emits light for a set duration and cuts itself off when the proper amount of light has reached the subject.

On many digital cameras, you can control the flash exposure with flash exposure compensation. This works like regular compensation in that you can increase or decrease the exposure. It can't control the flash as much as regular exposure compensation however, because once you get past a certain distance to the subject, the flash doesn't have enough power to make the photo brighter. And if you get too close, the flash may not be able to cut itself off fast enough to reduce exposure at a given f/stop.

One thing that will affect how you use the flash is its power. The power of a flash is given as a guide number, or GN. Guide numbers were once used to calculate exposure. The guide number was divided by the number of feet to the subject in order to get an f/stop. The number is usually based on an ISO of 100. This can be used as a rough guide for comparing the power of different flash units or to compare your built-in flash to an external unit. It is not an exact guide, since there is no absolute standard for measuring guide numbers that is consistent among manufacturers. Be aware that, while most guide numbers are given in feet, you will run across some guide numbers listed in meters, which will give totally different numbers, even if the flash power is the same. Guide numbers can only be compared when they are based on the same measurements and at the same ISO.

When it comes to comparing guide numbers, they act a little like f/stops. Full f/stops are related to each guide number—they double or halve the light reaching the sensor as you step through them. A set of full f/stop numbers is 2, 2.8, 4, 5.6, 8, 11, and 16. If you take a group of flash units and put them in order from lowest to highest power, you might find they had GNs of 28, 40, 56, 80, and 110. Each one of these is double the power of the previous unit and half the power of the next one.

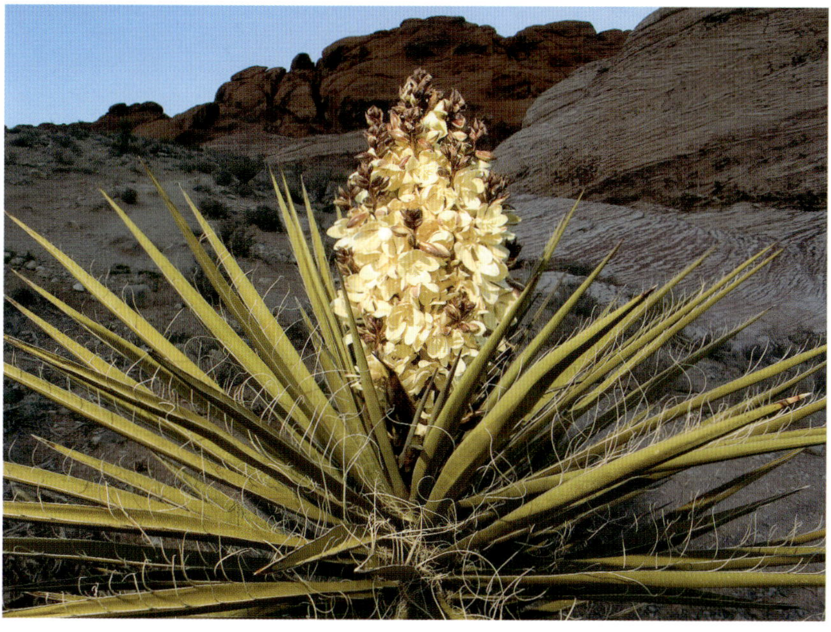

Flash offers many possibilities for stronger colors and tones. This yucca plant was shot at twilight with flash.

Red-Eye Reduction Flash Settings

Red-eye in flash photos of people is distinctly unattractive. A cute baby can be transformed into a devil child! It occurs in dark situations when flash is used. Those conditions result in the iris of the eye widening, which lets more flash into the eye. This light reflects off the back of the eye, causing the "red-eye." If the flash is at an angle to the subject compared to the camera, no eye reflection occurs. However, on small digital cameras with built-in flash, the flash is so close to the axis of the lens that red-eye is almost guaranteed.

Red-eye reduction settings will either cause the flash to "preflash" to make the subject's iris narrow or there can be a pre-flash that comes on to do the same thing. While this is helpful, it can also create photographic problems. Often the subject will react poorly to this camera function so that the photos may have less red-eye, but the photograph is distinctly unflattering. Sometimes it helps if you warn the subject that this red-eye reduction lighting will happen.

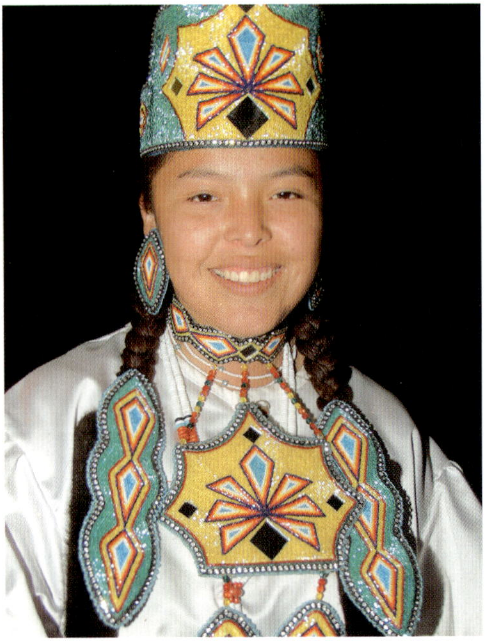

You can also get rid of red-eye by using an off-camera flash (described below). In addition, many software programs now include easy-to-use red-eye reduction tools that allow you to take the good shot and not worry about red-eye while you take it. There are even some new cameras today that include red-eye removal in the camera itself. The camera has smart processing that finds and corrects red-eye before the photo is saved to the memory card.

Easy Flash Options

Most photographers use a flash aimed directly at the subject, and this is certainly all that you can get from a built-in flash. This type of flash is useful when you need to see things in dark conditions. This is why paparazzi use direct flash—they want to be sure their celebrity prey are not lost in weak light. Also, you often need to use direct flash when your subject is some distance from you, as with sports or wildlife photography.

Unfortunately, a lot of flash photos look like those deer-in-the-headlights paparazzi images. This type of lighting isn't flattering to the subject, and can produce harsh, rather unattractive photographs when it is dark (this light looks just fine for filling in shadows in bright sun). The light is flat, very susceptible to glare from shiny surfaces, causes dark shadows right behind subjects, and is the most likely suspect for red-eye. If it sounds like this type of light is not something I like, you are right. I try to avoid it whenever I can.

This Navaho dancer was lit with off-camera, direct flash to give her form and still bring out the details in her clothing.

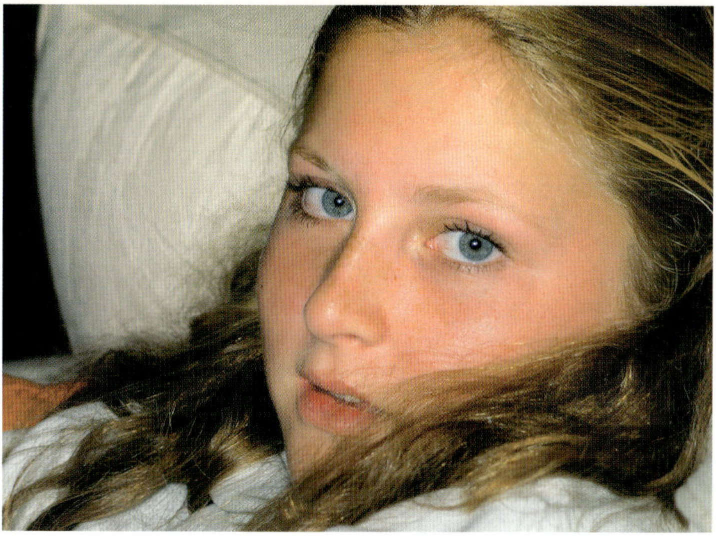

Red-eye can be a problem in low-light conditions and with direct flash. Using off-camera flash or red-eye reduction can eliminate the problem.

There is one thing you can do with your built-in flash to avoid this: allow some existing or ambient light to be exposed with your background (check your camera's manual to see the best way to do this, although if your camera has a night flash setting, this may work). This immediately makes the light from the flash look less harsh.

If you can use an accessory flash unit, there are two easy ways to get better photos with just a single flash unit and they don't require a lot of investment in money or time: off-camera and bounce flash. The digital camera makes these techniques a joy to use because you can see the results and quickly adapt and adjust the light if you don't like them.

Off-Camera Flash

Getting the flash off the camera immediately improves a number of things. It makes the light more dimensional, with natural-looking shadows, places shadows behind the subject, eliminates red-eye, and makes it less likely that shiny surfaces will bounce light directly back at the camera.

The easiest way to take the flash off your camera is with a dedicated flash cord. This is a cord that attaches between the hot-shoe of your digital camera and the flash. All of the dedicated flash automation is maintained. The dedicated cord allows the camera and flash to communicate and coordinate timing and settings electronically. This way, you can hold the flash up over the camera to the far left side (which is easier to reach because of the way a camera is designed to be held), to the right side, or even under the subject, for special effects. One challenge is aiming the flash at the subject for the best light direction. With a little practice you'll find it isn't that hard to hold and aim.

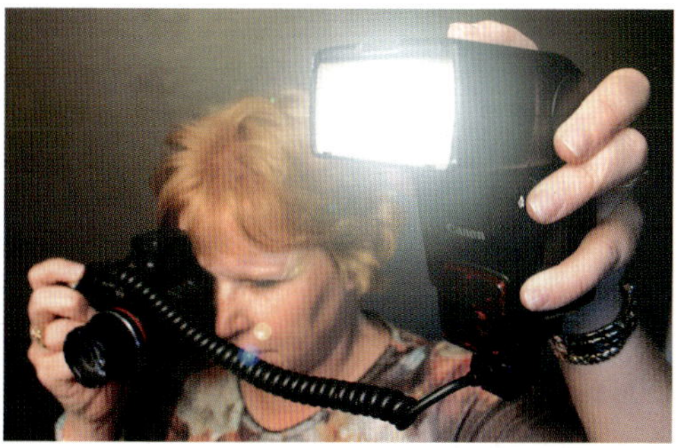

To use off-camera flash, practice holding the camera with your right hand, while you hold and aim the flash with your left.

Since you are using a digital camera, you will quickly see what the light from the flash looks like at that angle. Holding the flash high to the left is a comfortable way of creating a nice dimensional light with attractive shadows on the subject. When the flash is high, any shadows that might fall on a wall behind the subject will now drop down below the subject in a much better position than shadows from a camera-mounted flash. Since the camera is metering what it sees from the flash, exposure will generally be quite good (but of course you can vary it as needed).

By pointing the flash between the subject and background you can often get a more balanced light between subject and background (the background cannot be far behind, though, since light from a flash falls off quickly). If you can use a reflector on one side of the subject (and a white wall will work, too), you can point the flash so it just catches the subject but also heads to the reflector to add some nice fill light to the shadows.

The off-camera flash is really great for close-up work. You can put the flash in all sorts of positions related to the subject to get a whole range of lighting directions. When you are close, overexposure can be an issue, but a quick and easy way of dealing with this is to point the flash a little away from the subject so that the most direct light does not hit it. By checking the LCD, you can get a perfect exposure very quickly.

Bounce Flash

Bounce flash is another important flash technique. It can be used with any flash that tilts, or with off-camera flash. Here, you point the flash at a white surface (ceiling, wall, FomeCor, reflector, etc.). This spreads the light out and softens its edges. It can be a very attractive and natural looking light for interiors and is especially effective when photographing people.

You change the direction of the light for very attractive dimensional lighting by aiming the flash at surfaces angled to the subject. A common and easy technique is to use the flash on the camera and bounce the light from the ceiling. Be careful you are not too close to a person or the light will come from almost directly above, creating nasty eye shadows. Some flash units have little white reflectors that pop up to correct this.

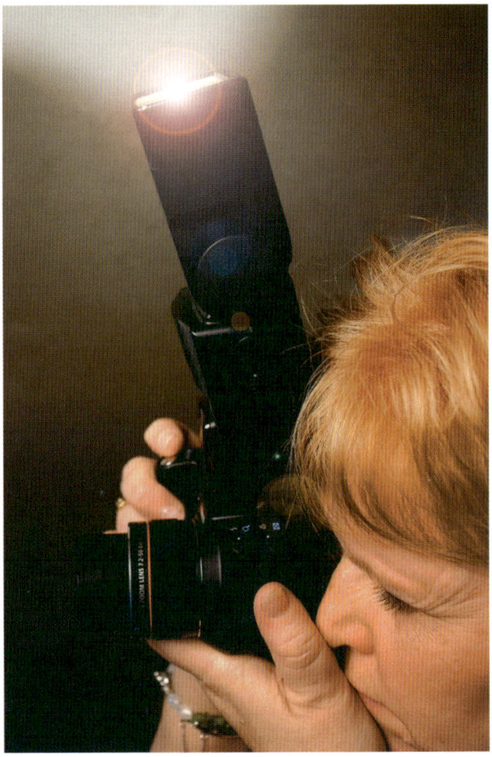

Most accessory flash units can be tilted for bounce flash. Angle the head of your flash unit up to bounce light off of a spot on the ceiling about halfway between you and your subject.

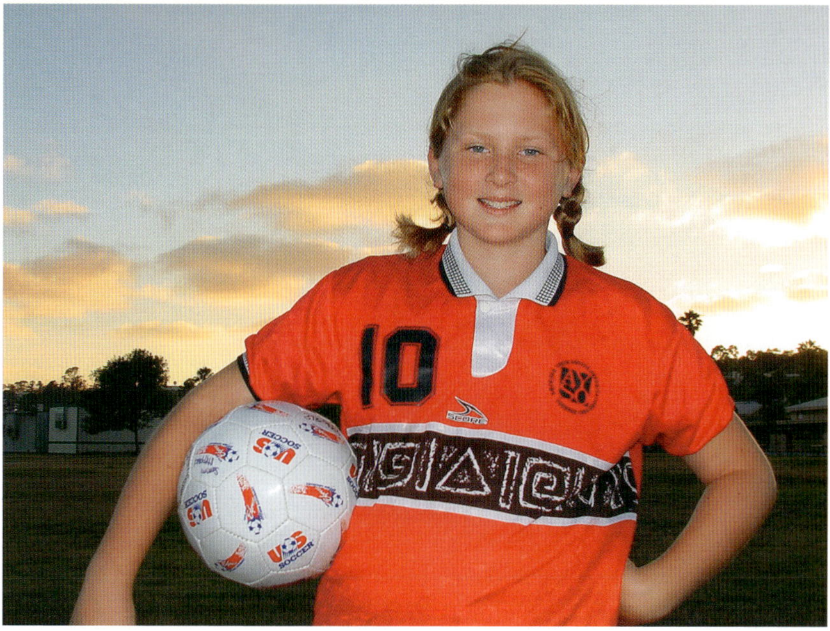

Mix flash with ambient light to capture a well lit soccer player against a beautiful sunset in the background.

Mixing Flash and Natural Light

Recent advances in technology have allowed for more and more photography in which a scene was subtly altered by flash mixed with the natural or ambient light. Ambient light is the light that already exists in a scene, also called existing light. It can be sunlight or artificial light. Pros use the technique of enhancing an exposure with flash because it is a way to capture the natural look of a scene in its "native" light and still have some control over the contrasts within it. Modern autoflash metering systems communicate very well with the camera's exposure system making this an easy, and very effective, technique.

The key to understanding this procedure is to realize that you are really creating a double exposure of two light sources—the natural light and the flash. Your camera creates an exposure for the existing light using both shutter speed and f/stop. The flash then creates a burst of light that matches the f/stop. The only requirement is that the shutter speed is at (or below) the camera's sync speed. You can shoot at as slow a shutter speed as needed to capture the natural light.

Fill Flash

The most basic form of mixing flash and existing light is called "fill flash." This allows the flash to brighten shadows in very contrasty light. It is an ideal use for a built-in flash. Watch people taking pictures of each other on a bright, sunny day. Notice the strong shadows on faces and under hat brims. Yet, although most of these people will have cameras with a built-in flash, the photographer rarely turns it on. A little bit of auto-flash would help immensely.

When you get close to the subject, you may find the flash overpowers the existing light. You might even want to tone down the flash (if you can) by adjusting the flash exposure compensation to -1 or more stops. This can make shadows appear more natural.

Use fill flash to illuminate a backlit subject. Add just a small amount of flash so the foreground subject doesn't look unnaturally bright.

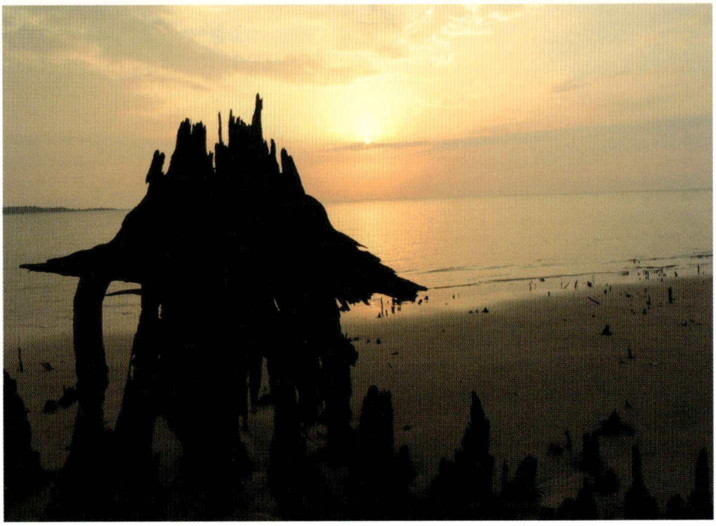

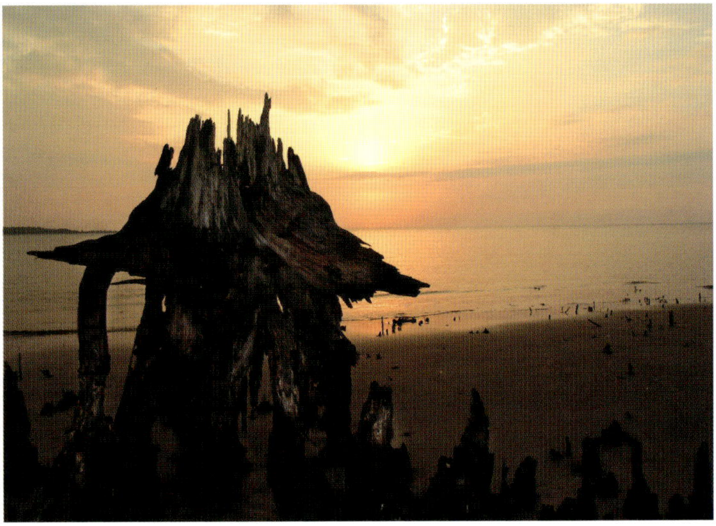

Unfortunately, every manufacturer makes different choices in how the metering system is set up for mixing flash and ambient light. On one camera, you may find it will not balance flash with existing light in the Program (P) mode because of the way shutter speed is set, but will work in the Aperture-priority (A or Av) mode. On another camera, all modes may work only if you hold a certain button during exposure. On yet another camera model, all modes work fine without any change. Check your camera's manual.

Fill flash does not have to be restricted to daylight. It will also help open up backlit subjects, including shooting something against a sunset (the silhouette will now gain color and detail). It can be used to brighten colors on gloomy days. It is a great technique to use to photograph a person at night and pick up details of the scene behind them. Some cameras have special exposure settings, called Night Flash or Slow Sync, that are designed to automate the process of balancing flash for a subject with a darker background.

Off-camera flash is another variation of the fill flash technique—you point the flash at parts of the scene that are in shadow and put light in very specific places. A good example of this would be a city scene that has nice light on the buildings across the street but only shadow on a street performer. By holding the flash off camera you get some nice modeling light and balance the subject to the brighter background. Landscape photographers use this technique to light up dark flowers when mountains or fields in the background are lit by the sunset.

If the movement is linear, however, you might not like the blur, as it will be in front of the subject. This is because the flash takes the picture at the first part of the exposure then the blur occurs afterward. To get the blur behind the subject, the flash has to go off at the end of the exposure. Some of the most advanced digital cameras have something called rear-curtain or second-curtain sync to do exactly that, which gives a different effect than standard sync for movement shots.

Slow Sync

Slow sync brings up another interesting technique—photographing motion with a flash. If you use a slow shutter speed to pick up the natural light on a moving subject while still using flash, you will get a photo with both motion blur and sharpness. This can be a fun and striking use of flash. It creates a sense of energy with the subject. Check your LCD to see what shutter speed works best for the movement.

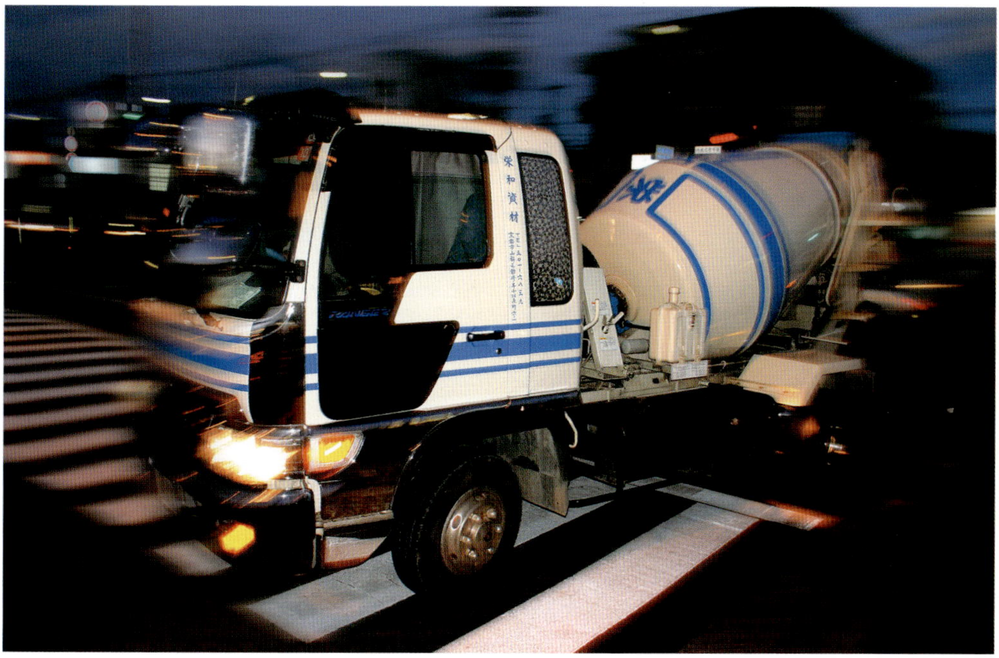

Some cameras have a Night Flash or Slow Sync setting. The camera sets the flash exposure for a subject in the foreground and sets a slow shutter to capture the dark background. This also works well for sunset scenes and city lights. If your subject is in motion or the camera is handheld, you can get some interesting blur effects.

picture taking in the field

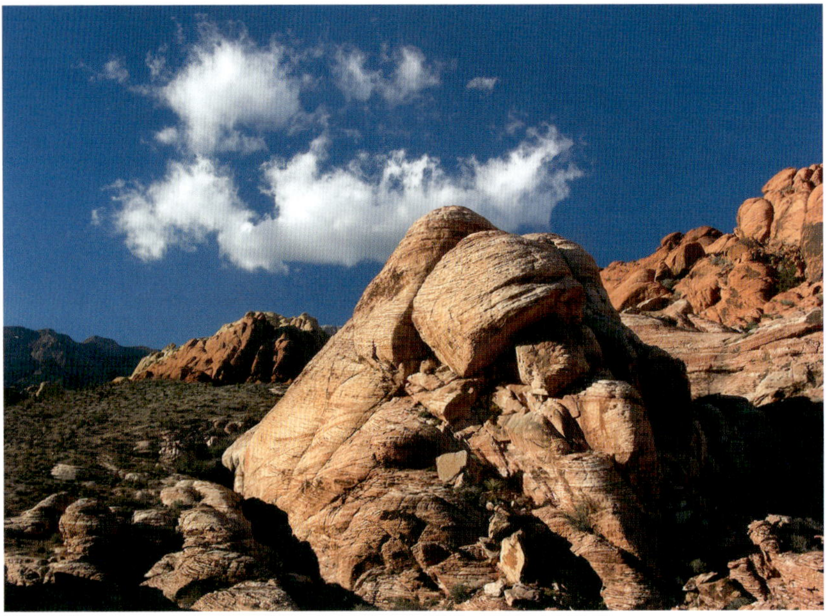

Why should you use filters with a digital camera? Your photos will look more natural if you capture the best image you can and tweak it a little with Photoshop. Too much manipulation can add noise and make your images look artificial.

Filters

Filters are absolutely essential to the photographer who wants to get the most from his or her photography. Personally, I cannot imagine going out with my digital camera without at least a polarizer or graduated ND filter in my camera bag. It is true that you definitely gain new control in adjusting exposure and contrast using an image-processing program. However, what you capture in the first place has a huge influence on how much you can do to improve an image later.

Filters can help a great deal to ensure you have the best possible image when you release the shutter, which will save time later at the computer. Plus, if you use a printer that allows you to connect directly with the camera (PictBridge compatible printers), this is the only way to guarantee detail in the critical parts of the photo. Remember, if you haven't captured detail in the first place you can't—except in a very artificial way—put it back in later. This has been true since the beginnings of photography—even before the advent of digital!

There are three basic types of filters that most photographers should own: polarizing, graduated neutral density, and full neutral density filters. There are certainly other filters on the market that can be of use to the digital photographer, but these are a good starter kit. For more information on filters, I recommend *Complete Guide to Filters for Digital Photography,* by Joseph Meehan.

Protective Filters

Many 35mm photographers use either a UV or skylight filter in front of the lens for "protection." Yet you'll find very few professional photographers using one (I don't even own one). And using one on most small digital cameras can be a challenge. For one thing, the way the lens collapses into the camera body may make such a filter difficult to leave on the camera. While there are reasons to use a protective filter on some occasions, you may be better off without it on your advanced digital camera most of the time for these reasons:

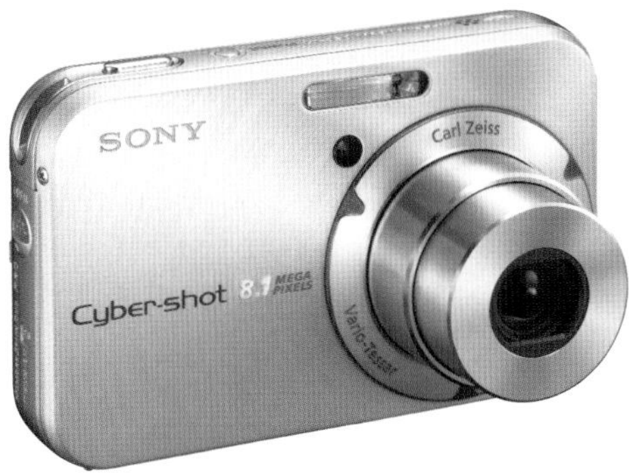

If your compact digital zoom camera has a retractable lens, you may not be able to leave a protective filter over the front element.

• Lens damage is rare.

• Lenses have hard coatings on the outside elements. Most photographers never put a camera in a position that could cause a scratch on the front lens. A hard impact to the front of the camera could be a problem, but if this happens, a filter probably won't help much.

• Filters give a false sense of security. I have noticed that photographers who don't use protective filters seem to take better care of their lenses. A dirty filter is no better than a dirty lens and I have seen far more dirty protective filters than dirty unprotected lenses.

• Inexpensive filters cause unsharpness. That little lens on your compact digital camera has very precisely arranged optics, and an inexpensive filter can throw this off. It is even possible for a cheap filter to transform an expensive high-quality lens into a soft-focus, poor-quality lens.

• Unnecessary filters increase the chance of flare. A filter is a flat surface. When you shoot toward the sun, a lot of light hits the front of the lens and its first elements. Some of this is reflected back at the subject. If a filter is in front of that lens, its flatness can act like a mirror and reflect ghosted images of that light.

• Too many filters on a lens cause sharpness problems and possible vignetting. If one filter sits on a lens all the time, any filter used for photographic reasons (such as a polarizer) can compound sharpness degradation. Also, stacking filters can cause the filter edge to be seen in the corners of the photo. This is called vignetting.

If you really feel safer with your lens protected, use a lens shade if your camera allows it—this is a protective tube that extends in front of the lens. It will block light from striking the front of the lens and cut down flare.

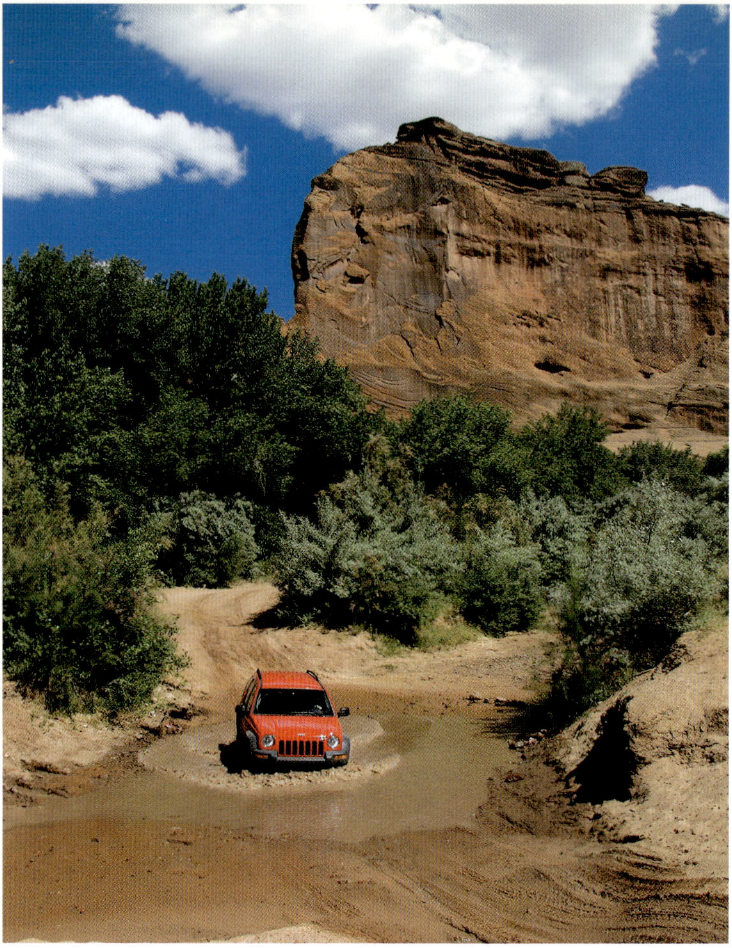

A polarizer is a key filter for the digital photographer. It will darken skies, enrich colors, and remove glare from water and other reflective surfaces.

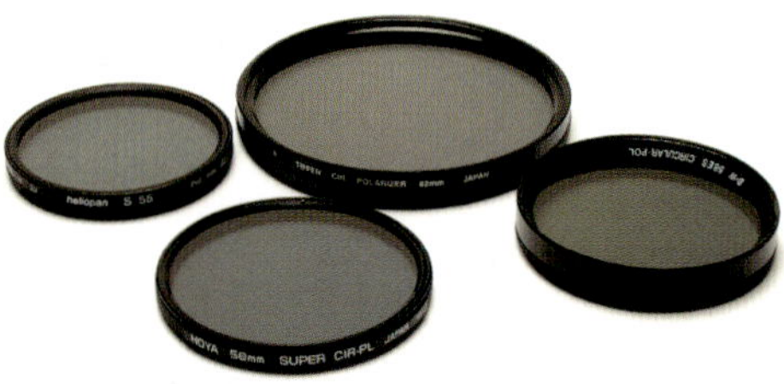

The effect of a polarizing filter can be adjusted by rotating the filter mount.

Polarizing Filters

This is one filter that every photographer should have. Some of its effects can be mimicked in the computer, but none can be exactly duplicated. This filter affects the way light goes through the lens and to the sensor, making the light waves "line up" instead of following a normal random pattern. The filter rotates in its mount, changing its orientation to the light waves, which changes its effect on the scene.

Exposure is generally pretty simple with modern TTL metering systems. The camera compensates for the darkness of the filter, which can act like a two-stop neutral density filter, and gives a correct exposure.

You will notice the image tones will change in the LCD or EVF as you adjust the filter. You may find that you prefer a brighter or darker exposure for certain scenes shot with this filter. Again, the LCD monitor will help you evaluate this.

A bigger issue is circular vs. linear polarizers. This does not refer to the shape of the filter—it has to do with how the polarization is achieved. So what is the difference? With most modern cameras, a linear polarizer can create a situation where the light does not properly reach the AF or AE sensors, causing focus and/or exposure problems. The best bet is to just use a circular polarizer. This prevents any issues arising between filter and AF or AE systems.

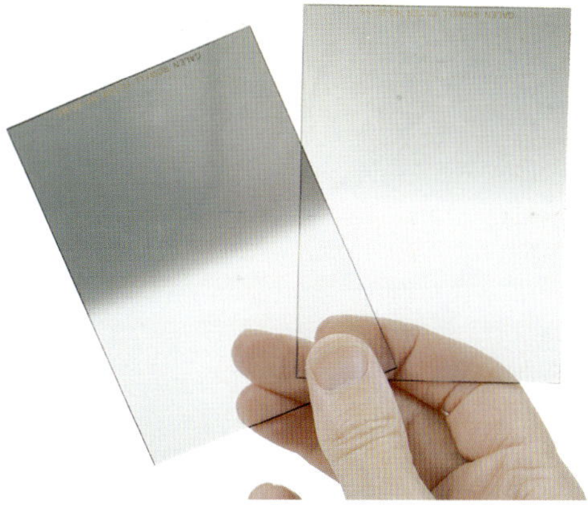

Graduated ND filters transition from dark gray to clear. Rectangular filters are used in a mount that allows the filter to be adjusted up and down or side to side.

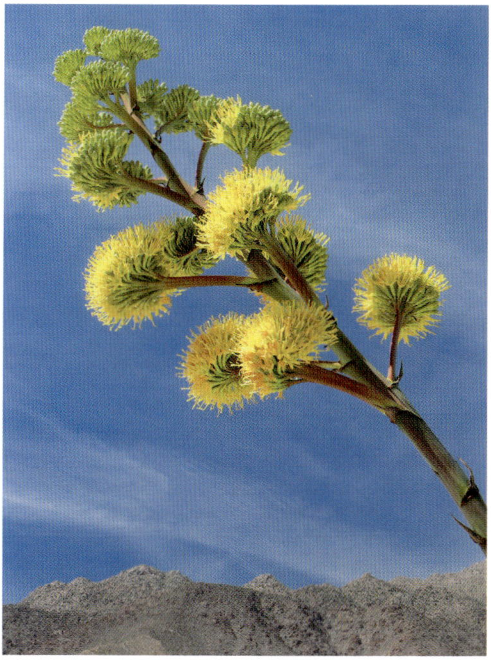

Using a polarizer made the yellow flowers richer and the sky darker, which also sets off the faint clouds.

Graduated Neutral Density Filters

I consider these filters to be among the most useful for any photographer—especially photographers who like to photograph landscapes or travel scenes. Also called grads, graduated ND, and split ND filters, they are made half clear/half dark gray, with a blend (the gradation) or transition so there is no sharp line of difference. They rotate in their mount (the rectangular versions will also move up and down or side to side) so that the dark and clear parts of the filter will cover different areas in the photo.

The grad filter allows you to bring widely differing brightness in a scene more in line with what the camera sensor can handle. The easiest way to explain this is to look at a landscape scene with green trees and bright white clouds in the sky. No camera is going to easily capture that range of tones. By rotating the filter so that the dark part is over the white clouds, that area of the photo will be darkened. This results with the overall exposure of the photo becoming increased so that the trees are revealed without washing out the sky.

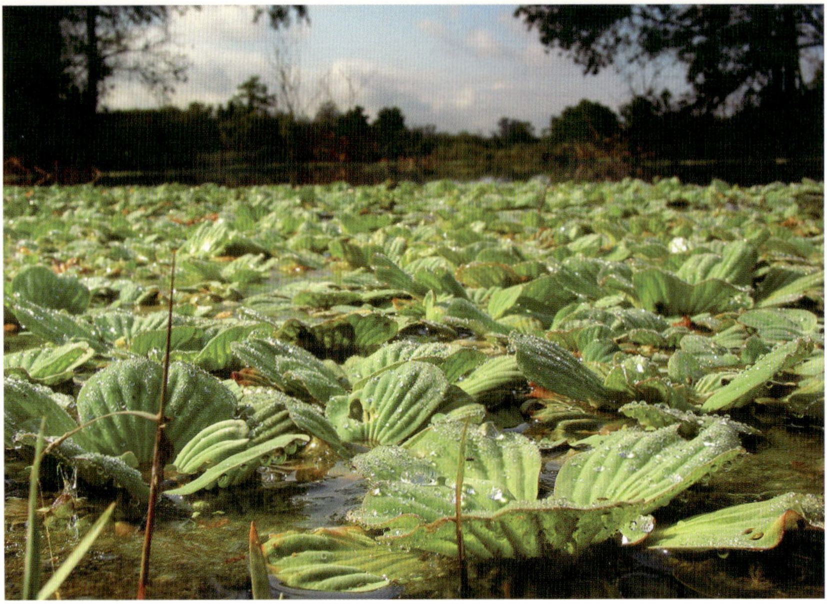

A graduated neutral density filter allows your sensor to capture the tonal range of a landscape with a bright sky.

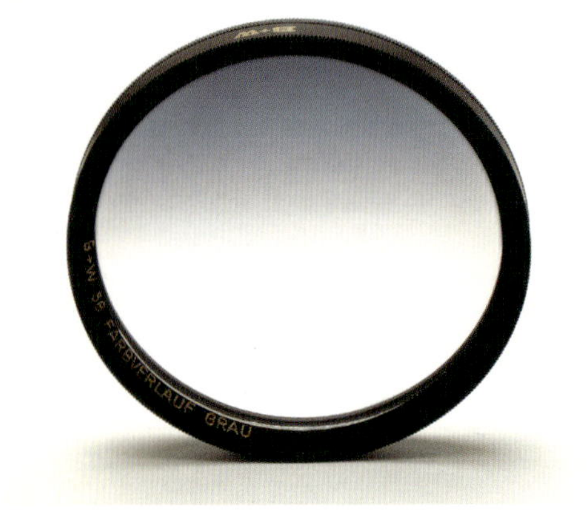

The mount on a round graduated neutral density filter rotates to position the filter effect.

While the computer can help balance bright and dark areas in a photo, it would be difficult—in this example—to take a single exposure that would provide enough detail in each area to allow the computer to show both trees and sky well. Sky is one of the prime subjects for the split ND filter since it is usually brighter than the ground. You can rotate the filter to compensate for hills and, with the rectangular version, you can raise it up or down to align with the horizon.

You can use a grad for any situation where one part of the photo is much brighter than another. Outdoors, this might mean toning down a field of grass next to a stand of shadowy trees or balancing a bright band of light on the water with the rest of the photo. Indoors, this could be a way of bringing a window in line with the rest of the composition or to tone down a bright area of lights next to a stage. A grad can also be used creatively to darken a part of a photo, so a brighter area of the composition is emphasized. Maybe you are photographing a big scene inside your school and you want to be sure the kids at the bottom are noticed. Throw on a graduated ND filter and darken the top of the photo.

These filters also come in colors—mostly in warm tones and blues. This will allow you to both darken a part of the photo and color it as well. They are mostly used for skies—a blue grad will darken and color a weak blue sky, and a warm-color grad will intensify a sunrise or sunset.

Exposure is not an absolute with these filters, and depends on what you want from the scene. For many situations just put the filter on and expose as you would normally.

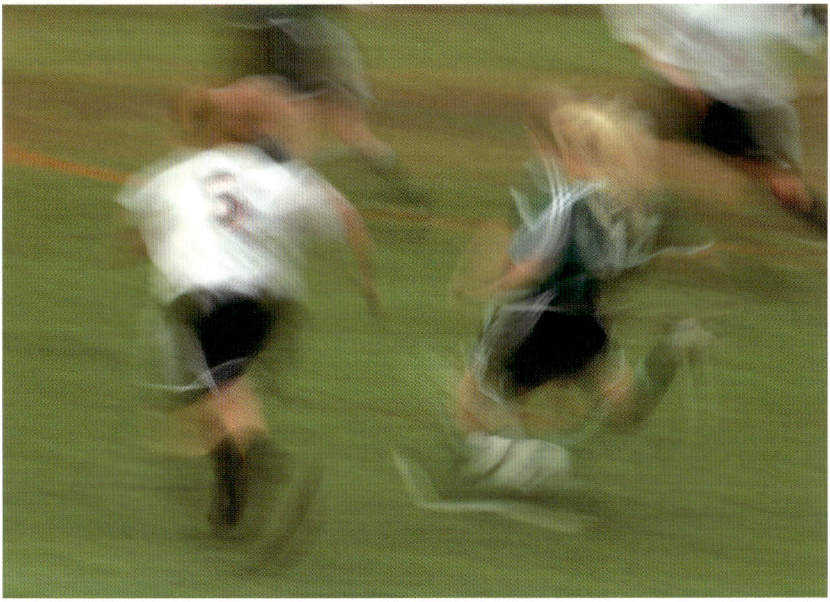

A neutral density filter may be required to use slow shutter speeds in bright sunlight.

For tricky conditions, try bracketing your exposure (giving the scene extra shots with more and less exposure). Luckily you have a real advantage over the traditional film photographer with your digital camera. You can now see what you are getting in your LCD, and even check the histogram to be sure.

Neutral Density Filters

These filters simply reduce the light coming through the lens without affecting color in any way (in essence, a dark gray filter). They come in different strengths from one stop to about nine stops reduction in light.

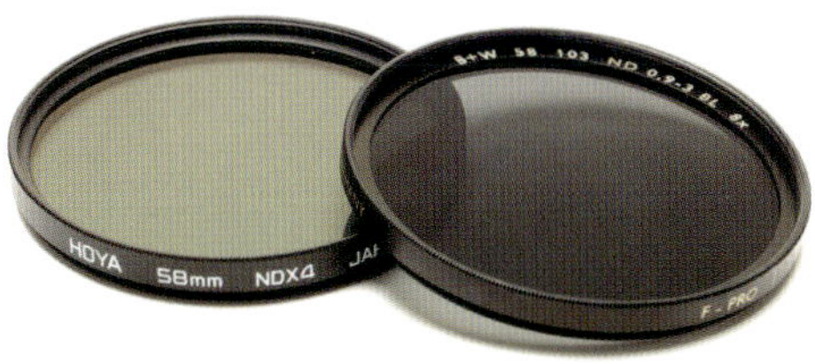

A neutral density filter reduces the amount of light that reaches the camera's sensor.

The ND filter can be very useful. If you like selective focus effects—shooting with a large aperture so that only the subject is sharp and everything else is out of focus—they can be a necessity on small digital camera lenses. (Remember their short focal length tends to give greater depth of field.) For example, in bright sun, if you want to use an aperture of f/2.8, you might have to shoot at 1/4000 second at an ISO setting of 100. If your camera does not have a shutter speed that fast, the only answer is an ND filter. A few cameras even include built-in ND filters that can be turned on and off in the shooting menu.

A main use of an ND filter is to allow slow shutter speeds so you can capture blurs. With an 8x filter (which gives a two-stop change), you can get exposures of shaded streams or waterfalls at shutter speeds of around 1 second. Bright sun requires a stronger filter. The fragmented movement captured by a faster shutter speed now blends to reveal flow patterns and water that appears smooth and milky. Many other subjects take on interesting looks when shot at slow shutter speeds. This offers great opportunities to experiment and push the envelope.

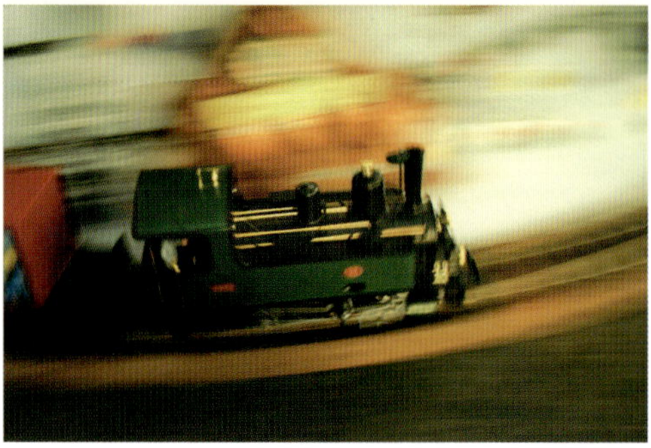

An ND filter lets you shoot at slow shutter speeds for creative effect.

There are also extreme ND filters offering nine stops of change (equal to 1/500 the amount of light). With a digital SLR, you can't focus or compose through this filter (it's too dark), but you have a live LCD on your compact digital camera so you can see something of the scene (though it may be so dark that you have to compose your shot before you mount the filter—you will need a tripod). This filter allows you to do some really unique photography. You can make exposures of many seconds—even in bright sun! This gives some fascinating blur and movement effects like the flow of a crowd. In the right light, you may even end up with exposures of 10, 20, or even 30 seconds, which will allow you to photograph a busy tourist location and make the tourists disappear! As long as no one stays in one spot very long the people will disappear from the scene.

Image Control with Depth of Field

We explained the effect of lens choice on depth of field in the previous chapter. Here we'll expand on two of the photographic variables that affect depth of field—f/stop and distance. You may remember that there are four things that affect depth of field (or the range of acceptable sharpness in a photograph from foreground to background): f/stop, distance, lens choice, and print size.

f/stop

As you reduce the size of the aperture in the lens (or go from a smaller f/number to a larger one), the amount of sharpness from front to back in a scene increases. So, for more depth of field, use a small lens opening; for less use a large lens opening. This is can be confusing because of the way lens openings are expressed.

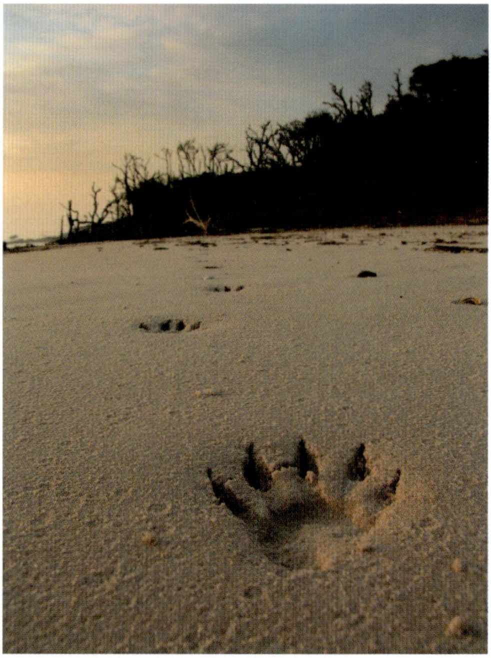

A small f/stop and a wide-angle focal length combine for maximum depth of field.

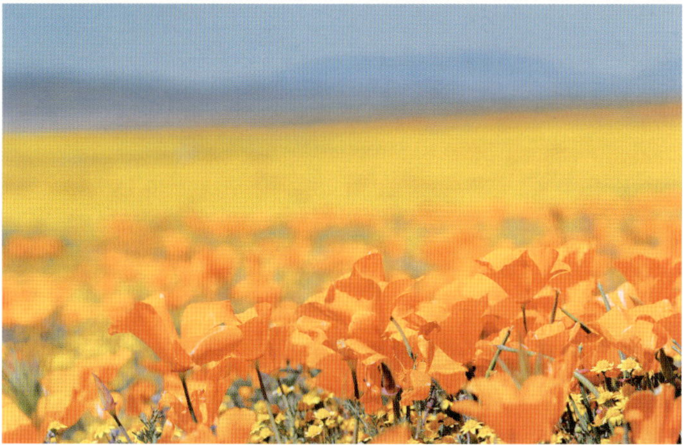

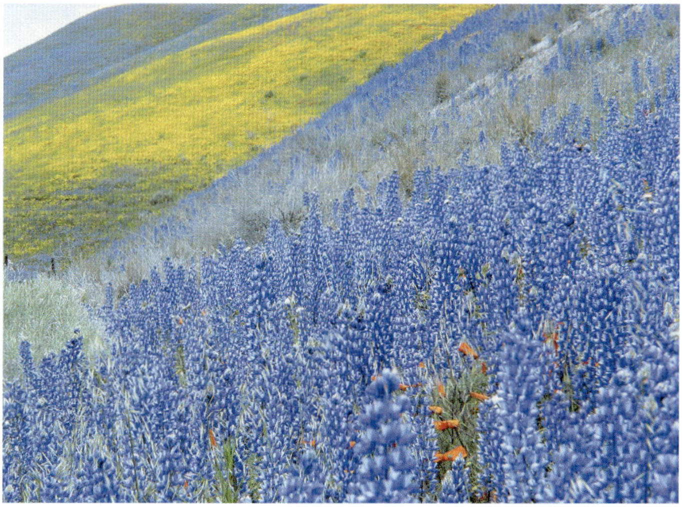

These two photos demonstrate the range of possibilities with depth of field. Using a large f/stop creates shallow depth of field (top), while a small f/stop gives deep depth of field.

A camera may offer a range of f/stops from f/4 to f/22. The number 22 is the largest number, yet the f/stop it represents is the smallest. On the other hand, f/4 is the largest f/stop, though the number is small. So, high numbers represent small lens openings and low numbers represent larger ones. Confusing, right?

The f/stop of a lens is actually a ratio or fraction related to the size of the lens and the opening inside the lens that lets light through. So f/8 is actually a fraction—1/8—which now does seem small, and f/2 is really a much larger fraction (1/2). Still, if you always had to remember all that, it could drive you crazy. An easy way to relate depth of field to f/stop is to realize that depth of field increases as the f/stop number increases.

Sometimes, you'll want a lot of depth of field for a landscape. Other times you may want minimal depth of field so that only your subject is sharp and the background is out of focus. This is called selective focus. In this example, you would deliberately choose a very shallow depth of field by using a wide lens opening such as f/2.8.

Distance

How close you are to the subject strongly affects depth of field. As you move closer to a subject (or focus closer), the zone of sharpness begins to shrink. As you move away the zone expands. The zone of sharpness for depth of field is not equal on both sides of the focus point. It actually extends one-third in front and two-thirds behind.

There are a number of practical ways to apply this information. At a distance—whenever the lens is focused on faraway objects—the depth of field basically covers everything at that distance to infinity. The actual f/stop used has little impact on sharpness in depth. Since you don't need a small f/stop, you could deliberately shoot at a higher shutter speed to minimize the blur due to camera movement

At middle distances, aperture rules. Slight changes in f/stop can have significant effects on depth of field. This is where using the depth-of-field preview button (if available) can help.

At the opposite end, depth of field will be severely limited as you focus closer. When you get to macro distances, depth of field can be measured in fractions of an inch. Taking advantage of this, you can do some really neat selective focus effects. For more depth of field, you are forced to use the smallest lens openings possible with your lens.

Distance between camera, subject, and background affects how sharply each of these elements will be rendered. This can be very important when you want a soft background that won't distract from your subject. When the subject is fairly close to the camera, it is easy to create an out-of-focus background. However, as the subject moves farther away from the camera, depth of field increases and it becomes more difficult to create a soft background. In this case, try opening the lens up or using a longer focal length, which will decrease the depth of field and soften the background.

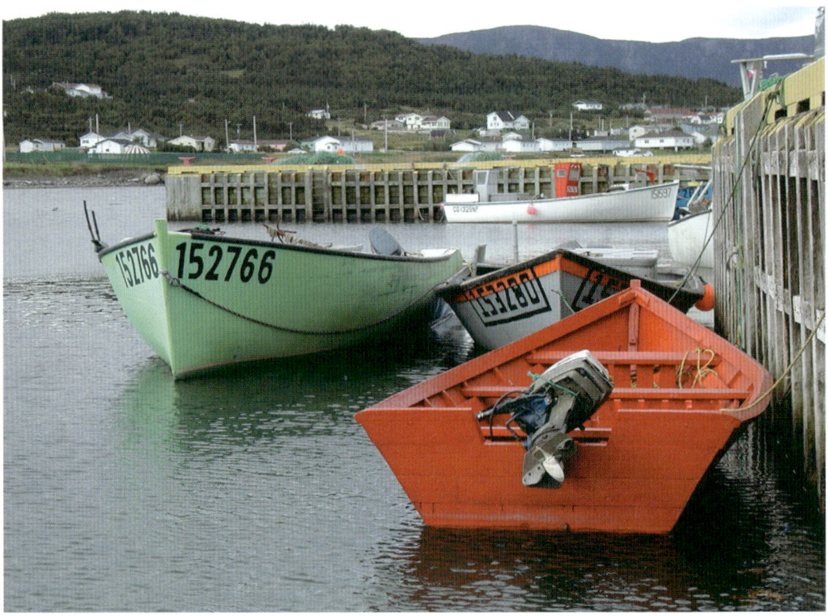

To maximize depth of field, avoid focusing on the object closest to the camera. Lock your camera's autofocus on an object about one-third back in the area that you want sharp in the photograph.

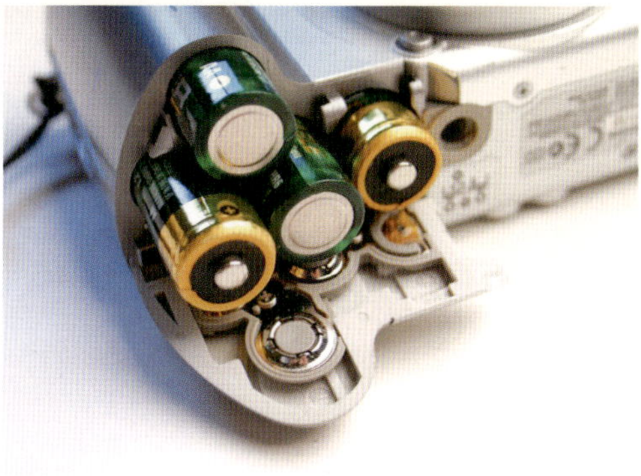

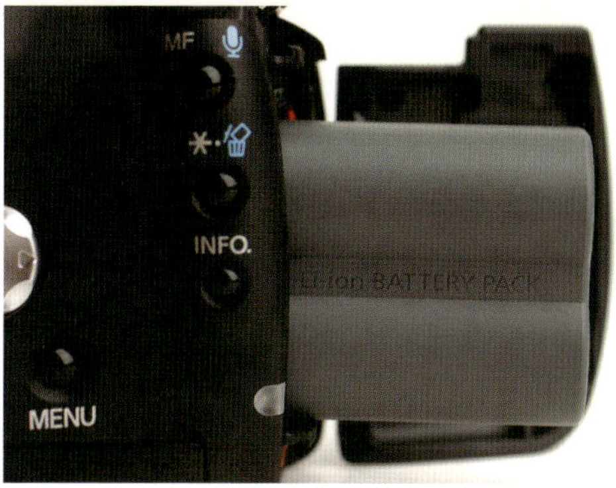

Batteries are critical for your camera to work. Most cameras use either AAs or a proprietary battery.

Batteries

Early digital cameras were terrible power vampires and gave digital photography a very bad rap regarding batteries. They'd go through common alkaline batteries so fast that you'd need multiple sets for even a few hours of shooting. Since digital cameras need more power and use it faster than film cameras, manufacturers have developed power-conserving technologies that have helped immensely. Still, batteries in a digital camera do quit in a very short time compared to film cameras (where you might replace batteries once a year).

Battery drain is affected mainly by three things: how you use your camera, the types of batteries, and how the camera is engineered. We have no control over the engineering except to know that newer cameras definitely have better power usage. We can, however, control how we use our cameras and, sometimes, the type of battery we use.

Everyone uses cameras differently. This is why manufacturers pull their hair out trying to give a "battery life" rating. There is no such thing as.a rating that will apply equally to all photographers. If you want to conserve your battery power, pay attention to how you use certain power-hungry parts of your camera, including the LCD monitor, built-in flash, and autofocus. A battery can actually start to show signs of low power (and the power bar shortens in the readout area) when multiple functions are happening at the same time—even though the camera may have enough power to shoot awhile longer.

The last point is a very important one that not everyone knows about. It is possible to have a camera read "empty" on the battery scale, but after the camera is turned off for a while, the battery starts to recover and the reading rises. This is especially true after power-intensive use, such as having the monitor on, the flash recharging, the lens autofocusing, and so forth—all in quick succession.

Battery Types

The right battery does make a difference in battery life, too. There are essentially two types of camera designs with regard to power supply—cameras that take a proprietary battery and cameras that AA-size batteries. Proprietary batteries fit only specific camera models from a single manufacturer. Typically, cameras that take proprietary batteries are using rechargeable lithium-ion batteries. Manufacturers choose these because the lithium-ion battery has a high power output for its size and is very stable. If your camera uses a proprietary battery, you do not have much choice. It is that battery or none. To purchase a spare battery, you need to go to a camera store and buy a battery made by your camera's manufacturer, or an independent manufacturer that makes replacement batteries.

Their disadvantage is inconvenience. If your proprietary battery dies and you don't have a spare, you are out of luck. You will not be able to walk into a local supermarket and buy a new one as you can with AAs. And for most of the lithium-ion batteries, there are no one-use back-ups available for you to keep in your bag for safety. (Some battery manufacturers are making one-use batteries for the very popular mini digital cameras—maybe they will for all digital cameras, too.)

For cameras that use AA-sized batteries, their wide availability is obviously a benefit. However, alkalines are really not of much use. They lose power quickly and they cannot be recharged. (The special alkalines marketed for digital products do last longer and could be used in an emergency.) Nickel-cadmium (NiCd) batteries can be recharged, but aren't usually recommended for digital camera use.

The two best AA battery types for photographers are rechargeable nickel-metal-hydride (NiMH) batteries and non-rechargable lithium batteries. NiMH batteries hold and release power well for digital cameras and can be recharged again and again. Their major disadvantage (true of all nickel-type batteries) is that they lose power just sitting. If you didn't use your camera for a month, you might discover your battery has no power—even though you just charged the batteries before you put the camera away. NiMH batteries will not give you their best right out of the package, either. They need to be charged and discharged a few times before they reach their full capacity. Sometimes photographers are disappointed in them after using them once, yet the batteries really aren't "conditioned" yet. Their capacity can even double after a few charging cycles.

Charging Batteries

How a battery is charged does affect its life. High-speed chargers are great when you are in rush but they will shorten the overall life of a battery. Sports photographers have discovered that they need to have back-up batteries if their rechargeables have been used hard for a while (both in the shooting and recharging) because they can just quit. Use standard chargers when you can to get the longest life from your batteries.

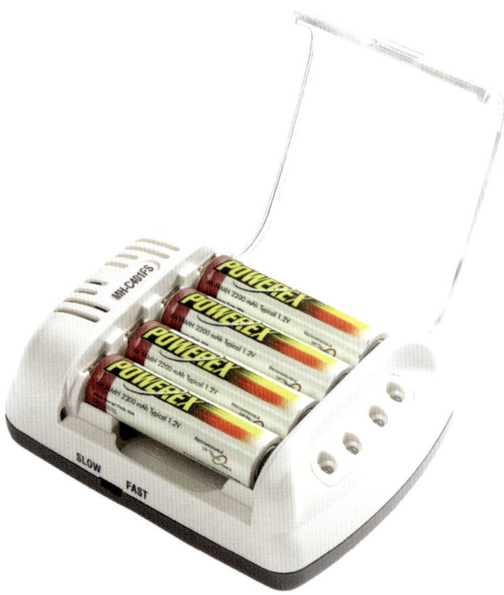

Check and charge your batteries before you need to go out and take photographs to ensure you have the power you need.

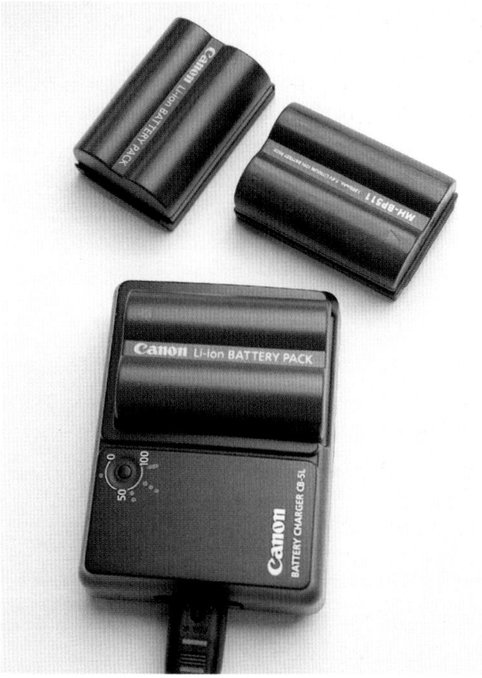

Three camera batteries (or sets of batteries) can be very helpful, because you'll always have a backup.

Backup Batteries

Lithium AAs are a great companion to NiMH and do hold their power just sitting—so you can buy a pack, throw it in your bag, and expect the batteries to work years later. They are more expensive for a one-use battery (typically 2.5 times the price of standard alkalines), but they have 5–7 times more life (and actually offer much more life than fully charged NiMH batteries). Lithium batteries are a great choice for backup and special conditions. They are lighter in weight than other AAs, work better in cold weather than most batteries, and will even last a long time under casual usage.

Since batteries are essential to digital camera operation, it is important to have multiple sets of batteries. Personally, I feel uncomfortable without at least three batteries (or sets of batteries) per camera; they don't take up that much space. I don't ever want to be caught with a dead battery just as I am ready to shoot.

Traveling with a Digital Camera

Your digital camera will give you some great new benefits for photographing when traveling. If you've traveled at all recent in recent years, you know how much security has changed at airports. Traditional film shooters really have a problem because film can be fogged by the big scanners used for checked bags. Yet carrying all their film for a trip through gate security can be a real pain. The digital camera comes to the rescue. It is actually a lot easier to get through the airport with one of these cameras. The gate security systems have no effect on memory cards and you don't need to be burdened with lots of film. Fogged film is no longer a concern since you have no film.

As I mentioned before, I like to have at least three sets of batteries per camera body. You can probably shoot a whole day while traveling, and maybe use up a single battery or battery set. (When traveling it is rare to be shooting constantly.) Having a second battery all charged becomes my backup—although for this type of shooting, I rarely use up the full charge of that battery in a day. Back at the hotel, the third battery is on the charger.

When I return that night, I take the fully charged battery from the charger and put it in my camera. I then put the most discharged battery on the charger to charge overnight. The next morning I take that newly charged battery for backup in my camera bag and put the third, partially used battery on the charger to start a whole new cycle that night.

Hint: If you have multiple camera bodies, consider getting a battery charger that can handle multiple batteries.

An important concern when traveling with your digital camera is protecting your photos. With memory cards available in gigabytes, you might just carry the biggest memory cards you can afford and keep images on them until you get home. Consider that there are also other ways that you can give your images added protection and ensure you get them home.

Do you travel with a laptop? You could download your images to its hard drive. You can use a PC-card adapter if your computer has a PC-card slot. Otherwise you can use a USB card reader. If your laptop has FireWire, go for that type of reader rather than USB, as it can be very fast.

I like to travel with a laptop that has a CD-burner, which allows me to make copies of all my images. This has become pretty much a standard way of working for pros. It can be funny to see a group of photojournalists with black hoods over their heads as they download images to their laptops outdoors during the day (the hood makes the screen easier to see). CDs are pretty durable, so they travel well and you can make duplicates as you go for even more security.

There are a number of other portable devices that allow you to download images to them as you travel. One type is built around a small and sturdy laptop hard drive. It has a slot for the memory card, battery power, and a monitor that either lets you see the device's menus or the photos themselves. Another type is the portable CD drive, which is becoming common in the market. It allows you to download images directly from a memory card to a CD.

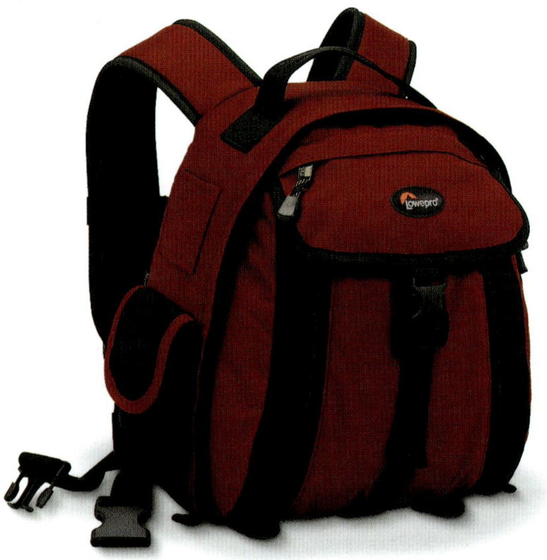

You can get a complete set of compact digital camera gear, from lenses to flash, and even an extra camera, into a small backpack camera bag.

glossary

A
See Aperture-Priority mode.

AA
Auto aperture. Refers to a Nikon flash mode in which the flash level is automatically adjusted for aperture.

aberration
An optical flaw in a lens that causes the image to be distorted or unclear.

Adobe Photoshop
Professional-level image-processing software with extremely powerful filter and color-correction tools. It offers features for photography, graphic design, web design, and video.

Adobe Photoshop Elements
A limited version of the Photoshop program designed for the avid photographer. The Elements program lacks some of the more sophisticated controls available in Photoshop, but it does have a comprehensive range of image-manipulation options, such as cropping, exposure and contrast controls, color correction, layers, panoramic stitching, and more.

AE
See automatic exposure.

AF
See automatic focus.

ambient light
See available light.

angle of view
The area seen by a lens, usually measured in degrees across the diagonal of the film frame.

anti-aliasing
A technique that reduces or eliminates the jagged appearance of lines or edges in an image.

aperture
The opening in the lens that allows light to enter the camera. Aperture is usually described as an f/number. The higher the f/number, the smaller the aperture; and the lower the f/number, the larger the aperture.

Aperture-Priority mode
A type of automatic exposure, which lets the photographer manually select the aperture and the camera automatically sets the shutter speed.

artifact
Information that is not part of the scene but appears in the image due to technology. Artifacts can occur in film or digital images and include increased grain, flare, noise, etc.

artificial light
Usually refers to any light source that doesn't exist in nature, such as incandescent, fluorescent, and other manufactured lighting.

astigmatism
An optical defect that occurs when an off-axis point is brought to focus as sagittal and tangential lines rather than a point.

automatic exposure
When the camera measures light and makes the adjustments necessary to create proper image density on sensitized media.

automatic flash
An electronic flash unit that reads light reflected off a subject (from either a preflash or the actual flash exposure), then shuts itself off as soon as ample light has reached the sensitized medium.

automatic focus
When the camera automatically adjusts the lens elements to sharply render the subject.

Av
Aperture Value. See Aperture-Priority mode.

available light
The amount of illumination at a given location that applies to natural and artificial light sources, but not those supplied specifically for photography. It is also called existing light or ambient light.

backlight
Light that projects toward the camera from behind the subject.

backup
A copy of a file or program made to ensure that, if the original is lost or damaged, the data is still available.

barrel distortion
A defect in the lens that makes straight lines curve outward away from the middle of the image.

bit
Binary digit. This is the basic unit of binary computation. See also, byte.

bit depth
The number of bits per pixel that determines the number of colors the image can display. Eight bits per pixel is the minimum requirement for a photo-quality color image.

bounce light
Light that reflects off of another surface before illuminating the subject.

bracketing
A sequence of pictures taken of the same subject but varying one or more exposure settings, manually or automatically, between each exposure.

brightness
A subjective measure of illumination. See also, luminance.

buffer
Temporarily stores data so that other programs, on the camera or the computer, can continue to run while data is in transition.

built-in flash
A flash that is permanently attached to the camera body. The built-in flash will pop up and fire in low-light situations when using the camera's automated exposure settings.

built-in meter
A light-measuring device that is incorporated into the camera body.

bulb
A camera setting that allows the shutter to stay open as long as the shutter release is depressed.

byte
A group of eight bits that is processed as one unit. See also, bit.

card reader
Device that connects to your computer and enables quick and easy download of images from memory card to computer.

CCD
Charge Coupled Device. This is a common digital camera sensor type that is sensitized by applying an electrical charge to the sensor prior to its exposure to light. It converts light energy into an electrical impulse.

chromatic aberration
Occurs when light rays of different colors are focused on different planes, causing colored halos around objects in the image.

chrominance
Hue and saturation information.

chrominance noise
A form of artifact that appears as a random scattering of densely packed colored "grain." See also, luminance and noise.

close-up
A general term used to describe an image created by closely focusing on a subject. Often involves the use of special lenses or extension tubes. Also, an automated exposure setting that automatically selects a large aperture (not available with all cameras).

CMOS
Complementary Metal Oxide Semiconductor. Like CCD sensors, this sensor type converts light into an electrical impulse. CMOS sensors are similar to CCDs, but allow individual processing of pixels, are less expensive to produce, and use less power. See also, CCD.

CMYK mode

Cyan, magenta, yellow, and black. This mode is typically used in image-editing applications when preparing an image for printing.

color balance
The average overall color in a reproduced image. How a digital camera interprets the color of light in a scene so that white or neutral gray objects appear neutral.

color cast
A colored hue that occurs in an image; often caused by improper lighting or incorrect white balance settings. Can be produced intentionally for creative effect.

color space
A mapped relationship between colors and computer data about the colors.

CompactFlash (CF) card
One of the most widely used removable memory cards.

complementary colors
In theory: any two colors of light that, when combined, emit all known light wavelengths, resulting in white light. Also, it can be any pair of dye colors that absorb all known light wavelengths, resulting in black.

compression
Method of reducing file size through removal of redundant data, as with the JPEG file format.

contrast
The difference between two or more tones in terms of luminance, density, or darkness.

contrast filter
A colored filter that lightens or darkens the monotone representation of a colored area or object in a black-and-white photograph.

CPU
Central Processing Unit. This perform principle computational functions and is the "brain" of a computer.

critical focus
The most sharply focused plane within an image.

cropping
The process of extracting a portion of the image area. If this portion of the image is enlarged, resolution is subsequently lowered.

dedicated flash
An electronic flash unit that talks with the camera, communicating things such as flash illumination, lens focal length, subject distance, and sometimes flash status.

default
Refers to various factory-set attributes or features, in this case of a camera, that can be changed by the user but can, as desired, be reset to the original factory settings.

depth of field
The image space in front of and behind the plane of focus that appears acceptably sharp in the photograph.

digital zoom
Cropping of the image at the sensor to create the effect of a telephoto zoom lens. The camera interpolates the image to the original resolution. However, the result is not as sharp as an image created with an optical zoom lens.

diopter
A measurement of the refractive power of a lens. Also, it may be a supplementary lens that is defined by its focal length and power of magnification.

download
The transfer of data from one device to another, such as from camera to computer or computer to printer.

dpi
Dots per inch. Used to define the resolution of a printer, this term refers to the number of dots of ink that a printer can lay down in an inch.

dye sublimation printer
Creates color on the printed page by vaporizing inks that then solidify on the page.

electronic flash
A device with a glass or plastic tube filled with gas that, when electrified, creates an intense flash of light. Also called a strobe.

electronic rangefinder
A system that utilizes the AF technology built into a camera to provide a visual confirmation that focus has been achieved. It can operate in either manual or AF focus modes.

EV
Exposure value. A number that quantifies the amount of light within an scene, allowing you to determine the relative combinations of aperture and shutter speed to accurately reproduce the light levels of that exposure.

EXIF
Exchangeable Image File Format. This format is used for storing an image file's interchange information.

exposure
When light enters the camera and reacts with the sensitized medium. The term can also refer to the amount of light that strikes the light sensitive medium.

exposure meter
See light meter.

extension tube
A hollow metal ring that can be fitted between the camera and lens. It increases the distance between the optical center of the lens and the sensor and decreases the minimum focus distance of the lens.

FAT
File Allocation Table. This is a method used by computer operating systems to keep track of files stored on the hard drive.

file format
The form in which digital images are stored and recorded, e.g., JPEG, RAW, TIFF, etc.

filter
Usually a piece of plastic or glass used to control how certain wavelengths of light are recorded. A filter absorbs selected wavelengths, preventing them from reaching the light sensitive medium. Also, software available in image-processing computer programs can produce special filter effects.

FireWire
A high speed data transfer standard that allows outlying accessories to be plugged and unplugged from the computer while it is turned on. Some digital cameras and card readers use FireWire to connect to the computer. FireWire transfers data faster than USB. See also, Mbps.

firmware
Software that is permanently incorporated into a hardware chip. All computer-based equipment, including digital cameras, use firmware of some kind.

flare
Unwanted light streaks or rings that appear in the viewfinder, on the recorded image, or both. It is caused by extraneous light entering the camera during shooting. Diffuse flare is uniformly reflected light that can lower the contrast of the image.

f/number
See f/stop.

focal length
When the lens is focused on infinity, it is the distance from the optical center of the lens to the focal plane.

focal plane
The plane on which a lens forms a sharp image. Also, it may be the film plane or sensor plane.

focus
An optimum sharpness or image clarity that occurs when a lens creates a sharp image by converging light rays to specific points at the focal plane. The word also refers to the act of adjusting the lens to achieve optimal image sharpness.

f/stop
The size of the aperture of a lens, also referred to as f/number or stop. The term is a ratio of the focal length (f) of the lens to the width of its aperture opening. (f/1.4 = wide opening and f/22 = narrow opening.) Each stop up (lower f/number) doubles the amount of light reaching the sensitized medium. Each stop down (higher f/number) halves the amount of light reaching the sensitized medium.

full-frame
The maximum area covered by the sensitized medium.

GB
See gigabyte.

gigabyte
Just over one billion bytes.

GN
See guide number.

gray card
A card used to take accurate exposure readings. It typically has a white side that reflects 90% of the light and a gray side that reflects 18%.

gray scale
A successive series of tones ranging between black and white, which have no color.

guide number
A number used to quantify the output of a flash unit. It is derived by using this formula: GN = aperture x distance. Guide numbers are expressed for a given ISO film speed in either feet or meters.

hard drive
A contained storage unit made up of magnetically sensitive disks.

histogram
A graphic representation of the tones in an image.

hot shoe
An electronically connected flash mount on the camera body. It enables direct connection between the camera and an external flash, and synchronizes the shutter release with the firing of the flash.

icon
A symbol used to represent a file, function, or program.

image-editing program
See image-processing program

image-processing program
Software that allows for image alteration and enhancement.

infinity
In photographic terms, the theoretical most distant point of focus.

interpolation
Process used to increase image resolution by creating new pixels based on existing pixels. The software intelligently looks at existing pixels and creates new pixels to fill the gaps and achieve a higher resolution.

IS
Image Stabilization. This is a technology that reduces camera shake and vibration. It is used in lenses, binoculars, camcorders, etc.

ISO
From ISOS (Greek for equal), a term for industry standards from the International Organization for Standardization. When an ISO number is applied to film, it indicates the relative light sensitivity of the recording medium. Digital sensors use film ISO equivalents, which are based on enhancing the data stream or boosting the signal.

JFET
Junction Field Effect Transistor, which are used in digital cameras to reduce the total number of transistors and minimize noise.

JPEG
Joint Photographic Experts Group. This is a lossy compression file format that works with any computer and photo software. JPEG examines an image for redundant information and then removes it. It is a variable compression format because the amount of leftover data depends on the detail in the photo and the amount of compression. At low compression/high quality, the loss of data has a negligible effect on the photo. However, JPEG should not be used as a working format—the file should be reopened and saved in a format such as TIFF, which does not compress the image.

KB
See kilobyte.

kilobyte
Just over one thousand bytes.

latitude
The acceptable range of exposure (from under to over) determined by observed loss of image quality.

LBCAST
Lateral Buried Charge Accumulator and Sensing Transistor array. This is an array that converts received light into a digital signal, attaching an amplification circuit to each pixel of the imaging sensor.

LCD
Liquid Crystal Display, which is a flat screen with two clear polarizing sheets on either side of a liquid crystal solution. When activated by an electric current, the LCD causes the crystals to either pass through or block light in order to create a colored image display.

LED
Light Emitting Diode. It is a signal often employed as an indicator on cameras as well as on other electronic equipment.

lens
A piece of optical glass on the front of a camera that has been precisely calibrated to allow focus.

lens hood
Also called a lens shade. This is a short tube that can be attached to the front of a lens to reduce flare. It keeps undesirable light from reaching the front of the lens and also protects the front of the lens.

lens shade
See lens hood.

light meter
Also called an exposure meter, it is a device that measures light levels and calculates the correct aperture and shutter speed.

lithium-ion
A popular battery technology (sometimes abbreviated to Li-ion) that is not prone to the charge memory effects of nickel-cadmium (Ni-Cd) batteries, or the low temperature performance problems of alkaline batteries.

long lens
See telephoto lens.

lossless
Image compression in which no data is lost.

lossy
Image compression in which data is lost and, thereby, image quality is lessened. This means that the greater the compression, the lesser the image quality.

low-pass filter
A filter designed to remove elements of an image that correspond to high-frequency data, such as sharp edges and fine detail, to reduce the effect of moiré. See also, moiré.

luminance
A term used to describe directional brightness. It can also be used as luminance noise, which is a form of noise that appears as a sprinkling of black "grain." See also, brightness, chrominance, and noise.

M
See Manual exposure mode.

Mac
Macintosh. This is the brand name for computers produced by Apple Computer, Inc.

macro lens
A lens designed to be at top sharpness over a flat field when focused at close distances and reproduction ratios up to 1:1.

main light
The primary or dominant light source. It influences texture, volume, and shadows.

Manual exposure mode
A camera operating mode that requires the user to determine and set both the aperture and shutter speed. This is the opposite of automatic exposure.

MB
See megabyte.

Mbps
Megabits per second. This unit is used to describe the rate of data transfer. See also, megabit.

megabit
One million bits of data. See also, bit.

megabyte
Just over one million bytes.

megapixel
A million pixels.

memory
The storage capacity of a hard drive or other recording media.

memory card
A solid state removable storage medium used in digital devices. They can store still images, moving images, or sound, as well as related file data. There are several different types, including CompactFlash, SmartMedia, and xD, or Sony's proprietary Memory Stick, to name a few. Individual card capacity is limited by available storage as well as by the size of the recorded data (determined by factors such as image resolution and file format). See also, CompactFlash (CF) card, file format.

menu
A listing of features, functions, or options displayed on an LCD screen that can be selected and activated by the user.

microdrive
A removable storage medium with moving parts. They are miniature hard drives based on the dimensions of a CompactFlash Type II card. Microdrives are more susceptible to the effects of impact, high altitude, and low temperature than solid-state cards are. See also, memory card.

middle gray
Halfway between black and white, it is an average gray tone with 18% reflectance. See also, gray card.

midtone
The tone that appears as medium brightness, or medium gray tone, in a photographic print.

mode
Specified operating conditions of the camera or software program.

moiré
Occurs when the subject has more detail than the resolution of the digital camera can capture. Moiré appears as a wavy pattern over the image.

MOSFET
Metal Oxide Semiconductor Field Effect Transistor, which is used as an amplifier in digital cameras.

noise
The digital equivalent of grain. It is often caused by a number of different factors, such as a high ISO setting, heat, sensor design, etc. Though usually undesirable, it may be added for creative effect using an image-processing program. See also, chrominance noise and luminance.

normal lens
See standard lens.

operating system (OS)
The system software that provides the environment within which all other software operates.

overexposed
When too much light is recorded with the image, causing the photo to be too light in tone.

pan
Moving the camera to follow a moving subject. When a slow shutter speed is used, this creates an image in which the subject appears sharp and the background is blurred.

panorama
An image having wider proportions that the normal 3:4 image ratio.

PC
Personal Computer. Strictly speaking, a computer made by IBM Corporation. However, the term is commonly used to refer to any IBM compatible computer.

perspective
The effect of the distance between the camera and image elements upon the perceived size of objects in an image. It is also an expression of this three-dimensional relationship in two dimensions.

pincushion distortion
A flaw in a lens that causes straight lines to bend inward toward the middle of an image.

pixel
Derived from picture element. A pixel is the base component of a digital image. Every individual pixel can have a distinct color and tone.

plug-in
Third-party software created to augment an existing software program.

polarization
An effect achieved by using a polarizing filter. It minimizes reflections from non-metallic surfaces like water and glass and saturates colors by removing glare. Polarization often makes skies appear bluer.

pre-flash
A series of short duration, low intensity flash pulses emitted by a flash unit immediately prior to the shutter opening. These flashes help the TTL light meter assess the reflectivity of the subject. See also, TTL.

Program mode
In Program exposure mode, the camera selects a combination of shutter speed and aperture automatically.

RAW
An image file format that has little or no internal processing applied by the camera. It contains 12-bit color information, a wider range of data than 8-bit formats such as JPEG.

RAW+JPEG
An image file format that records two files per capture; one RAW file and one JPEG file.

rear-curtain sync
A feature that causes the flash unit to fire just prior to the shutter closing. It is used for creative effect when mixing flash and ambient light.

red-eye reduction
A feature that causes the flash to emit a brief pulse of light just before the main flash fires. This helps to reduce the effect of retinal reflection.

resolution
The amount of data available for an image as applied to image size. It is expressed in pixels or megapixels, or sometimes as lines per inch or dots per inch.

RGB mode
Red, Green, and Blue. This is the color model most commonly used to display color images on video systems, film recorders, and computer monitors. It displays all visible colors as combinations of red, green, and blue. RGB mode is the most common color mode for viewing and working with digital files onscreen.

S
See Shutter-Priority mode.

saturation
The intensity or richness of a hue or color.

sharp
A term used to describe the quality of an image as clear, crisp, and perfectly focused, as opposed to fuzzy, obscure, or unfocused.

short lens
A lens with a short focal length—a wide-angle lens. It produces a greater angle of view than you would see with your eyes.

shutter
The apparatus that controls the amount of time during which light is allowed to reach the sensitized medium.

Shutter-Priority mode
An automatic exposure mode in which you manually select the shutter speed and the camera automatically selects the aperture.

slow sync
A flash mode in which a slow shutter speed is used with the flash in order to allow low-level ambient light to be recorded by the sensitized medium.

SLR
Single-lens reflex. A camera with a mirror that reflects the image entering the lens through a pentaprism or pentamirror onto the viewfinder screen. When you take the picture, the mirror reflexes out of the way, the focal plane shutter opens, and the image is recorded.

small-format sensor
In a digital camera, a sensor that is physically smaller than a 35mm frame of film.

standard lens
Also known as a normal lens, this is a fixed-focal-length lens usually in the range of 45 to 55mm for 35mm format (or the equivalent range for small-format sensors). In contrast to wide-angle or telephoto lenses, a standard lens views a realistically proportionate perspective of a scene.

stop
See f/stop.

stop down
To reduce the size of the diaphragm opening by using a higher f/number.

stop up
To increase the size of the diaphragm opening by using a lower f/number.

synchronize
Causing a flash unit to fire simultaneously with the complete opening of the camera's shutter.

telephoto effect
When objects in an image appear closer than they really are through the use of a telephoto lens.

telephoto lens
A lens with a long focal length that enlarges the subject and produces a narrower angle of view than you would see with your eyes.

thumbnail
A miniaturized representation of an image file.

TIFF
Tagged Image File Format. This popular digital format uses lossless compression.

tripod
A three-legged stand that stabilizes the camera and eliminates camera shake caused by body movement or vibration. Tripods are usually adjustable for height and angle.

TTL
Through-the-Lens, i.e. TTL metering.

Tv
Time Value. See Shutter-Priority mode.

USB
Universal Serial Bus. This interface standard allows outlying accessories to be plugged and unplugged from the computer while it is turned on.

vignetting
A reduction in light at the edge of an image due to use of a filter or an inappropriate lens hood for the lens.

viewfinder screen
The ground glass surface on which you view your image.

wide-angle lens
A lens that produces a greater angle of view than you would see with your eyes, often causing the image to appear stretched. See also, short lens.

Wi-Fi
Wireless Fidelity, a technology that allows for wireless networking between one Wi-Fi compatible product and another.

zoom lens
A lens that can be adjusted to cover a wide range of focal lengths.

index

A

aberration 116, 147, 148
Adobe Photoshop 46, 47, 55, 56, 91
Adobe Photoshop Elements 91, 147
AF-assist beam 42
AF point (see AF sensor)
AF sensor 27, 41–42, 74, 137
ambient light 44, 72–73, 126, 129, 131–132, 147, 148, 156
aperture 22, 36–37, 43, 44, 68, 72, 91, 107, 121, 124, 139, 140, 142, 147, 149, 150, 151, 152, 153, 154, 156
Aperture-Priority mode 26, 68, 69, 74, 147, 148
artifact 37, 46, 147, 149
autofocus (AF) 27, 33, 39–40, 74, 108, 137, 143, 150
automatic exposure bracketing (AEB) 74, 79

B

backlit 66, 132
battery 10, 27, 39, 61, 101, 104, 143–146, 153
Bayer pattern 37, 38
blur 18, 44, 69, 71, 78, 100, 113, 117, 122, 133
bounce flash (see flash, bounce)
buffer 38, 40–41, 95, 148
built-in flash (see flash, built-in)
bulb exposure 29, 78–79, 148

C

card reader 59, 98–99, 101, 104
CCD sensor (see sensor, CCD)
CD 101, 102–103, 104, 146
center-weighted metering (see metering, center-weighted)
close-up lens (see lens, close-up)
Close-Up mode 71, 114
close-up photography 109, 114, 121, 130, 149
CMOS sensor (see sensor, CMOS)
color cast 24, 84, 85, 88, 149
color temperature 55, 83
CompactFlash (see memory card)
compression 53, 54, 96, 149, 157
continuous focus 27, 41
continuous shooting 39, 40
cropping 105, 118, 119, 150

D

default settings 48, 150
delete (see erasing images)
depth of field 22, 26, 36, 37, 43, 69, 71, 110, 114, 121, 124, 139, 140–142, 150
depth-of-field preview 142
digital lens (see lens, digital)
download 10, 40, 59, 88, 97–99, 100, 104, 146, 149, 150
dpi (dots per inch) 50–53, 150
DPOF (Digital Print Order Format) 99
drive speed 40
DVD 102, 103, 104

E

electronic viewfinder (EVF) 28, 31, 34, 108, 114, 137
enlarge (see magnification)
enlargement 56, 57
erasing images 13, 19, 40, 63, 96, 100, 103, 104
EXIF 91, 150
exposure compensation 26, 43, 68, 70, 74–75, 79, 127, 131

exposure,
combining 79–81
long 10, 29, 45, 47, 71, 78–79

F
file format 53–58, 59, 105, 149, 150, 151, 153, 156, 157
fill flash (see flash, fill)
filter 24, 28, 36, 37, 38, 86, 87, 89, 90, 109, 115, 134–140, 150, 151, 154, 155
FireWire 98, 99, 102, 146, 151
flash 11, 18, 24, 28, 29, 33, 34, 43, 44, 61, 68, 69, 72, 91, 126–133, 143, 148, 150, 152, 155, 156, 157
bounce 129, 130
built-in 29, 33, 44, 126, 127, 128, 129, 131, 143
close-up 130
fill 44, 131–133
off-camera 128, 129–130, 133
flash exposure compensation 127, 131
flash sync 18, 29
focus 20, 22, 27, 32, 33, 37, 41–42, 67, 69, 70, 75, 88, 114, 115, 116, 121, 137, 139, 140, 141, 142 150, 151
formatting 100, 104

G
grain 37, 43, 44, 46, 47, 51, 147, 149, 154, 155
guide number (GN) 127, 152

H
hard drive 58, 59, 93, 97, 101, 104, 105, 146, 152, 154
portable 101, 102, 146
histogram 26, 66, 76–78

I
image stabilization 117, 152
International Organization for Standardization 25, 43, 152
ISO 10, 13, 25, 27, 32, 33, 37, 38, 43, 44–45, 47, 91, 127, 139, 152, 155

J
JPEG 23, 29, 46, 53, 54–55, 56–58, 95, 96, 105, 149, 151, 153, 156

L
LCD 10, 11, 12, 16–18, 26, 27, 28, 29, 39, 41, 42, 58, 60–63, 65–66, 73, 75, 76–78, 85, 88, 90, 104, 114, 117, 122, 125, 126, 130, 133, 137, 139, 140, 143, 153
Landscape mode 71
lens,
close-up 109, 115
macro 109, 114, 115, 124, 154
telephoto 22, 32, 35, 36, 42, 44, 69, 73, 106, 108, 109, 112–113, 114, 115, 116, 117, 118, 119, 120, 121, 123, 124, 157
wide-angle 22, 35–36, 106, 108–109, 110–112, 114, 115, 115, 116, 117, 118–119, 120, 121, 123, 157
zoom 34, 35, 36, 44, 107, 111, 116, 117, 120, 123, 150, 157

M
macro lens (see lens, macro)
magnification 35, 113, 118, 123
manual exposure 25, 33, 67, 68, 72–73, 74, 154
megapixels 10, 20, 23, 28, 32, 33–34, 38, 40, 46, 50–52, 95, 103, 124, 154, 156
memory card 10, 16, 19, 23, 4, 38, 40, 41, 46, 54, 58, 59, 64, 92–102, 104, 128, 145, 146, 154
metadata 87, 88, 90–91
metering 26, 42, 43, 65, 66, 67, 68, 73, 74, 78, 126, 130, 131, 132, 136
center-weighted 73
multi-point 67
partial 73
spot 73
microdrive 92, 93, 154
motor drive 40
MPEG 59

N
natural light 131, 133
Night Flash mode 71, 129, 132, 133
noise 13, 21, 22, 25, 29, 38, 43, 44–47, 66, 78, 79, 134, 147, 149, 152, 154, 155

O
off-camera flash (see flash, off-camera)
overexposure 22, 66, 77, 130, 155
alert 78

P

panoramic 72
parameters 48, 91
partial metering (see metering, partial)
PCMCIA card slots 98
Photoshop (see Adobe Photoshop)
portable hard drive (see hard drive, portable)
Portrait mode 71
ppi (pixels per inch) 50–52
predictive AF 41
pre-focus 41
preflash 126, 128, 155
print 10, 12, 20–21, 24, 28, 32, 33–34, 48, 50–53, 55, 56, 75, 92, 97, 99, 105, 121, 122, 140
Program mode 26, 68, 132, 156
protecting images 102, 104

Q

quality (see resolution)

R

RAW 29, 54–58, 85, 90, 91, 95, 96, 103, 105, 151, 155
red-eye 128, 129, 156
reformatting 100
resolution 10, 20, 21, 23, 28, 33, 50–53, 58, 150, 152, 156

S

sensor,
  CCD 38, 149
  CMOS 38, 149
shutter lag 29, 40
Shutter-Priority mode 26, 68, 69, 156, 157
single-shot AF 27, 41
Slow Sync 132, 133, 156
Sports mode 71
spot metering (see metering, spot)
storage 10, 59, 64, 93, 94, 97, 101–103, 152, 154
sync speed 131

T

telephoto lens (see lens, telephoto)
TIFF 46, 53, 56, 57, 58, 105, 151, 157
tripod 62, 78, 79, 113, 122, 123, 124–125, 140, 157
TTL 136, 156

U

USB 97, 98, 102, 146, 157

V

vignetting 109, 135, 157

W

white balance 11, 13, 14, 24, 26, 32, 33, 55, 60, 61, 70, 82–90, 104, 114
wide-angle lens (see lens, wide-angle)
workflow 54, 104–105

Z

zoom lens (see lens, zoom)